RENAISSANCE DRAMA

New Series XVI ᴄᴈ 1985

Renaissance Drama

New Series XVI

Renaissance Plays: New Readings and Rereadings

Edited by Leonard Barkan

Northwestern University Press

EVANSTON 1985

The front-cover illustration is "The sacred chase," from Otto van
Veene's *Emblemes of Love* (1608) (p. 131, STC 24627a.5 copy 1). By
permission of the Folger Shakespeare Library.

The back-cover illustration is the title-plate for John Speed's *The History of Great Britaine* by Jodocus Hondius STC 23045 copy 1). By
permission of the Folger Shakespeare Library.

Publication of this volume was made possible by a grant from the College of Arts and Sciences, Northwestern University.

200293

Editorial Note

R ENAISSANCE DRAMA, an annual publication, provides a forum for scholars in various parts of the globe, wherever the drama of the Renaissance is studied. Coverage, so far as subject matter is concerned, is not restricted to any single national theater. The chronological limits of the Renaissance are interpreted liberally, and space is available for essays on precursors, as well as on the use of Renaissance themes by later writers. Editorial policy favors articles with some scope. Essays that are exploratory in nature, that are concerned with critical or scholarly methodology, that raise new questions or embody fresh approaches to perennial problems are particularly appropriate for a publication that originated from the proceedings of the Modern Language Association Conference on Research Opportunities in Renaissance Drama.

The Editor gratefully acknowledges his debt to the members of the Editorial Committee, and similar warm thanks are due to the editorial assistant, Nancy Arnesen, and to our administrative assistant, Jamie O'Connor. The efficient and expert help of the assistant editor, Janice Feldstein, has been absolutely indispensable.

With this volume the editor concludes his decade-long tenure with *Renaissance Drama* and places the journal in the capable hands of Mary Beth Rose of the Newberry Library. A few sentences cannot do justice to all the retrospective feelings that emerge at this moment of transition. Suffice it to say that it has been a great intellectual and personal pleasure to publish essays by both highly established scholars and new voices fresh from graduate school, to meet (in mind and sometimes in person) experts in Renaissance Drama from around the world, and to engage in a kind of ten-year postgraduate seminar in the field with hundreds of fellow students.

Volume XVII of *Renaissance Drama* will concern itself with "Renaissance Drama and Cultural Change." Correspondence, submissions, and enquiries regarding future volumes should be addressed to Mary Beth Rose, The Newberry Library, 60 West Walton Street, Chicago, Illinois 60610.

Contents

RENAISSANCE DRAMA

New Series XVI 🙠 1985

The Death of Castile in The Spanish Tragedy

JAMES P. HAMMERSMITH

"**M**UCH CRITICAL INK has been spilled," it has recently been observed, "in seeking reasons for Hieronimo's murder of Castile," a comment which naturally makes one flinch from the entire question. But it is no less discomfiting to let pass unremarked the conclusion that "the point is precisely that there is *no* reason for it—it is a mad act, an act of cruelty and of waste, and one dramatically calculated to differentiate the justice of nature from earthly or heavenly justice."[1] Fredson Bowers has long ago pointed out that in the classical tradition upon which Kyd drew "revenge is collective as well as personal, in that it extends to all descendants of the injurer and to all his collateral kindred." This is so because "the guiltless must fall with the guilty, for they cannot avoid profiting by the sin, and so have committed the sin too."[2] It is my purpose here to show how Kyd worked through this principle of collective guilt and vengeance in *The Spanish Tragedy*, so that the satisfaction of poetic justice, if not strictly of retributive jus-

1. Charles A. and Elaine S. Hallett, *The Revenger's Madness: A Study of Revenge Tragedy Motifs* (Lincoln, Nebr., 1980), p. 158.
2. Fredson Bowers, *Elizabethan Revenge Tragedy 1587–1642* (Princeton, N.J., 1940), pp. 44,45.

1

tice, is achieved in the death of Castile; it is a corollary purpose to show as well that the author of the additions to the play also understood Kyd's play in these terms and consequently wrote several passages which clarify and reinforce the necessity of the Duke's death.[3]

The movement of the play, even in its original form, is arrested not only by Hieronimo's madness but by his search for the most effective means to redress his wrongs, a search which culminates in his turning to the art of drama, through which he is able to control and to direct to his own uses the otherwise intractable brute facts of reality. The main point of the Painter additions is to heighten the significance of Hieronimo's choice of drama by introducing alternative forms of art from which he might choose, so that his "search for a more complete medium will end when he turns to drama."[4] In one way of looking at it, the play is a play about coping, about discovering the best means of coming to grips with an external reality which, despite one's efforts to control it directly, consistently and frustratingly eludes one's grasp. In this sense, Hieronimo's "quest for justice is made to include a quest for knowledge, and the combination of these two quests broadens the scope of the play by making Hieronimo ask about the relation of appearance to reality and about the nature of reality itself."[5] In nature there are wills opposed to one's own, so that the behavior of forces outside oneself is not only uncontrollable but unpredictable. Hieronimo ultimately comes to terms with the unpredictable elements of nature, the brute reality, by becoming an artist, the consummate dramatic artist— playwright, director, and actor. By drawing the elements of nature into the framework of art, the artist achieves a measure of control over nature through the art which is, to him, predictable and de-

3. The identity of the author of the additions is of no real consequence for my purposes, since I am concerned with the design of the results of those additions no matter who wrote them. The issue has, however, its own interest and significance, and it remains still unresolved. The leading candidates for authorship have been Jonson and Kyd himself, but difficulties stand in the way of accepting either of them unequivocally. For a concise review of the complexities, see Andrew S.Cairncross, ed., *The First Part of Hieronimo* and *The Spanish Tragedy* (Lincoln, Nebr., 1967), pp.xxi–iv; he concludes as I would conclude: "The problem remains baffling."

4. Donna B. Hamilton, "*The Spanish Tragedy*: A Speaking Picture," *English Literary Renaissance*, IV(1974),215.

5. Peter B. Murray, *Thomas Kyd* (New York, 1969), p.22.

termined. The author of the additions, however, brings Hieronimo to this conclusion only after affording him a consideration of the forms of art available to him.

Thus much has long been fairly well recognized, but its application to the task Hieronimo has set himself has not been much noticed, especially as it bears upon the "gratuitous" deaths of the catastrophe. Before turning to Hieronimo's specific problem, however, it is important to observe that the thematic design of the play, not the plot, generates the inevitability of Castile's death. That is, an outline sketch of the action would indicate that Castile's death is altogether adventitious, whereas an exploration of the thematic relationship of art to nature as the play presents it reveals that his demise completes the conceptual design. The main action of *The Spanish Tragedy* treats the aftermath of the war between Spain and Portugal, and in skeleton form the plot is not exceptionally complicated: the initial action following the induction shows us that Lorenzo, the son of the Duke of Castile (Spain), and Horatio, son of the Marshal Hieronimo (Spain), are rivals for the honor of having captured Balthazar, son of the Viceroy of Portugal. Balthazar distinguished himself in the war by dispatching Don Andrea, Horatio's friend and the lover of Bel-imperia, Lorenzo's sister. Bel-imperia and Horatio promptly fall in love in the process of planning vengeance for Andrea's death, while Lorenzo seeks a match between Bel-imperia and Balthazar in order to bring himself closer to the united thrones of Spain and Portugal. Hence, Lorenzo and Balthazar kill Horatio, who represents an obstacle to the match, and Hieronimo ultimately avenges the death of his son by mounting a court play in which he and Bel-imperia transform fiction into reality by stabbing Lorenzo and Balthazar, respectively. Bel-imperia commits suicide on the instant, but Hieronimo delays his intention to do the same until he has explained himself to the courtiers who have witnessed his performance. Then, moments before the conclusion, "*He with a knife stabs the Duke [of Castile] and himself.*" Nothing in the plot, apart from the revenge tradition upon which it is based, prepares for this assault on Castile, but thematically the act consummates the whole design of Hieronimo's plan.

As the plot-sketch indicates, Castile has little do with the action of the middle part of the play, but he is throughout an important character simply by virtue of his being a key figure in the relationships between the other characters: he is the brother to the King of Spain, and he is the father of both Lorenzo and Bel-imperia. He is thus critical to the fortunes of the nation because the King, as it happens, is childless. Castile's role is therefore one of cumulative significance, acquired as the action unfolds around him; hence, before taking up the meaning of his death it is necessary to examine in detail the thematic context of the play in order to determine just how that significance accrues to him.

Kyd's strategy is to build the play around physical places which assume thematic significance by association of ideas. The two focal points of "place" are the Court, associated with art, and the Garden, associated with nature. These loci, though they are radically opposed at the outset of the play, become more and more specifically paralleled as the play progresses. The parallels, however, are generated by the association of symbols within the play rather than by the logic of the plot movement, with the result that, as Peter Murray has it, "the play implies that men must perceive parallel relationships as well as those of cause and effect if they would understand reality and their place in it."[6]

The Garden typically signifies a place of peace, harmony, and generation, and it is there that Horatio and Bel-imperia meet to celebrate their blossoming love in "safety." The Garden as a natural emblem of generation is signaled not only by the references to Flora (II.iv.*25, 26*),[7] but by Horatio's image of the elm and vine: "Nay, then, my arms are large and strong withal: / Thus elms by vines are compass'd, till they fall" (II.iv.*44–45*). The vine is a "symbol of ideal love," and "in most emblems, the elm and vine also connote fertility as the vine supported by the elm produces grapes." Hence, "Kyd's use of the elm and vine topos accentuates the atrocity of Lorenzo's crime,"[8] but it also re-

---

6. Ibid., p.55. See also Donald R. Wineke, "Hieronimo's Garden and 'The Fall of Babylon': Culture and Anarchy in *The Spanish Tragedy,*" in *Aeolian Harps: Essays in Honor of Maurice Browning Cramer,* ed. Donna G. and Douglas C. Fricke (Bowling Green, Ohio, 1976), p.71.

7. The edition I cite throughout is that of Andrew S. Cairncross (see note 3). For additions he provides line numbers in italics, a convention I preserve in my citations.

8. Stephen Watt, "Emblematic Tradition and Audience Response to Kyd's *The Spanish Tragedy,*" *Studies in Iconography,* VI (1980), 100, 101. Wineke points out that the

inforces the point that the perpetuation of bloodlines, as we shall see, is a crucial aspect of both the original crime and of Hieronimo's revenge; it is therefore also a critical feature of Bel-imperia's choice of a husband. Such love as Horatio and Bel-imperia share is supposed to be fruitful, and it is fitting therefore that they meet in the bower, in the arbor of fruit trees.

The Court too is concerned with a kind of love, in this case a political match between Balthazar and Bel-imperia. The primary consideration of this marriage is also its fruit, for, as the King explains, "if by Balthazar she have a son, / He shall enjoy the kingdom after us" (II.iii.*20–21*). Bel-imperia thus forms the nexus binding the natural to the artificial, and the issue is this: if she follows the natural course of love, she aligns herself with Horatio, and her proper place is in the Garden with him; if she follows the dictates of an arranged match the concern of which is not natural affection but political expediency, then she is bound to Balthazar, and her rightful place is in the Court, as she becomes little more than a vehicle to bear an heir to the state which will result from the union of Portugal and Spain. What makes this context radical, and what gives it its particular urgency, is the fact that both the men involved are sole heirs—Horatio is Hieronimo's only son as Balthazar is the Viceroy's; hence, the bloodlines of each family rest with these young men, so that the prospects for the future, for bearing the "fruit" of the "family tree," so to speak, reside in them alone. Not only is there something therefore ultimate in Bel-imperia's choice, but the lives of the men come to signify "life" in a much larger sense—in the sense of hope, in the sense of prosperity, in the sense of heritage, and in the sense of lineal or ancestral continuity.

Horatio and Balthazar are apt representatives of the Garden and the Court, respectively, for, "although Horatio's speech is courtly, it is natural and easy compared with that of Balthazar, whose consistent artificiality in speech and behavior suggests that he is governed by conventions."[9] We have, then, two suitors whose characters are reflections of

---

Garden "is conceived by Hieronimo as a 'sacred bower' and by the young lovers . . . as a garden of love. But it becomes a place of death, the scene of a tragic reversal" (p.66). As I hope to show, however, this reversal of significance is not complete until it is accomplished in the Court as well.

9. Murray, *Thomas Kyd,* p.16.

their attitudes toward the aims of love itself. As Murray adds, Horatio's approach to Bel-imperia "is as physically direct as it well can be" (p. 16), which suggests that he is the exponent of natural impulse, whereas Balthazar, an element in an arranged match of state, approaches her with all the distance, refinement, and artifice of the courtly lover.

In this context, then, Lorenzo's brutal murder of Horatio in the Garden acquires a much broader significance; as Balthazar's champion, Lorenzo becomes an agent of the Court point of view, and when he steps into the bower to assault Horatio he crosses over into the "other realm," the realm of nature, and imposes upon it values inimical to it. Before doing Horatio in, the murderers *"hang him in the arbor,"* and Lorenzo grimly punctuates the proceedings with, "These are the fruits of love" (II.iv.53–55) as he stabs him. The intrusion of Court values, a denial of natural love, has transformed the Garden into a grisly perversion of itself; the tree upon which Horatio hangs bears dead fruit, the fruit of Hieronimo's bloodline, and with him the family's hope for the future is dead as well. This, then, is the context within which Hieronimo himself must work in the rest of the play, and the tension between the Court and Garden pervades the unfolding action and its symbols. Hieronimo's task is to find in the Court the correlative to this murder in the Garden, but not only must he kill the courtly perpetrators of this deed, he must invest his own act of revenge with the same significance as this in the Garden. That is, the metaphorical force of the act is that the fruit of love is death, the ultimate consequence a barren Garden; therefore, Hieronimo must find the means to transform the fruit of the Court's arranged match into death as well, the ultimate consequence a barren Court.

Upon discovering the corpse hung in the arbor, Hieronimo is overcome with grief, and he laments with Isabella the death of the "lovely rose, ill-puck'd before thy time," before the two of them "bear him in from out this cursed place" (II.v.46, 65). The sense of a curse upon this Garden hangs heavily over the rest of the play, but rather than Hieronimo it is Isabella, the other parent, who eventually articulates this curse and acts upon it. She too understands the symbolic significance of what has transpired in the Garden, and her strategy is to act directly upon nature itself, to take her case directly to the Garden. Between Hieronimo's casting of his play (Act IV, scene i) and the performance of it (Act IV, scenes iii-iv) Isabella enters the Garden with a weapon and destroys the arbor. "I will revenge myself upon this place," she vows (IV.ii.*4*), and she mounts an assault upon pure nature, slashing the arbor to pieces and reducing the place of harmony and order to a chaotic rubble. In her rage, she issues a curse of sterility upon the place itself:

> Fruitless forever may this garden be,
> Barren the earth, and blissless whosoever
> Imagines not to keep it unmanur'd'!
>
> (IV.ii.*14–16*)

She is insuring that the Garden bear nothing, that it remain ever perverse, sterile, "fruitless forever," as she herself has been rendered fruitless since the Garden bore her dead son, and she guarantees the efficacy of her curse by cutting off the "branches" and the "loathsome boughs," finally burning "the roots from whence the rest is sprung" (IV.ii.*6, 9*). The parallel to the branches, boughs, and roots of a family is made explicit when she turns the attack upon herself:

> And as I curse this tree from further fruit,
> So shall my womb be cursed for his sake;
> And with this weapon will I wound the breast,
> The hapless breast, that gave Horatio suck.
>
> (IV.ii.*35–38*)

Isabella is herself the tree, and she too has borne the same dead fruit; like the tree, she will be forever barren in death. But she was Horatio's source as well, one of the "roots" out of which was to have prospered finally the "branch" of the family tree, Horatio. The metaphorical relationship is thus complex rather than simple, but there seems to be a clear sense in which the tree in the Garden is likened in her mind to a family tree the source of which is barren and useless, itself dead once the fruit for which the tree existed has fallen.

Isabella's assault on nature—an attack on vitality and fertility—is, as an act of revenge, utterly futile; it is a random, chaotic, impulsive act which fails to accomplish its end and which leaves the real object of revenge, the Court, untouched. "Helpless to destroy those who took her son's life, Isabella takes her revenge against the sources of life in the arbor and herself,"[10] but the metaphorical equation which she draws in her mind, that between the tree and herself, finds no expression in her literal action: she sees only the brute facts, the tree upon which Horatio was hanged, the Garden in which the murder took place, and the mother who bore the son like the tree. "In literal terms, of course, Isabella's assault on the garden as a substitute for revenge against her son's murderers is merely pathetic, the action of a grief-crazed woman frustrated by her inability to obtain justice. But in symbolic terms it stands as a vivid renunciation of a world gone bad."[11] The symbolic renunciation, however, is ineffectual; it has yet to be worked out in the *real* world gone bad, namely, the Court. Although Isabella does proceed to the level of meaning in her own mind, she is unable to translate the significance she understands theoretically into significant action of the same metaphorical order. Instead, she equates herself directly with the tree, understanding both herself and the tree to be creatures of nature which somehow bore lifeless, hopeless fruit, and her response is to attack the natural elements themselves, as though Horatio's death were a freak of perverse nature, an aberration which can be prevented in the future by annihilating the generative features of a nature run amok. But the real sources of Horatio's death are freakish, unnatural elements of a *society* run amok, of a Court the artifice of which obscures its essential perversity. As Wineke adds, the Garden "symbolizes social and moral order. And by reducing it to rubble Isabella converts it from a false mirror to a true one, reflecting the chaos that actually exists in Spain" (p. 74). In the imaginative terms of the reflection, this is exactly the case, but Isabella's action does not cross contexts from the Garden to the Court; the murderers escape her furious attack and remain alive, which is precisely the motive for her continued grief (IV.ii.*29–33*). Indeed, she herself recognizes the futility of her attempt in that respect: "And none but I bestir me—to no end!" (IV.ii.*34*).

Given Isabella's distinctive approach to the matter, we must suppose that she wants Hieronimo to kill the murderers directly, to avenge Horatio's death by the simple expedient of walking up to the actual perpetrators and running them through, just as she marched

10. Ibid., p.140.
11. Wineke, "Hieronimo's Garden," p. 65.

into the Garden and slaughtered the plants. That, to Isabella's way of thinking, would probably be the correlative act in the Court to hers in the Garden; that Hieronimo does not do that seems to be the source of her despair that "none but I bestir me." But Hieronimo instead seeks a form of action which will give significance to his revenge, an act which will present and illuminate the meaning of the parallel between the Garden and the Court. As the Garden is an emblem of nature, so Isabella's impulsive, instinctual action is appropriate to it; as the Court is an emblem of the art of society, so Hieronimo's action through conscious artistry will be appropriate to it. He must meet the artifice on its own terms, transferring the meaning of Isabella's attack on the Garden to an attack on the Court which will bear the same meaning in its particular context. Their actions have the same ends, but Isabella's is misdirected because it is aimed at the wrong context—she does not perceive that Lorenzo and Balthazar crossed contextual lines in effecting their murder in the Garden; she is still seeking Horatio's murderers in the Garden somehow, but Hieronimo recognizes the need to cross contexts again. That is, his revenge must reverse the process of the original crime, crossing from the Garden into the Court; he must take over the meanings inherent in nature and body them forth in art.

"We may assent to the deaths of Balthazar and Lorenzo," Murray allows, "but we cannot feel that the death of the Duke is a just consequence of the murder of Horatio. The Duke is entirely innocent of that crime, and insofar as he is tainted by having fathered the villainous Lorenzo, we must remember that he is also the father of Bel-imperia" (p. 50). Murray contends as well that "the impression that he is an innocent is maintained to the very end" (p. 50), and the Halletts too call Castile "an innocent bystander" (p.158). Of the original crime he is indeed innocent, but justice in the matter entails, as Bowers reminds us, an assessment also of the consequences of the original crime. Castile stands to profit much by the murder of Horatio, and the profit is actually less the result of his having fathered Lorenzo than of his having fathered Bel-imperia, for it is she, after all,who is to be made queen of Spain and Portugal, and, moreover, it is her child, Castile's grandson, who "shall enjoy the kingdom after us." The Duke is therefore to gain exactly that of which Hieronimo has been deprived through the larger significance of the crime, namely, a means to carry on his bloodline so that his lineage shall flourish. Hence, for Hieronimo's revenge to be complete he must act in the Court in such a way that he too may "burn the roots from whence the rest is sprung"; he must transfer Isabella's curse from the Garden to the Court, lopping off the branches and boughs—Lorenzo, Balthazar, and Bel-imperia—but insuring the future sterility as well by destroying the roots—Castile—whence those branches were sprung. That the King and the Viceroy escape the holocaust more emphasizes the hopelessness of their future than diminishes the sense of completion in Hieronimo's action. The King is childless from the outset, and the final line he speaks in the play registers his recognition of the dismal bleakness which lies in. the future hopes of Spain: "I am the next, the nearest, last of all" (IV.iv.*207*). And it is made as plain as can be that the Viceroy has no hope of further children; the depth of his despair when he thinks Balthazar dead early in the play can leave no doubt that the prosperity of his future rests with this only son:

> My breach of faith occasion'd bloody wars;
> Those bloody wars have spent my treasure;
> And with my treasure my people's blood;
> And with their blood, my joy and best beloved,
> My best beloved, my sweet and only son.
>
> (I.iii.*34–38*)

And again his lament just before discovering that Balthazar has actually survived the wars names his son as "the only hope of our successive line" (III.i.*14*). It seems quite clear that there can be no expectation of another "hope" for the continuance of his line.

The desolation in the Court is therefore utter, and Hieronimo leaves the King and the Viceroy alive to contemplate the full significance of the deaths of Lorenzo, Balthazar, and Bel-imperia, just as he himself has had to endure the pain of this same awareness, as the author of the additions makes explicit: "He was my comfort, and his mother's joy, / The very arm that did hold up our house: / Our hopes were stored up in him" (III.xi.*31–33*), a speech which echoes the Viceroy's "my joy and best beloved" and "the only hope of our successive line." The death of the fruitful Castile leaves only the King and the Viceroy, who are, in effect, dead roots already. In this respect, the play is true to its title, for it is the tragedy of Spain, of an entire state laid waste and barren by the necessary expulsion of evil.

Dead sons figure prominently in the play, and the author of the additions was apparently much alert to the larger significance of only sons. Kyd's Senex, who petitions Heironimo for justice, has also had a son murdered, but it is not specifically made clear whether it was an only son or a last son. The Painter, whom the additions' author added evidently to parallel the Senex, has had a son murdered, too, and he explicitly points out, "I had no more but he" (III.xiiA.95). At stake in these murders, then, are not only the present grief and injustice but the hopes for the future as well. If we accept from the design of the play, reinforced by the addition of the Painter, that the Senex's son was very likely intended to have been an only son, too, then we have at the end of the play five fathers whose hopes for the future have been terminated with the deaths of their children—and in this sense all of them are dead, Castile and Hieronimo literally, the Senex, the Painter, and the Viceroy metaphorically.

The Painter's function is similar to Isabella's in that he, too, is a link between the natural and the artificial; through him Hieronimo comes to recognize the futility, dramatically exhibited in Isabella's attack on the Garden, of approaching the Court directly, as though it were a simple element in nature. Rather, the emphasis comes to fall upon Hieronimo's "search for order and relief through artistic responses," not upon his search for a means to act in order to change the conditions of experience.[12] In the Senex Hieronimo is able to see "the lively portrait of my dying self" (III.xiii.85), the exact correlative in nature to the experience of his own condition. But merely observing the condition recur elsewhere in nature is small comfort and less help in redressing his wrongs; the Senex can offer no means to transcend the condition in order to correct it. Through this lively portrait there is no access to the Court that Hieronimo does not already possess; that is, he himself is just such a lively portrait of grief and wrong, and his very presence is a presentation of the portrait to the Court, which, however, has remained throughout the play indifferent to and untouched by his experience and condition.

12. Hamilton, *"The Spanish Tragedy,"* p. 205.

The Painter, on the other hand, can offer another mode of experience through which to present the grief and wrong: art, a mode more
in accord with the experience and condition of the Court itself. Hieronimo begins to test the Painter's capacity for rendering the experience in his art, asking whether he can "paint me a tear, or a wound, a
groan, or a sigh" (III.xiiA.*107–108*) and eventually whether he can
"paint a doleful cry" (l. *122*). The Painter replies, "Seemingly, sir," but
that does not satisfy Hieronimo's needs. Seemingly is not good enough:
"Nay, it should cry," Hieronimo insists. Finally, he catalogues for the
Painter the whole sequence of events in Horatio's death (ll. *138–154*),
events impossible to depict in a single painting—"he is asking not for
interpretive painting, but history in painted form,"[13] and consequently "he keeps pushing the Painter beyond the limits of his art."[14]
He is asking, in short, that the Painter paint the events we ourselves
have just seen in the play, and "the conclusion inevitably emerges that
drama is the form most capable of expressing the human experience
because it is both *poesis* and *pictura,* and has, as well, real sound and
action."[15] In drama the doleful cry can cry in deed. Drama takes over
the elements of nature—the "lively portrait" of the Senex—and gives
to them the organizing framework of art. What an audience sees in
drama "is not to be confused with 'reality'; rather, it is to be perceived
as a determinate construct ordered by principles which are not necessarily those which govern the world of nonartistic experience."[16] But
the material cause of drama is, nevertheless, nature. Still, in drama the
natural actions of human beings are not impulsive or instinctive, as
they can be in nonartistic experience; rather, they are ordered by principles which govern the world of the play. This is, in a sense, what a
courtly society accomplishes as well. It takes the natural man and re-
fines him, placing random, impulsive behavior into a framework of artificial rules—either of etiquette or of law—resulting in the cultured
aspects of civilized living, the most extreme example of which is
Balthazar himself. The whole social mode is a kind of drama. Baltha-

13. Ibid., p.214.
14. Murray, *Thomas Kyd,* p.158.
15. Hamilton, *"The Spanish Tragedy,"* pp.204–205.
16. Barry B. Adams, "The Audiences of *The Spanish Tragedy," JEGP,* XVIII (1969),
227.

zar's stylized behavior in love is as remote from nature as Horatio's direct behavior in love is as close to it as can be and yet remain within the confines of social rules. When it is working properly, the Court provides a framework within which the social and fine arts, refinements of natural impulses, can find their places in daily, civilized life.

By turning to drama for his revenge, then, Hieronimo accomplishes two ends: he finds for his grief a mode of expression which corresponds to the courtly mode of experience, and he is able to incorporate from the Garden Isabella's expression of natural impulses, giving them artistic shape and significance which the Court, in its particular mode, will be more disposed to see and to understand. Isabella's rage and frustration vented in her literal assault on the branches and roots of the tree become transferred to Hieronimo's metaphorical assault on the "branches" and "roots" of the Spanish "family tree." By this means he conveys to the Court his and Isabella's grief over their own lost hopes for the future by making the courtiers experience the same grief through a reversed process: actions which ought to be metaphorical in Hieronimo's play become literal in the Court. The movement in Hieronimo is from nature (the Garden and the Senex) to art (the Painter and the play); the movement in the courtiers is from art (mannered society and metaphorical death) to nature (the devastating chaos of literal death). Through the medium of art the members of the Court are brought exactly to the experience of Hieronimo's own condition—the dramatic portrait becomes, for them, a lively portrait, themselves the embodiment of it. The nexus is Horatio's body, which Hieronimo found literally hanging in the Garden but which he also displays as a part of his art in the Court; we know that Horatio is dead, but in this "spectacle" dramatic death and real death become indistinguishable for the courtiers. Art and nature converge in a powerful display of individual death rendered universal through art:

> See here my show; look on this spectacle!
> Here lay my hope, and here my hope hath end!
> Here lay my heart, and here my heart was slain!
> Here lay my treasure, here my treasure lost!
> Here lay my bliss, and here my bliss bereft!
> But hope, heart, treasure, joy, and bliss,
> All fled, fail'd, died, yea, all decay'd, with this.
>
> (IV.iv.*89–95*)

These lines also echo the Viceroy's laments, lexically and rhetorically, opening the significance of Horatio's death outward to that of the deaths of all children, a point Hieronimo drives home explicitly to the condition of the Spanish Court:

> And grieved I, think you, at this spectacle?
> Speak, Portuguese, whose loss resembles mine:
> If thou canst weep upon thy Balthazar,
> 'Tis like I wail'd for my Horatio.—
>
> (IV.iv.*113–116*)

The spectacle the Court here beholds is identical in its significance to the spectacle Hieronimo beheld in his Garden, a spectacle transferred now from the context of the Garden to the context of the Court through the medium of dramatic art. Consequently, his grief is now theirs as well; as Hamilton puts it, Hieronimo "has presented them with a lively image of his own grief, which in turn is a product of his acquaintance with a cruel universe" (p.216), which is to say that his experience of nature has been projected into the Court through the artistic experience of the play.

The final step in completing the correlative experiences is the death of Castile, as Hieronimo burns the roots of the Court and deprives it of its source of vitality. His last task is to bring home to the courtiers the ultimate effect upon parents of the deaths of their children, an effect he articulates in the commentary upon Horatio's body: "From forth these wounds came breath that gave me life; / They murder'd me that made these fatal marks" (IV.iv.*96–97*). That the death of Castile is thus a necessary and inevitable consequence of the chain of events emerges clearly from the design of the play as a whole and is an aspect emphasized in the additions; the problem with this reading, however, is that so few of Hieronimo's words and actions in the catastrophe point to this conclusion or prepare for the stabbing of the Duke. Indeed, in Kyd's version Hieronimo seems to be satisfied that his revenge is complete long before the assault on Castile: "My guiltless son was by Lorenzo slain, / And by Lorenzo and that Balthazar / Am I at last revenged thoroughly" (IV.iv.*170–172*). And even earlier he claims that with the deaths of Lorenzo and Balthazar "my heart is satisfied" (IV.iv.*129*). On the face of it, these declarations appear to justify the Halletts' conclusion that Hieronimo's revenge is actually completed with the killing of the original murderers (p.159). Still, if the killing of Castile does seem wanton and cruel, its significance is not lost upon the King, who links the death of the Duke with the deaths of the others in the larger scheme of state considerations—"My brother, and the whole succeeding hope / That Spain expected after my decease!" (IV.iv.*202–203*)—before uttering his recognition that he himself is "last of all."

There are, then, two ways of viewing Kyd's conclusion: that Hieronimo himself never explicitly articulates his own understanding of the need for Castile's death may be seen as a flaw in the completion of the design of the play; or Hieronimo's lack of self-awareness may be taken to indicate that the killing of Castile is a desperately wanton, irrational act. That the former, not the latter, is the case seems to have been the understanding of the author of the additions, who gave Hieronimo a speech which brings him much closer to an awareness of the larger meaning of Horatio's death and of the deaths of the other children as they bear upon the Duke:

> You [the Viceroy] had a son, as I take it; and your son
> Should ha' been married to your [Castile's] daughter.
> Ha, was't not so?—You [Castile] had a son, too;
> He was my liege's nephew. He was proud
> And politic; had he lived, he might 'a' come
> To wear the crown of Spain. I think 'twas so—
>
> (IV.iv.*199–204*)

The primary focus of these lines is upon Castile and upon the implications that the original crime had for him. Hieronimo's thought goes beyond the prospect of the marriage between Balthazar and Bel-imperia to encompass as well the possibility that Lorenzo's machinations might not have stopped at that but would have pressed forward until he himself had worn the crown. This line of reasoning increases substantially the likelihood that Castile's descendants would have profited handsomely from the death of Horatio, either through Bel-imperia's state marriage (to which Horatio was an obstacle) or through Lorenzo's policies for his own advancement (in which Horatio was initially a sharer by virtue of his prowess in the wars). Here Hieronimo perceives that both Bel-imperia and Lorenzo represented "branches" by which Castile's line would certainly have flourished in the royal house, and in this speech there is a clear sense of Hieronimo's awareness that Castile stood to profit considerably, in terms of the advancement of his family, by Horatio's death. And that, I take it,is why Hieronimo continues on and makes such a point—directly to Castile—that he himself avenged Horatio upon Lorenzo: " 'Twas I that killed him; look you, this same hard, / 'Twas it that stabb'd his heart—do ye see? this hand— / For one Horatio, if you ever knew him" (IV.iv.*205–207*).

In the revenge tradition the Duke of Castile must not remain alive to enjoy the spoils of the original crime; in some respects, that condition is actually satisfied by the deaths of his children, but through the parallel between the Garden and the Court the design of the play itself imposes another condition which makes the Duke's death necessary and inevitable, namely, that poetic justice be satisfied by depriving the Court of its heritage through the revenge just as Hieronimo was deprived of his heritage through the original crime. By heightening the equivalency between Lorenzo and Horatio the author of the additions made plain the equivalency between Castile and Hieronimo as fathers deprived of vital lineage, a parallel made clear in the Garden image and reinforced in the addition of the Painter scenes. Hieronimo's claim that he himself died in his son thus makes Castile's literal death a legitimate element in the satisfaction of poetic justice.

Multiple Plotting in Friar Bacon and Friar Bungay

CHARLES W. HIEATT

IN THE SECOND CHAPTER of *Some Versions of Pastoral,* William Empson acknowledges Robert Greene's "invention" of the double plot in *Friar Bacon and Friar Bungay* and proceeds to establish the first recorded claim for a rationale for this device. In his view, the independent stories of Friar Bacon and Margaret, the fair maid of Fressingfield, imply an equation of the special powers of the two characters: "the power of beauty is like the power of magic; both are individualist, dangerous, and outside the social order. . . . The process," claims Empson, "is simply that of dramatizing a literary metaphor."[1]

Although briefly stated, and although now some fifty years old, this appraisal of the use of implied cross-reference for developing theme in *Friar Bacon* has endured. Empson is cited in virtually all discussions of the matter, and there has been almost unanimous agreement with him to the present day. I would argue, however, that Empson's view entails a partial and distorted interpretation of the play, partly because his identification of its basic structural components (its "plots") is incomplete. Bacon and Margaret do not become full-fledged protago-

1. William Empson, *Some Versions of Pastoral* (London, 1935), p. 33.

nists until scene ix, and their independent stories of the failure of magic
and beauty to produce desired ends terminate in scene xiv, leaving
substantial segments of action at the beginning and end unaccounted
for. I would also claim that Empson did not identify the full significance of Greene's method. It is true that the play employs what Richard Levin calls "equivalence plots," in which "characters and actions
are drawn from very different aspects of life that must in some sense
be equated on the formal level."[2] But important as it is, equivalence is
only part of a larger issue here. Multiple plots typically establish similarities as a context for introducing significant differences; they depict
persons whose attributes and experiences are roughly alike in order to
develop theme through the use of contrast, and hence the implied
comparisons in *Friar Bacon* will probably do more than simply prove
a literary metaphor. In seeking an accurate interpretation of this most
important of the pre-Shakespearean comedies, one must therefore
reappraise its structure and the significance of its implied comparisons
in an effort to gain an improved understanding of Greene's use of the
multiple plot. But because of the critical position of *Friar Bacon* in
the development of the multiple plot, such understanding will have
the additional benefits of enabling us to gauge the influence of
Greene's use of the device on later playwrights, to perceive how they
succeeded where he failed, and to answer the old question of how and
from whence the device entered English literature.

I

One critic, Peter Mortenson, departs from the Empsonian view
when he claims that *Friar Bacon* has not only two but "four interact-
ing lines of action": the "magic plot," the "garden-of-Eden or pageant
plot," and the two "love plots" involving "Margaret-Edward" and
"Margaret-Lacy."[3] But while this view goes beyond Empson's to take
in the whole of the play, it is faulty on grounds other than his, failing to

2. Richard Levin, *The Multiple Plot in English Renaissance Drama* (Chicago, 1971),
p. 148.
3. Peter Mortenson, "*Friar Bacon and Friar Bungay:* Festive Comedy and 'Three-
Formed Luna,' " *ELR,* II (1973), 196–197.

identify component parts as complete, organic actions within an over-all scheme. To speak of a Margaret-Edward as distinct from a Margaret-Lacy plot is to neglect that the rivalry between Edward and Lacy unites these relationships in a single action that ends when one man gets the girl. To refer to a "magic plot" as a single action is to neglect that Edward and Bacon cause the latter's magical powers to be brought into use for different purposes on entirely separate occasions: Edward employs Bacon as an aid in his campaign to obtain Margaret; but Bacon has his own ambitions, and most of his magical feats are performed without reference to the Prince. In short, Empson's approach to structure in terms of the individual character and his aspirations is appropriate to this play, but the approach requires more precise definition and a wider application than he provides. The Margaret and Bacon stories are properly regarded as separate plots in that they are identifiable sequences focusing on a character's pursuit of his motivating desire. But the motivating desires of Edward and Henry also impel discrete lines of action for substantial periods before being resolved, and one must therefore look to four rather than two character-defined plots.

In effect, these plots are set before us at the very beginning in separate introductions of the four major characters: in the first scene Edward plans to seduce Margaret; in the second Bacon reveals his wish, as Clement says, to "eternise" himself by his art; in the third Margaret falls in love with Lacy; in the fourth Henry looks to his son's marriage with Eleanor of Castille and to the forthcoming contest between Bacon and Vandermast, both of which will bring greater glory to his country. At the same time that they introduce the play's component or static structure, these scenes roughly anticipate its sequential structure (the ordering of the components in fictional time), being themselves part of an initial "movement" dealing with the Edward plot. The governing force in the first eight scenes is the Prince's unbecoming desire for Margaret, the introduced desires of the other characters taking second place as everyone participates chiefly in relation to his efforts to seduce her. Included is a quantity of farce and purely introductory material, but Edward initiates nearly all of the action, sending Lacy as his intercessor to Margaret, enlisting Bacon in the same cause, and incidentally attracting Henry to Oxford where the King expects to join him. Lacy poses a threat to Edward when he wins Margaret's love and causes the plot to assume the shape of a competition between two

men for the same woman. But with the aid of Bacon's magic, Edward
prevents the lovers from marrying, and although Lacy eventually gets
Margaret, he does not take the protagonist's role from the Prince. The
climactic meeting in scene viii begins as a confrontation between rivals, but it ends as a contest between the Prince's worse and better
halves. The meeting provides a dramatic occasion for Edward to recognize the nobility of true love in contrast to his own unworthy, unre-
ciprocated desire: "Is it princely to dissever lovers' leagues, / To part
such friends as glory in their loves?"[4] The focus in the first movement
of the play remains on the Prince, ending only when his exemplary
victory over himself causes him to relinquish control over the lovers
at the close of the scene.

At this point Greene temporarily abandons the technique of presenting a single plot in a relatively unbroken line of action. Released
from Edward's demands at the end of scene viii, Bacon and Margaret
become involved in entirely separate concerns, the one winning the
contest with Vandermast before failing to eternize himself with the
brazen head, the other attracting new rivals in the Suffolk squires,
Lambert and Serlesby, before losing her beloved Lacy. But these two
lines of action are presented together, receiving regularly alternating
treatment from scene ix until they terminate at the end of xiii and the
beginning of xiv, where Bacon and Margaret forgo the world and give
over their protagonist roles. As a result, we are forced to experience
the two plots simultaneously as a second movement in the sequential
structure of the play; and this impression of oneness is increased by a
palpable connection between the two plots that Greene clearly goes
out of his way to establish. It is most unlikely that the squires would
have sons studying under Bacon and thus available at the right time
and place for the second duel in scene xiii, but by bringing in these two
new characters Greene is able to transfer the quarrel over Margaret
from one plot to the other. Bacon's scholars do not compete for Margaret, of course; but she is the basic cause of the controversy between
them as she is between their fathers, and hence the two plots are connected by their identification with the same issue. Greene further en-
hances our impression of oneness by presenting the two duels as if

4. *Friar Bacon and Friar Bungay,* ed. J. A. Lavin (London, 1969), viii.116–117. Quotations in my text are from this New Mermaid edition of the play.

they were occurring in the same place. We watch the Oxford scholars, who with the aid of Bacon's magic glass watch their fathers fighting in Suffolk; in other words, as J. A. Lavin points out, we see all four men on stage together.[5] Consequently, when the scholars fall to fighting and shortly die as a result of their fathers' behavior, we are likely to perceive the two duels as a single action momentarily uniting the separate plots.

In the third and last movement Greene returns to focusing on a single protagonist, the King now being at the center of things and always conspicuously in charge. The greater part of this movement is confined to the last scene, which takes place after the wedding during a momentary pause in what Henry calls "a march in triumph." Necessarily, however, the Henry plot reaches backward to encompass earlier events, in that we have been prepared to understand the present knitting-up of the play's scattered action as a demonstration of the King's control over all of the major characters. Edward acknowledges obedience to his father's choice at the end of the first movement when he says that "I must go see and view my wife" (viii.148), and subsequent glimpses of him with Eleanor in scenes ix and xii assure us of a happy outcome to this dutiful beginning. After some discussion of Margaret in scene xii, Henry tells Lacy to "hie thee to Fressingfield and bring home the lass" (xii.56), and thus the couple's second decision to marry may also be said to prepare for the third movement, being a result of the King's recognition of Margaret as a suitable bride for one of his courtiers and a worthy representative of English beauty in the approaching solemnities. For Bacon the third movement begins in the same scene, when Rafe gives Henry the idea to "send for Friar Bacon to marry" Edward and Eleanor (xii.24). We do not see Bacon deciding to come out of retirement, but he surely does so in response to the King's request that he officiate at the wedding. Henry also causes Bacon to reverse the decision to abandon his art. Toward the end of the last scene, the King asks, "what shall grow from Edward and his queen?" (xvi.41), and Bacon's mystical prediction of the reign of Elizabeth I is thereby made to originate with Henry, again casting him as the ultimate controller of the play's action.

5. Ibid., p. xvii.

II

Considering the four plots without regard to their peculiar sequential structure for the moment, one can see that they are related according to what was to become the usual practice of multiple plotting. Margaret and Bacon are comparable in that they are superior beings whose
unusual powers endow them with a kind of royalty in their respective
spheres. To the maid of Fressingfield, "the flower of all towns," "great
lords have come and pleaded for my love" (iii.66); to the Master of
Brasenose, "the wonder of the world," come a prince, an emperor,
two kings, and distinguished colleagues to petition and admire. But
the aura of superiority that associates Margaret with Bacon also links
them with actual royalty. The glowing descriptions of English Henry
and his legendarily handsome, heroic son, for whom Eleanor, having
but heard of his fame and viewed his picture, dared to "cut through
the seas" (iv.10), complement those of Bacon and Margaret to remind
one of the sort of folktale that brings together impossibly glamorous
individuals from opposite ends of the social spectrum. More specifically, the several plots utilize the comparability of their protagonists in
a series of related actions that treat the theme of the proper use of extraordinary power. The Edward, Bacon, and Margaret plots are arranged in parallel, all three characters being engaged in self-seeking
enterprises in which they plan to benefit from their superiority. Having begun successfully, they are all betrayed by their closest associates,
Edward and Margaret by Lacy, Bacon by his servant Miles. Subse-
quently, all three cause extreme danger to others, are appalled by the
effects of their powers, reconsider their motives, find them wanting,
and renounce their desires, thereby giving up their protagonist roles
and terminating their respective plots.[6] In the Henry plot the theme is
resolved as the King reverses the earlier unsuccessful action, manipulating the three lesser powers so that everyone may realize his personal desire while benefiting the country at large. For Edward, Henry
secures a diplomatic marriage and a wife even more appealing than
Margaret; he allows Margaret to have Lacy, thereby enriching his court

6. Empson observes that the rivalry of Margaret's new suitors is "the repetition of a
situation with new characters to show all its possibilities," but he notes neither pattern
nor meaning in this. See *Some Versions, p. 32.*

with her beauty and virtue; recognizing Bacon's value, Henry finds appropriate employment for his art and for his extraordinary prestige.

The play, then, presents a series of implied analogies that involve the powers not only of magic and beauty (Empson), but of Edward's royalty as well. Furthermore, however "individualist" and "dangerous" they may be, none of these powers is seen as necessarily "outside the social order." On the contrary, the play illustrates how the three subjects' powers are well employed *within* the social order when controlled by the monarch, the only member of society with the authority and wisdom to manage them for the common good. On the other hand, it is essential to see that the several plots do not interrelate solely on the basis of their equivalence; while indicating equivalence, parallel action in *Friar Bacon* also provides a context for indicating critical differences, both in the quality of power and in the behavior of those who wield it. Chief among these differences are those that distinguish the first three plots from the Henry plot to illustrate the proper administration of power. Henry utilizes magic, beauty, and the royal prerogative selflessly and safely, without anyone's betraying him, and his protagonist role will in a sense continue forever. But Greene is equally concerned with employing the multiple plot to discriminate among the powers and the behavior of the King's three subjects, and in this the play's peculiar sequential structure assumes a vital part.

Lavin describes the pattern of alternating locations that I have noted in the second movement of *Friar Bacon* as occurring throughout most of the play: "after the opening scene the shift in action from one group to the other is accompanied by an almost equally regular shift in location, from Oxford to the environs of Fressingfield and back."[7] While this is true, it is important to see that the pattern is organic in the first movement, artificial in the second. Through scene viii, most of the shifting back and forth is necessary for our following a single line of action dominated by Edward and involving competition between him and Lacy for Margaret; if we are to be kept abreast of related developments we must know what is occurring in the separate locations. From scene ix onward, however, the oscillation between Oxford and Fressingfield, while becoming even more regularized, is no longer functional in these terms; indeed, it would be a positive disadvantage to

7. *Friar Bacon*, p. xxiii.

our following the two stories were we not already accustomed to it and acquainted with Margaret and Bacon.

One reason Greene continues this tandem arrangement is that by rendering the Margaret and Bacon plots as a single movement he can create the impression that the Edward plot is occurring all over again, in terms not only of its pattern of alternating locations but also of its connection between the locations. Conceivably, Margaret and Bacon might have retraced Edward's path of self-seeking, betrayal, reconsideration, and renunciation in entirely separate, uninterrupted lines of action. But the malign conjunction of their powers that brought the first movement to its climax cannot recur if the activities of the two characters remain isolated in the "end-to-end" arrangement made necessary by uninterrupted plots; and hence the tandem deployment, which presents the two lines of action within the same time scheme and allows Greene to bring them together under familiar circumstances. As a a result of seeing the lovers together in Bacon's glass, Edward had been drawn from Oxford to Fressingfield in scene viii, poniard in hand, ready to kill Lacy in order to have Margaret for himself. In scene xiii, Margaret's beauty and the glass perspective again act together to provoke hostility between friends, and with the two confrontations seeming to occur in the same place, the climax of the first movement is repeated in recognizable fashion. By imitating the structural pattern as well as the sequence of events of the first movement, Greene is able to show that magic and beauty combine to produce the same peril under Bacon and Margaret's individual control as they had under Edward's, thus indicating the similarity of the powers of all three characters with striking force and economy.

But the two scenes are not precisely alike, of course. The second goes beyond the danger of death to death itself, the point here being that while proving equivalence, the dueling scene also provides one in a series of variations on the first movement that show Margaret and Bacon's situations to be similarly different from Edward's. The Prince acts deliberately and must therefore be blamed for any ill effects of his behavior; but his power, being superior, is controllable, and he is exonerated when he governs his desire, avoids violence, and otherwise shows his kingly potential by anticipating Henry's giving Margaret to Lacy. Margaret and Bacon do not intend to endanger anyone. The harm they cause is inadvertent, and that magic and beauty combine a second time in so unlikely a way implies that these powers have a sinister energy beyond the control of their possessors. Paradoxically, however, the element of repetition could also imply a measure of responsibility on Margaret and Bacon's part, in its suggestion that they should have recognized the uncontrollable nature of their powers as the means and provocation to danger; at the least, it poses the question whether they should have suppressed their powers before there was occasion for further danger, and this question follows naturally from another difference between the Prince and the two commoners that is established at the beginning of the second movement. In scene ix Bacon's playfulness takes on an increasingly arrogant tone as he scornfully out-magics Vandermast and stages impudent pranks on his betters. In scene x Margaret disdains her new conquests, Lambert and Serlesby, in favor of a more worthy lover who will "check the pride of these aspiring squires" (l.98), thus reminding us of her admiration of courtly behavior and her pleasure at being wooed by great lords ("Who but the keeper's lass of Fressingfield?," says Margaret smugly: iii.67). The emphasis on vanity and willingness to benefit from power provides an altered perspective on Margaret and Bacon, while the proximity of the two scenes links them in contrast with Edward to imply that a longer-standing, more ingrained sin than his momentary lapse prevents their achieving the saving self-recognition that he did in scene viii.

But the close similarity of Margaret and Bacon is also the basis for illustrating their differences in greater detail than that used to indicate the differences between them and Edward, and this, too, is facilitated in the second movement, by the telling juxtapositions of the tandem structure. Margaret's prideful attitude is much less pronounced than Bacon's, and even as she scorns the squires she regrets the effect of her Helen-like beauty on them and looks to marriage as a means of canceling it. Under the circumstances she can apparently do nothing to prevent the effects of her power, nor can she be blamed for not having relinquished it sooner since she sees marriage as a means of doing precisely that. Her vanity is still discernible, however; although she no longer relishes the random effects of her beauty, the expectation of capturing a lord of the land encourages her to retain her self-importance and regard any lesser offer as unworthy. Furthermore, her great love for Lacy, which prompts her to curb her power in marriage, and which was seen as ennobling in the first movement, is now seen as a major source of blame. The very strength of her devotion constitutes the lover's classic error of allowing feelings for the beloved to crowd all else from her spiritual horizon. She as much as admits this in the same scene on hearing of Lacy's betrayal: "If Lacy had but loved, heavens, hell, and all, / Could not have wronged the patience of my mind" (x.145–146). Margaret's sin is the overvaluation of worldly things, specifically her beauty and the rewards she expects it to bring; and the inevitable punishment for this sin in a changing world arrives even before her expectations can be realized, though in her case punishment proves to be immediately beneficial when she overcomes her anger, forgives Lacy, rejects his money, and vows to become a nun. Recognizing the instability of the world, Margaret perceives the error of overvaluing it and consequently puts away both her pride and her power to achieve worldly reward.[8]

In the next scene Bacon enters with all the paraphernalia of the sorcerer to restate his expectations of the brazen head and impress upon Miles the importance of watching over it in his absence. Contrasting strongly wilth the previous scene, this one emphasizes that Bacon's is an entirely selfish goal that involves an increase rather than a reduction of power. It also reminds us that, unlike Margaret's, Bacon's is an acquired power whose effect on others, whether intended or not, depends on its active employment. Moreover, a *portion* of Bacon's power *is* outside the social order in that it is inherently evil. Bacon tells Miles that he has "dived into hell / And sought the darkest palaces of fiends" in order to enhance his art (xi.7–8). Like Faustus, he uses black magic to become something greater than God made him, and in so doing he liberates the forces of evil to act against both God and man.[9] A greater,

8. Mortenson sees Margaret's tribulation as a means of justifying her marriage with someone who is her social superior: "like patient Griselda, Margaret is tested before she can be elevated in the new civil order": "Festive Comedy and 'Three-Formed Luna,'" p. 201.

9. Bacon is cast in the tradition of the benevolent magician in literature, and we do not actually see him practicing black magic. But there is no question that he does so, as Frank Towne shows in his article, " 'White Magic' in *Friar Bacon and Friar Bungay?*," *MLN*, LXVII (1952), 9–13.

more stubborn worldliness than Margaret's is further illustrated in this scene when it is Bacon's turn to be deprived of the rewards of power. Let down by Miles, he shows none of her forgiveness and self-deprecation, but flies into a rage, vilifies his servant, and mourns his loss of "fame and honour." Unlike Margaret, he fails to relinquish his power in recognition of the folly of earthly aspiration, with the consequence that his black magic brings further mischief to others and greater punishment to himself.

So far as the deaths of the squires and their sons are concerned, Margaret would thus appear to be entirely blameless. This is borne out in the next scene (xii), where Henry's telling Lacy to retrieve Margaret from Fressingfield *before* the duels signifies that her punishment (her apparent loss of Lacy) has nothing to do with them, and it is also borne out in the dueling scene itself. For one thing, Bacon's active part in the confrontation of the scholars contrasts with Margaret's relatively passive role during the squires' initial confrontation in scene x. For another, Margaret witnesses neither of the duels and, as far as we know, never learns of them, there being no occasion for charging her with them. And for another, Bacon assumes a measure of responsibility for the duels when, having watched the men kill each other, he points to his magic glass and addresses first Bungay, then himself:

> See, Friar, where the fathers both lie dead.
> Bacon, thy magic doth effect this massacre.
> This glass prospective worketh many woes;
> And therefore, seeing these brave lusty brutes,
> These friendly youths, did perish by thine art,
> End all thy magic and thine art at once.
> The poniard that did end the fatal lives
> Shall break the cause efficiat of their woes.
>
> (xiii.74–81)

Bacon clearly blames himself for the sons' deaths, which would not have occurred at this time were it not for his magic, and he blames himself for the fathers' deaths as well. Were he referring only to the sons, as Empson claims,[10] there would be no reason for naming Lambert and Serlesby in the first line and using so large a word as "massa-

10. *Some Versions*, p. 33,

cre" in the second. We are to understand that in blaming his magic for the fathers' deaths Bacon refers to the occasion on which Bungay had attempted to marry Lacy and Margaret in order to "avoid ensuing jars" (vi.135). Bacon had prevented the marriage with his magic, thereby opening the way for the renewed competition for Margaret that Bungay had feared, and hence he correctly sees himself as culpable in the matter of the fathers as well as the sons.

Bacon is not primarily to blame, of course, since those who do the actual fighting are fundamentally responsible for their actions. On the other hand, the quarrel over Margaret is not important in itself; we know nothing about the new rivals, even less about their offspring. Moreover, although secondary, beauty and magic are equally direct— as Bacon says, "efficiat" (efficient)—causes of the four fatalities, and hence the contention in the second movement poses the question of which (if either) of the two characters is the more censurable. The indicated answer is that Margaret is not personally to blame, since she neither by intention nor through negligence provokes the duelists and is apparently unable to stop them. Her sin is to lose sight of eternal values in permitting her beauty to impart an inflated idea of herself and of the joy that it can bring. In her confession, which provides a formal definition of her trespasses, she admits that "beauty used for love is vanity," and that she had "doted more on him [Lacy] than on my God" (xiv.14, 18). In contrast, Bacon stands measurably guilty of the four fatalities, and his active participation bespeaks a state of iniquity more profound and less easily absolved than Margaret's. As the climax of Bacon's story, the dueling scene brings about his self-recognition as one who has allied himself with forces actively hostile to the Almighty. In his confession, which is juxtaposed to Margaret's for our better comparison, Bacon does not refer specifically to the squires and their sons, but to the sin that made the fatalities possible and that includes his desire to alter divine purpose to suit himself: "Bacon must be damned / For using devils to countervail his God" (xiii.96–97). It is true that Bacon's faults are forgiven; on repenting his sins and forgoing his pride and his art, he too is allowed a privileged position and the exercise of the beneficial aspects of his power. But the extremity of his wickedness requires that he continue a downcast penitent at the end of the play, finding joy only in what he foresees of his country's golden future.

III

In the Introduction to his edition of *Friar Bacon,* Lavin names the two most praised qualities of the play: the combination of a multiplicity of literary ingredients to produce "the first successful Romantic Comedy," and the use for the first time in English drama of the "true double-plot (as opposed to a comic sub-plot)."[11] Lavin also calls the play a *mélange,* and this too represents a widely held opinion; in Wolfgang Clemen's words, "Greene's play is built up out of small units, and it can scarcely have presented itself to his mind as a complete whole."[12] Aside from changing "double-plot" to "multiple plot," I would agree with these opinions; but if they are individually just, it is nonetheless mistaken to see the phenomena they describe as isolated from one another. In another article I have demonstrated that Greene in writing the first movement of *Friar Bacon* adapted Lyly's *Campaspe,* popularizing that relatively austere humanist work by exchanging Alexander for Edward, a celebrated English hero, and elevating romantic love from something to be shunned by the exemplary Prince to an ideal that governs his behavior.[13] Greene ensured further popular appeal by introducing an English monarch in the person of Henry, a folk hero in Bacon, and a Cinderella figure in Margaret, and the same thing may be said of his use of physical knockabout, parodic role-playing, and various other Vice-like tricks of Rafe and Miles. To please a larger, more heterogeneous audience than Lyly's, Greene furnished a profusion of elements, including royalty, patriotism, magic, heroically sustained love, farce, and the social promotion of lowborn characters, and this extraordinary diversity required an extraordinary means of control, which he found in his use and development of the multiple plot. Rather than expanding *Campaspe,* Greene retained Lyly's basic plot and built new ones around it, contriving an implied interrelation of character and incident that was intended to unify the finished prod-

---

11. *Friar Bacon,* p. xxi.

12. Wolfgang Clemen, *English Tragedy Before Shakespeare,* trans. T. S. Dorsch (London, 1961), p. 185.

13. Charles Hieatt, "A New Source for *Friar Bacon and Friar Bungay," RES,* XXXII (1981), pp. 185–186.

uct.[14] But the universal complaint of a lack of coherence in *Friar Bacon* rightly denies the success of Greene's endeavor. However firm one's understanding of its unifying techniques, a reading of the play yields the impression of literary ingredients that fail to coalesce, the reasons for this being the hybrid nature of Greene's multiple plotting and the intransigence of the materials he brought to it.

Certain of the techniques of multiple plotting are to be found in rudimentary form in plays that appeared during the medieval and early Tudor periods, but the wide dispersal of these plays in time and an obvious continuity within Greene's own work indicate that he was drawing upon a much more immediate source. After the failure of his first play, *Alphonsus of Aragon,* Greene turned from imitating Marlowe's *Tamburlaine* to the more varied and conventionally popular materials of *Friar Bacon* noted above, and in seeking a way of organizing these materials he naturally turned to prose romance, the genre with which he had started literary life and which he had practiced almost exclusively for some ten years. He had often begun his prose tales with a long sequence that focused on a single character, pursued the adventures of the same or other characters in loosely related stories that branched from the main stem, and accounted for everyone at the end in a brief resolution to the overall narrative. He had also used theme as a kind of skewer on which to transfix his tenuously related series of stories, at times going so far as to parallel the events in one story with those of another. These techniques are used in his best-known tale, *Pandosto,* for example,[15] and they are transferred from the narrative to the dramatic medium with some success in *Friar Bacon.* What is different in *Friar Bacon* is the device of interleaving separate plots within the same fictional time span, thereby achieving the

14. The Henry plot is apparently entirely Greene's; the rest arises from two sources: Lyly's *Campaspe,* from which Greene got the Edward plot, and the anonymous *Famous Historie of Fryer Bacon,* which furnished the Bacon plot and most likely inspired the parallel story of Margaret in the second movement. For additional treatments of sources see P. Z. Round, "Greene's Materials in *Friar Bacon and Friar Bungay,*" *MLR,* XXI (1926), 19–23; Waldo F. McNeir, "Traditional Elements in the Character of Greene's Friar Bacon," *SP,* XLV (1948), 172–179; *Friar Bacon,* pp. xiv–xvi.

15. *Pandosto* has a tripartite structure, its three plots being arranged in parallel and each illustrating passion overcoming reason to produce a false judgment. See Charles Hieatt, "The Function of Structure in *The Winter's Tale,*" *YES,* VIII (1978), 242–243.

means for a proximate, detailed comparison. This is Greene's specific contribution to the art of play-making, and it is regarded as the critical ingredient in the true Elizabethan multiple plot today,[16] a fact that partly explains why the Margaret and Bacon stories have for so long been considered in isolation from the rest of the work.

It is reasonably certain that the idea for this innovation originated within *Friar Bacon* itself. I have described how the first movement utilizes a back-and-forth shifting from Oxford to Fressingfield primarily to keep an audience abreast of separate developments contributing to a single action or plot. With the first movement well in hand, Greene must have noted this pattern as a ready means for repeating the fatal combin: tion of magic and beauty; and although he would have planned from the beginning to interrelate all four plots, at some stage in composition he must also have identified this pattern as an efficient means for achieving a direct, point-by-point comparison of Margaret and Bacon. He may have seen it as a way of keeping a pleasing change of material before his audience as well.[17] While illustrating his genius for organization, however, Greene's use of the tandem method of the second movement with the "end-to-end" method of the first and third movements combines a dramatic with an essentially prose technique to place unrealistic demands on a viewing audience. The multiple plot is not perceivable as a functioning mechanism until the middle of the play, where at the beginning of the second movement one must abruptly come to grips with implied comparisons between the interleaved plots while at the same time recognizing the individual and joint relevance of these to the lengthy Edward plot. Granted, in bringing all three plots into the same plane of reference, the dueling scene provides a

16. Richard Levin notes that even such cross-referential structures as that of the "*Secunda Pastorum* are not really multiple plots in our sense, since their components are almost invariably arranged in serial order and are conceived as successive incidents in a single linear progression, rather than as independent lines of action occurring over the same span of time." See *The Multiple Plot in English Renaissance Drama,* p. 23.

17. The regular alternation of locations and groups of characters may originate in the practice of doubling parts among small troupes of traveling actors. David Bevington refers to the influence of this practice as an "indigenous structural heritage" that was "employed and transformed by Marlowe, Greene, Dekker, and Shakespeare": *From "Mankind" to Marlowe: Growth of Structure in the Popular Drama of Tudor England* (Cambridge, Mass., 1962), p. 199.

relatively obvious point of recognition. But this occurs late in the second movement, and in any case the identification of one system of
parallels and contrasts as existing within a larger, composite system is
more than can be expected of auditors at a play. Such a degree of complexity would be more at home in prose romance, which allows one to
proceed at one's own pace, and in which the cryptic expression of
simple truths was often part of the appeal.

Yet more seriously undermining the operation of the multiple plot
in *Friar Bacon* is a second practice that Greene brought from his earlier
writing: the celebration of conflicting standards of behavior within
the same work. The Margaret and Bacon stories are (like the latter's
source) conventional Morality tales that illustrate the wrong and the
right attitudes toward God as the two protagonists turn from their
worldly ways and conform to His will before it is too late. In the Edward plot romantic expectations are fulfilled; but their fulfillment depends upon a controlling protagonist's turning from a guilty to a virtuous attitude toward love, and thus the story is not strictly a Romance
but a secular Morality supporting romantic principles. The Henry plot
celebrates the ideal of good rulership; but as it leads to a happy ending
for those who, having failed to achieve happiness on their own, place
themselves under his sway, it too is a secular Morality in its illustration
of the correct relationship between the ruler and the ruled.[18] Greene
arranged the four Moral tales in the comic rhythm of stability, confusion, and resolution to all difficulties, and he attempted to impart generic unity with techniques that anticipate those in Shakespeare's so-
called Festive Comedies. As Mortenson has shown, in *Friar Bacon*
"the dramatic pattern of experience . . . moves from release to clarifi-
cation, from holiday to a new vision of everyday, from a denial of limit
and inversion of rule to rediscovered limit and triumph of an inclusive
rule."[19] Other earmarks of Festive Comedy are to be seen in Greene's
use of disguise and in the way the farcical scenes make light of Edward
and Bacon's sins, waylaying our moral judgment and inviting us to
perceive human folly as human nature. The holiday atmosphere is en-

18. J. A. Lavin identifies a number of "Morality elements" in *Friar Bacon* and notes
that they have been generally overlooked, but he does not see the play as a series of
Morality tales. See *Friar Bacon*, pp. xxi, xxix–xxxi.

19. "Festive Comedy and 'Three-Formed Luna,' " p. 195.

hanced by frequent use of words such as "frolic" and "revel," and the play ends with the festive elements of pageantry and a reassuring return to order. But despite evidence of this sort of comedy, the major characters' eventual self-recognition and remorse for their sins contrast sharply with the alliance of seriousness and levity described by Professor Barber. The overridingly ethical view of human error in the four Morality tales displaces the ironic view of Festive Comedy and requires that the characters be fully responsible for their behavior. At the same time, however, competing demands of fidelity to God, to the monarch, and to the principle of romantic love make it impossible for the characters to submit themselves convincingly to any one of these; on the contrary, the presence of three different governing ideas in the same work fragments character and subverts continuity and overall development.

Lacy alters between the first and second movements from a sincere, dedicated lover to a shallow courtier whose euphuistic letter to Margaret proves the inconstancy of the world, and he changes again to a less than fervent lover who, like Edward, woos at the bidding of King Henry. Lacy's poor behavior cannot be explained as a test of Margaret's "constancy" to him (xiv.73), since her clear rejection of all earthly love, and his in particular, means that she would fail such a test. The efforts of critics to make her into a Griselda figure are no more successful than the bad joke about women loving "to die in a man's arms" (xiv.104), which is an attempt by Greene to make light of her unseemly haste in returning to Lacy as part of the holiday atmosphere.[20] Margaret loses nothing in stature when she turns away from the world, but in returning to it she sinks from a noble heroine to a doting, weak-willed girl who cannot resist Lacy's "enchanting face," despite his new take-it-or-leave-it attitude. Characters in *Friar Bacon* may thus be forced to undergo illogical shifts in personality according to the shifting requirements of the three movements through which they pass, and this manifest confusion of purpose is equally damaging to the op-

20. The whole of scene xv, in which one of Bacon's conjured devils discovers the jolly, Vice-like Miles and departs with him on his back, has a similar purpose. Chronologically, this belongs after scene xi—at the end of which Bacon adjures "some fiend or ghost" to haunt Miles and transport him to Hell—and before Bacon renounces his art in scene xiii. But Greene needs it later as a traditional means of making fun of serious matters that will lift the tone of the play in preparation for a festive ending.

eration of the multiple plot. In the first movement Edward appears wickedly self-centered in acting against romantic love, an absolute value that prompts the lovers to offer their lives for each other's safety, but in the second movement the giving over of oneself to romantic love is regarded as a selfish neglect of God. There is no true effort to readjust the first attitude toward love. Margaret adopts the orthodox Christian attitude toward temporal values, but we are not asked to think of her actions in the first movement as anything less than admirable and morally valid. Greene simply makes equal commitments to contradictory standards of ideal behavior, and hence the basis for comparing Edward and Margaret (their equivalent use of power for selfish purposes) is undermined. At the end of the play everyone demonstrates well-beseeming obeisance to Henry, but in turning to him they revert to acting against principles that they had come to regard as inviolate. Having arbitrarily claimed Margaret for himself, Edward surrenders her to Lacy in recognition of the free choice required by romantic love, but he then surrenders his own choice of a mate to his father; having sinfully overvalued the world, Margaret and Bacon see their error and submit their powers entirely to God, only to reemploy them for worldly purposes,[21] and hence the implied assertion that the behavior of all three characters under Henry stands in estimable contrast to their previously sinful ways is logically unsound. We must experience the play's individual movements in isolation from one another, or else acknowledge their inherent contradictions, and in either event the implications of their cross-referential actions are subverted and, in consequence, will probably go unnoticed.

21. Another way of saying this is that Margaret and Bacon should not allow Henry to forgive sins that they have committed against God—though the latter is less blameworthy in this regard. In reverting to his art in the last scene, Bacon uses only natural (white) magic, and in any case such political predictions about Elizabeth's reign were conventional, as Lavin points out: see *Friar Bacon,* xvi.42–62n. It is also worth noting that Bacon's pledge to spend the remnant of his life in "pure devotion" (xiii.107) is not as strong as that of his counterpart in Greene's source, whose fulfilled vow of seclusion until death would have prevented his coming to court, either as priest or magician. See *The Famous Historie of Fryer Bacon* in *English Prose Romances,* ed. Henry Morley (London, 1889), pp. 327–328.

The Worlds of Edward II

SUSAN McCLOSKEY

A MONG MARLOWE'S WORKS for the stage, *Edward II* strikes most critics as the odd play out. For the first and only time, Marlowe
turned to the English chronicles as his source, and found in Edward
not an overreacher, but a hapless victim. To accommodate this unlikely
protagonist, he chastened his usually luxuriant verse and turned away
from spectacle. These puzzling departures from the Marlovian norm
have prompted widely different responses: some critics regard *Edward* as a sign of Marlowe's increasing artistic maturity, others as an
indication of waning power.[1] Even *Edward*'s admirers react ambiva-
lently to the play, praising its power while citing its enervated language, inconsistent characterizations, and incoherent structure—signs,
usually, that a playwright's reach has exceeded his grasp.[2] But while
Edward II warrants these divided responses, Marlowe just as surely
deserves the benefit of the doubt. The play's anomalous characteristics may well be evidence of Marlowe's intentions, rather than unfortunate accidents. And *Edward*'s peculiarities may derive from those
intentions as they are realized in the play.

1. Those who regard the play as an advance over earlier work cite the skill of its con-
struction and the integration of its elements; see, for example, David M. Bevington,
From "Mankind" to Marlowe (Cambridge, Mass., 1962), p. 234. By contrast, Muriel Bradbrook, *Themes and Conventions of Elizabethan Tragedy* (1935; rpt. Cambridge, Eng.,
1973), p. 160, thinks the play overrated even on these scores. Most critics reach Michel
Poirier's conclusion, in *Christopher Marlowe* (London, 1951), that *Edward II* is Marlowe's most skillful play, but that "the author of *Tamburlaine* and *Doctor Faustus* is a
more original writer, a greater genius than that of *Edward II*" (p. 192).

2. Most critics have commented on what Harry Levin, in *The Overreacher: A Study of
Christopher Marlowe* (Cambridge, Mass., 1952), p. 97, calls the "pedestrian stretches"
and "minor harmonies" of Marlowe's verse in the play; J. B. Steane, *Marlowe: A Critical
Study* (Cambridge, Eng., 1964), p. 207, rightly observes that a "hard, colloquial realism"—not lyricism—"is the distinctive 'music' of the play." For criticism of *Edward*'s
inconsistent characters and structural discontinuity, see notes 3 and 9, below.

At the very least, Marlowe's particular choice of Edward's story from those contained in the chronicles suggests his discovery of material suited to his vision, to the ideas he wished to express in dramatic form. In the context of his other plays, this choice indicates a challenge to his former, confident view of the world-altering efficacy of human action. For Edward's is emphatically *not* the career of an astoundingly successful Scythian shepherd or Maltese trader, remaking the world in the image of his dreams. Edward's story illustrates quite the reverse: how circumstances in the world constrain human action and conspire to destroy human agents. Unlike Tamburlaine, that is, Edward does not long proceed, on the strength of his will and in spite of the odds, to be frustrated only by death; unlike Barabas, he does not respond with astonishing nimbleness to a world in flux. He is from the outset what Dido and Faustus become only at the ends of their lives: one to whom things *happen,* the victim of forces he cannot control.

The decision to present a protagonist who illustrates the world's, not his own, controlling influence inevitably sets *Edward II* apart from Marlowe's other plays. Defining that world and dramatizing his characters' relationships to it offered Marlowe an unprecedented challenge. In order to emphasize the world's central role in the action, he presented it not once, but twice. The structure he devised for the action, along with the details of his stagecraft, initially distinguish the world of the first two acts from that of the last three. In the early acts, he shows the world blocking his characters' attempts to realize their intentions in action; in the later acts, by contrast, the world seems indiscriminately to favor each character's purposes, no matter how opposed. After Edward, Isabella, Mortimer, and Kent cross from a hostile world into one more obliging, however, Marlowe reveals that these two different worlds turn on the same axis. Having misunderstood the freedom they were briefly permitted to exercise, his characters—with the single exception of Edward III—end in circumstances even more constrained than those in which they began.

I

Edward II is often criticized for its structural incoherence, the apparent discontinuity between the action of the first two acts and the last three.[3] Marlowe's evident care in articulating this divided structure, however, suggests that it is deliberate, the consequence of choice rather than artistic mishap. He uses it to distinguish the two versions of the play's world, and to express through his characters' experience what it means to live in that world. In order to understand those experiences, we need first to deal with the context in which they occur and the structure through which Marlowe defines it.

Marlowe presents the play's world, in which frustration and failure become the disabling rule, in two stages, by dividing the play and shaping each part according to a different principle. Most of the scenes in Acts I and II are causally connected; the events of one scene directly occasion those of the next. The world defined by the shape of the action is a closed system, in which experience, no matter how various, finally conforms to a single pattern. After Gaveston's death at the opening of Act III, however, Marlowe attenuates the direct connections between the scenes, dramatizing an altogether different causal order. A loosely episodic structure allows him to present a world suddenly vulnerable to external forces. Here, effects spring from causes either immediate or remote, which may or may not in turn become the causes of subsequent action.

In the stalled world of the play's first two acts, a great deal happens at breakneck speed, but little changes.[4] The action quickly reaches an impasse, in part because the characters live in thrall to the past. Edward wants Gaveston to share his life now as he did before his exile; Isabella wants Edward as he was in the first, happy days of their marriage; as the representative of the rebel lords, Mortimer wants to banish Gaveston, thereby securing noble privilege. Because these goals are at odds, the action of the first part becomes a strenuous tug of war,

3. Most of Marlowe's critics address the question of the play's division. See, for example, Levin, *The Overreacher*, p. 98. Steane thinks the break more apparent than real, arguing that Edward's third-act ascendancy over the barons is a "point of equilibrium" holding "the balance between the two main blocs" of the play (p. 205). Robert Fricker, "The Dramatic Structure of *Edward II*," *English Studies*, XXXIV (1953), 214, maintains that "in spite of a certain weakness of the link between the two movements of the action, the play forms an organic whole." My own view is that the play breaks radically at Gaveston's death, achieving coherence only in its final moments.

4. On the play's rapid pace, see Toby Robertson's remarks in "Directing *Edward II*" (an interview conducted by John Russell Brown), *TDR*, VIII (Summer 1964), 174–183.

in which the contestants can hope to gain only momentary advantage. Edward briefly attains his end with Gaveston's return at the play's outset, only to encounter the lords' fierce opposition. The lords in turn gain their objective with Gaveston's banishment, only to retreat when Isabella pleads for his recall. The second act duplicates the pattern of the first. Edward and Gaveston are again reunited; Isabella is again estranged from Edward; the lords again oppose the minion's influence. In such a world, where action immediately triggers counteraction, progress is unlikely.

Indeed, Marlowe structures individual scenes to forestall real progress or change, thereby emphasizing the closed system in which his characters act. For instance, the events of Act I, scene iv, the longest scene in the play, advance the action hardly at all. Marlowe constructs the scene as a neatly connected series of exchanges, in which A acts on B, who then acts on C. At the scene's outset, the lords force Edward to banish Gaveston; Edward then forces Isabella to plead for Gaveston's recall. Isabella performs this feat in the middle of the scene when she persuades Mortimer to intercede with his peers. Her success brings about her reconciliation to Edward, who then reconciles himself to his lords. This deliberate symmetry counters the scene's apparent movement from confrontation to harmony. What takes place after Isabella persuades Mortimer to relent merely undoes what was done before, returning all the runners in this curious relay race back to the starting line. Isabella regains Edward's love by restoring to him her rival; the lords abandon the hard-won political advantage of Gaveston's exile by calling him home. The considerable energy these characters devote to change, in other words, merely re-creates the circumstances that made change so desirable.

By the end of Act II, it is plain that if the characters' baffled energies are ever to issue in action unchecked by counteraction, some new element must emerge to break the stalemate. That element is Warwick's "wit and policie," which results in Gaveston's murder at the opening of Act III.[5] Providing the release of violence for pent-up energies, Warwick's act redefines in an instant the ground rules of the first two acts, changing what had seemed an unalterable state of affairs. Unable to ab-

---

5. *Edward II*, II.v.96, *The Complete Plays of Christopher Marlowe*, ed. Fredson Bowers (Cambridge, Eng., 1973), vol. 2. All citations refer to this edition.

sorb these new energies, the first version of the play's world shatters, along with the structure through which Marlowe defined it. Immediately after the event, he relaxes the tight connections between scenes characteristic of the play's first part. The episodic structure of the last three acts presents a world governed by chance, rather than by direct causality. Random events coincide for no apparent reason, and the consequences of actions become increasingly difficult to foresee.

Act III, scene ii, the first scene after Gaveston's murder, demonstrates the world's new dispensation. In it, Marlowe moves us as far as possible from the clockwork regularity of Act I, scene iv. Characters whom we have never seen before, such as Spencer Senior, drop into the action unannounced, illustrating that the closed system of the first part is now open to forces from without. While Edward awaits news of Gaveston's fate, other messengers arrive at the camp, bringing more news than the distracted king had bargained for. Isabella reports the French king's seizure of Normandy, Arundel the news of Gaveston's death, and an anonymous messenger word of the barons' opposition to Spencer Junior's elevation. These messengers arrive in no particular order; that they have news to bring at the same moment is entirely a matter of chance. The outcome of the scene's chaotic action is even less predictable: Edward, who began the scene listless with fear, ends by rousing his forces to battle.

The rest of Act III and all of Act IV elaborate this scene's elements of surprise and coincidence, and the world's altered circumstances. Quite against the odds, Edward's army—which seems entirely to consist of Spencer Senior's "band of bowmen and of pikes, / Browne bils, and targetiers, foure hundred strong" (III.i.36–37)—overcomes the combined might of the rebel lords. Whim undercuts Edward's tardy subscription to the dictates of political expediency: when the rebels' brutal suppression seems likeliest to restore order to his kingdom, he exempts Mortimer from death. Traitors crop up from unexpected quarters: Edward's own brother aids Mortimer's escape from prison and flight to France; Edward's own wife finds in Sir John of Henolt an unexpected friend and a fresh supply of rebel troops. When Isabella's army defeats Edward, forcing his flight, the sheerest coincidence leads to his capture. A Mower outside the abbey at Neath just happens to recognize under Edward's disguise the figure of the king and the lucky means to rich reward.

II

Marlowe reinforces the distinction between the world of the first two acts and that of the last three through the details of staging contained in the text's explicit and implicit stage directions. The indications of time and place, of sound effects, costuming, and the use of the playing space characteristic of the first two acts suddenly change after Gaveston's murder. The pattern and specificity of these details suggest Marlowe's plan that the play's two-part structure be both visible and audible in performance.

References in the text, for instance, indicate that all the scenes in Acts I and II occur in the daytime. After Gaveston's death in Act III, darkness descends over nearly half the scenes—a fact indicated in Marlowe's theater both by spoken reference and by the presence onstage of torches. The sun with which Edward early associates himself first fades, then disappears. "The day growes old" as he is led captive from the abbey (IV.vii.85); "dayes bright beames dooth vanish fast away" during the scene of his abdication (V.i.69). His humiliation at Matrevis's and Gurney's hands, and Kent's failed attempt to rescue him, occur in the depths of night. In his last scene, he is drawn from his dungeon's darkness by the unfamiliar gleam of a torch, and calls out to Lightborn to discover "what light is that?" (V.v.42).

Marlowe uses place as well as time of day to underscore the difference between the play-world's two versions. The first two acts infrequently shift locale, an index, even on a bare stage, of the world's stalemated condition.[6] Act I takes place in Edward's court. After a brief scene at Gloucester's residence, Act II moves to Tynemouth. In the third act, however, Marlowe sets this static world in motion. Act III moves from the forest where Gaveston is murdered, to Edward's camp, to the battlefield. Act IV begins in England, shifts to France, and returns to Edward's court, the battlefield, and the abbey at Neath. In the last act, such restless movement becomes a part of Edward's tor-

6. Glynne Wickham, *"Exeunt to the Cave:* Notes on the Staging of Marlowe's Plays," *TDR,* VIII (Summer 1964), 184–194, reviews Marlowe's theatrical resources, arguing persuasively for his access to emblematic scenic elements. Use of such elements would make even clearer the contrast between the stasis of Acts I and II and the frequent shifts of place in Acts III-V.

ture, as Matrevis and Gurney carry out Mortimer's order to move the king "still from place to place by night" (V.ii.59).

The only sounds we hear until the end of the second act are those of human voices, usually expressing either anger or grief—a range of feeling as narrowly restricted as the variety of the action or the characters' mobility. Even the few moments of joyful exchange quickly collapse into acrimony. Edward and Gaveston, for instance, conclude their ecstatic first reunion by abusing the Bishop of Coventry. In the last three acts, however, Marlowe extends the range of speech. We begin to hear new voices and unfamiliar accents: young Prince Edward's, old Spencer's, the abbot's, those of the Frenchman Levune and the Welshman, Rice ap Howell. To these human voices, Marlowe adds in the play's second half sounds unheard before the outbreak of civil war at the close of Act II: drums and fifes to signal battles waged offstage; trumpet blasts to mark the new king's coronation; relentless drumbeats to keep the captive Edward from sleep. Marlowe reserves for Edward's death scene the play's most harrowing sound: the anguished scream that penetrates the castle's walls, and alarms the surrounding town.

The text also encourages the use of costuming to underscore the difference between the play's two worlds. Through the first two acts, characters should be dressed in mourning, for Edward I's, then for Gloucester's death.[7] Such uniformly sober clothing lends point to Mortimer's distaste for Gaveston's "short Italian hooded cloake, / Larded with pearle" (I.iv.413–414). With the outbreak of civil war, in II.iv, black robes yield to the silvers and grays of chain mail and armor, in which the belligerents remain until the close of Act IV. Marlowe clearly intends Edward's dress in the play's second half to express his swift descent from regal eminence. At the end of Act IV, Edward exchanges battle gear for a monk's robes. In Act V, after surrendering his crown, he is stripped of the signs not only of kingship, but of manhood as well. We last see him as a man of sorrows, his beard shaven off, his robes reduced to filthy tatters. Just as clothing marks the stages of Edward's decline, it might suggest the countering pattern of his enemies' rise. Mortimer should assume in the play's second half the in-

7. Because the text prescribes only a few details of costuming, my remarks here are necessarily more tentative than those dealing with other indicators of staging. Another interpretation of the play would dictate different choices.

creasingly splendid clothing of England's would-be king; Isabella should abandon her mourning for costumes to express the womanliness Edward so consistently disdained.

All these details of stagecraft indicate that the tensions beneath the uneasily calm, uniform, and static surface of the play's first part explode in the second—in the fitful gleam of torchlight, the impression of motion, the sounds of battle, the sight of a king in rags. These distinctions in turn warrant an equally distinctive use of the stage in each of the play's two parts. All scenes in Acts I and II, for instance, can easily be played on the platform; the script requires entrances and exits only through the doorways at stage left and right. Acts III through V, by contrast, invite the use of the entire stage. The above might be used for the beginning of Edward's abdication scene and for Edward III's coronation. Matrevis, Gurney, and Lightborn might enter through the curtained recess when Mortimer summons them to their grim work. A downstage trap could function as Edward's dungeon prison.[8] Such expanded use of the playing space, like the other features of Marlowe's dramaturgy, signals the characters' changing relation to the world Marlowe changes around them.

III

Marlowe relies on *Edward*'s different theatrical styles and divided structure to define the play-world's two versions. Through the experience of the characters who inhabit this world, he expresses the play's thematic focus on human constraint and limitation, the delusion of power and efficacy. In the first two acts, his characters appear to be tightly contained within their roles. Edward is the ineffectual king, Isabella the distressed wife, Mortimer the aggrieved lord. After Gaveston's death, those who were once bent on recovering the past break free of it altogether, and work feverishly to revise their identities and destinies. The playboy king becomes a warrior, then a victim; Isabella, an adultress and accomplice in regicide; Mortimer, an unprincipled ty-

---

8. Wickham's reconstruction of the kind of stage on which Marlowe's plays were probably first presented would support most of the staging suggestions I make in this paragraph. His evidence precludes only the use of a trapdoor in the platform.

rant. Having achieved these startling metamorphoses, however, they discover in their "new" selves the crippling limitations of the old. No better able now than before to bend circumstances to their desires, they are finally crushed by the world they had hoped to reshape.

Marlowe has often been criticized for these "inconsistent" characters, as if he had aimed for consistency and missed.[9] One of the play's curious features, however, is that Marlowe offers so few characters even the opportunity for self-contradiction. He splits his dramatis personae, like the play, into two parts.[10] Few both witness and survive the pivotal event of Gaveston's murder, which divides the world of the early acts from that of the last. Many characters, such as Mortimer Senior, the Bishop of Coventry, and Margaret, appear only in the early scenes. Once Gaveston and the lords responsible for his death have been killed in Act III, new characters—such as Spencer Senior, Prince Edward, Sir John, and a second group of lords—emerge to fill their places. Of the minor characters, only Spencer Junior and Baldock successfully cross the third act's divide, making Gaveston's death the occasion of their rise. But even their success is fleeting; both die at the close of Act IV.

By so distinguishing the characters of the play's early acts from those of the later, Marlowe focuses our attention on the only four who remain active throughout the play: Edward, Isabella, Kent, and Mortimer. Of these, Kent is the least complex. His allegiance, not his character, changes in the course of the play. In presenting Edward, Isabella, and Mortimer, however, Marlowe works out detailed variations on the pattern of experience central to his play's meaning: the discovery that, in this play's world, the exercise of freedom after long constraint results only in more severe forms of bondage.

Marlowe begins to articulate this pattern in Act III, as Edward, Isabella, and Mortimer once again watch old circumstances replicate themselves in new forms. Having believed through the play's early acts that their fates depended on Gaveston's, all three learn immedi-

9. An instance of this common complaint is Bradbrook, *Elizabethan Tragedy*, p. 161. F. P. Wilson, *Marlowe and the Early Shakespeare* (Oxford, 1953), pp. 95-98, sensibly counters the charge.

10. Bevington, *From "Mankind" to Marlowe*, pp. 236–239, discusses Marlowe's handling of the dramatis personae, his practical and artistic solution to the problem of a large number of roles for a small number of actors.

ately after his death how greatly they were mistaken. Edward quickly replaces Gaveston with Spencer Junior; Isabella again fails to recapture Edward's love; Mortimer's contempt for sycophants merely finds a new target. The energies each one had devoted to securing Gaveston's presence or absence, life or death, suddenly appear to have been woefully misdirected.

The act of murdering Gaveston, however, turns out to have made a greater difference than the fact of Gaveston's death. By releasing the pent-up energies of the first two acts, Warwick's violent deed gives to the few who survive its bloody atonement a heady sense of their power to *act,* to do what they had formerly only dreamed of doing. In the aftermath of Gaveston's death, Edward, Isabella, and Mortimer quite literally set themselves in motion, as if shaking off the lethargy induced by their former restraint. Edward rouses himself to victorious battle, and becomes in his execution of the rebels the brutal king he had threatened to be. Isabella promptly departs for France, assumes leadership of the rebel forces, and becomes Mortimer's lover. Mortimer breaks out of prison, and abandons his principled opposition to Edward in order to seize power for himself. Each behaves, in other words, as if Gaveston's death had sealed the past from the present. What each one was has little or no bearing on what each might be in a world newly defined by an apparently limitless freedom to act.

Isabella's experience in the second half of the play, however, reveals the delusory nature of this newfound freedom. As with Edward and Mortimer, her sense of power and possibility in a chance-governed world expands only to contract. Once she breaks free of her role as Edward's wife, she tries on a series of new identities, all of which offer only fleeting or partial satisfaction. She seeks her brother's aid in France, only to discover a sister's role as ungrateful as a wife's. Empowered by a fresh supply of rebel troops, she then acts for a time as England's war-faring queen. But Mortimer soon checks her power. She "dare[s] not speake a worde," for instance, when Mortimer orders Kent's execution (V.iv.96). Mortimer's preoccupation with power—the limiting trap into which *he* has fallen—vitiates even her role as his mistress. When she tells him that he is "the life of *Isabell,*" he responds by wondering whether Edward has surrendered his crown (V.ii.15). What she creates with Mortimer is merely a criminal version of her relationship with Edward. Believing herself free, Edward's loving wife ends as his murderer's lover. When her son later sends her to prison as an accomplice in Edward II's murder, even her role of last resort fails her:"He hath forgotten me, stay, I am his mother" (V.vi.90).

This description of Isabella's futile exertions might elicit the sympathetic response that her actual presentation in *Edward* does nothing to provoke. With Isabella as with all his characters, Marlowe resists our impulse toward empathy. Indeed, a less appealing cast of characters would be hard to find. Unable to translate intention into action, the best become jealous of their prerogatives, disposed to complaint and dejection. Wishing to block Mortimer's rise to power, for instance, Kent is reduced to an unedifying tug of war over Prince Edward's guardianship. In the next scene, he reacts to his bungled attempt to rescue his brother as if failure had been his sole expectation. On the other hand, the few who succeed in matching desire to deed do so at the expense of their own humanity. By the time Mortimer has secured his power by cowing Isabella and the prince, and murdering Kent and Edward, he aptly compares himself to "*Ioves* huge tree," impervious to attack, incapable of feeling (V.vi.11).

Only late in the play does Marlowe's purpose in preventing our engagement with these characters become clear. Act V focuses on Edward as he traces the pattern of Isabella's experience. Like her, he witnesses the rapid contraction of what had seemed boundless possibility, and undergoes the alienation from self that it entails. In Edward's case, however, Marlowe images this pattern in visible, physical terms—as the experience of a human body subjected to torment. At Mortimer's order, Edward is hurried from one stronghold to the next, denied food and drink, bathed in channel water, and forcibly shaved. The king who had once claimed an entire country as his own is finally confined to the stench, filth, and darkness of Killingworth's dungeon, where the guards pound a drum to keep him from sleep. There he experiences the slow erosion of his human faculties: "My mindes distempered, and my bodies numde, / And whether I have limmes or no, I know not" (V.v. 64–65). This self-estrangement renders Edward at once more affectingly human and oddly anonymous—no longer Edward, but a representative victim. For this victim, Marlowe finally enlists the feelings he has restrained in his audience, by presenting onstage the death scene reported in Holinshed. We last see Edward clinging to what remains of his life while Matrevis and Gurney crush him between a mattress and a table. Then, in a brutal parody of sexual intercourse, Lightborn thrusts a red-hot spit into Edward's anus.

The action of the play reaches its climax in this image of almost unimaginable cruelty, of men behaving as beasts toward a man so reduced that only his articulate agony marks him as human. When Edward's words yield to a harrowing scream and then silence, Marlowe ends the exploration he began in Act I. In Kent's and Isabella's disintegration, in Mortimer's secondhand cruelty, in the sight and sound of Edward's physical suffering, he has shown us what the world of the play's second part enables the survivors of the first to become. It is difficult to imagine a vision bleaker than this, a more despairing estimate of human possibility.

IV

Marlowe's staging of Edward's death is an instance of risk-taking characteristic of the play and the playwright. A scene from which recovery seems unlikely, it threatens to turn what follows into the merest coda, the winding up of an action that has already exhausted its energies and meanings. But by the close of *Edward II,* Marlowe has taken another sort of risk, which the final scene must justify. His rendering of *Edward's* world—through a divided structure, different styles of presentation, and characters who revise their identities midway through the play—threatens the play's coherence. The division he has so carefully maintained requires that the closing moments perform a doubly complex task: they must not only resolve the action, but locate the two versions of the play's world within *Edward's* final thematic design.

Marlowe sets about both tasks at once, presenting a scene significantly without precedent in the play, except by way of contrast. Immediately after Mortimer hears of Edward II's murder, young Edward III enters to punish him and Isabella for their crime. Surrounded by the lords whose "aide and succour" he has sought, he is no longer the uncertain boy of previous scenes (V.vi.21). In one swift movement, he brings Mortimer and Isabella to grief in the world they have failed, like

Kent and Edward II before them, to reshape. His speed is as striking as his self-possession. Earlier scenes have accustomed us to a different rhythm and result—of characters forming their intentions in one scene, attempting to enact them in another, and confronting their failure in a third. Edward III, by contrast, no sooner thinks than acts, no sooner acts than succeeds. His apparently effortless command, made all the more striking by his youth, seems to be Marlowe's point.

As his conduct in the scene suggests, Edward III escapes his elders' difficulty in realizing intention in action by defining his relationship to his world in terms different from theirs. Choosing to accept his world's constraints, and to act with rather than against its grain, he quietly defies his elders' precedents. More confidently than his mother, whose identity shattered in her efforts to forge it, he identifies himself as Edward's son and England's king, and acts to punish his father's murderers. Unlike his father, who confused freedom with the unchecked exercise of personal whim, Edward subdues his inclinations to the demands of justice by sending his beloved mother to the Tower. Unlike Mortimer, who understood freedom as absolute power, Edward honors the law's dictates in dealing with Mortimer's crime. As he beats the play's earlier estimate of the odds against anyone's success, he reveals the truth that his elders first misunderstood and then denied: that the world, to be commanded, must be obeyed. In enacting that truth, he draws together the two opposed versions of the play's world in his rejection of both. They become, in effect, the single thesis to which he and the order he creates are the unexpected antithesis.

The play that began as an exploration of failure and inefficacy draws to its close with an instance of successful action. Edward III seems to present an alternative to the play's bleak vision, proof that the world is not always opposed to human purposes, nor bent on destroying its would-be masters. No sooner does Marlowe offer this optimistic view, however, than he takes pains to qualify it. The final moment of *Edward II* emphasizes the fragility of Edward III's order, the powerful forces it must hold in check. The last ten lines focus our attention on a single image, in which Marlowe recapitulates the play. While Edward mourns over his father's hearse, he puts on funeral robes like those Edward II had worn at the play's outset. With one hand, the young king holds aloft the grisly offering of Mortimer's head, recalling the earlier beheadings of Gaveston and the rebel lords. In his other hand, he grasps the ambiguous warrant for Edward II's death, which he presented earlier in the scene as evidence of Mortimer's crime.[11] Like the other properties, this letter looks back across the play, to the opening scene of Gaveston reading Edward II's invitation to return to England and *"share the kingdom with* [his] *deerest friend"* (I.i.2.). That promise of delight disrupted the kingdom, and initiated the chain of events leading to Gaveston's murder. Mortimer's letter leads through a second act of bloodshed to an order that has met only its first challenge. This image of Edward III, in gathering together the play's most powerful symbols of death, grief, violence, love, and hatred, recalls the passions barely contained in the play's first part and out of control in the second. Having brought them all to a single moment of delicate poise, Edward III fittingly greets his triumph with tears.

11. There is good theatrical, although no specific textual, support for the letter's appearance in the last image. Edward III produces it at l. 44; the text offers him no convenient means to dispose of it. A director worth his or her title would hesitate, I hope, to have Edward stuff so significant a prop into his pocket.

"What resting place is this?" Aspects of Time and Place in Doctor Faustus (1616)

ROY T. ERIKSEN

HOW THEN," Sir Philip Sidney asks, "shall we set forth a story, which containeth both many places and times?"[1] The problem of how to lodge a unified dramatic action within a coherent loco-temporal setting vexed *cinquecento* poets and commentators on Aristotle's *Poetics* to an equal degree.[2] The question is likely to have crossed Marlowe's mind, too, judging by his decision in the Prologue to *Doctor Faustus* to give to his account of the protagonist's multifarious career a distinct form: "the form of *Faustus* fortunes, good or bad" (l. 9). A plausible interpretation of this phrase is that Faustus's actions and their outcome ("fortunes") are combined into *one* unified, but deliberately ambiguous, shape. The situation is complicated, however, by the fact that by traditional standards Marlowe seems to have failed to fashion such a desired unity. The extremely episodic nature of *Doctor Faustus* contrasts manifestly with anything we readily associate with the pseudo-Aristotelian ideal of "the three unities." If we take into account the play's time scheme of twenty-four years, its insistent mix of serious and comic materials, and the protagonist's extensive travels, *Doctor Faustus* appears at first (to continue in Sidney's phrase) to be "inartificially imagined" with regard to action, time, and place.[3] This

1. *An Apology for Poetry,* ed. Geoffrey Sheppard (London, 1973), pp. 134–135.
2. T. W. Baldwin's massive effort to prove that Elizabethan dramatists, and Shakespeare in particular, were influenced by Italian theoreticians along these lines has not won general acceptance; see *Shakespeare's Five-Act Structure: Shakespeare's Early Plays on the Background of Renaissance Theories of Five-Act Structure from 1470* (Urbana, Ill., 1947). John M. Steadman takes a more viable route in his cogently argued study *Epic and Tragic Structure in Paradise Lost* (Chicago and London, 1976).
3. *An Apology for Poetry,* p. 134.

should not induce us to dismiss the play in a common textbook phrase as "dramatically a mess"[4] or to compare its structure to the "barrenness of the fifteenth-century *Everyman.*"[5] I recognize that it at times is very uneven in terms of stylistic finish, but this should not prevent us from appreciating the sophistication that characterizes its loco-temporal organization. Goethe's famous verdict on the play alerts us to some degree of conscious planning ("Wie gross ist alles angelegt!"[6]), but without providing any clues to the kind of planning intended. My principal concern here is Marlowe's treatment of time and place and its implications for our reading. The play's loco-temporal structures reveal, I propose, that he worked with a plan of hitherto unsuspected integration and symbolic import, when reshaping the episodes of *The English Faust Book (EFB).*

I have chosen a *topomorphical* approach to the text, which—as I define it—is a type of rhetorical analysis involving the study of the distribution of topoi, or textual segments devoted to specific topoi, with particular reference to their structure (morphe) and the interrelationships they form.[7] The method applies to individual segments within a work (speeches, scenes, stanzas), to groups of such segments (acts, cantos, books), or again to the whole configuration of segments within a work. Figurative rhetoric is essential to the method, because various rhetorical repetitions often signpost important stages in the texts and establish links between parts. In the Renaissance, poets could combine an overall plan with highly patterned segments, such elaborate units then usually holding an especially important episode or theme. By allocating an important episode to an acknowledged central or "trium-

4. Robert Barnard, *A Short History of English Literature* (Oslo and Lund, 1984), p. 18.

5. J. B. Steane, *Marlowe: A Critical Study* (Cambridge, Eng., 1964), p. 156; see also his views in *The Complete Works of Christopher Marlowe* (Harmondsworth and Baltimore, 1969), pp. 261–262.

6. Henry Crabb Robinson, *On Books and Their Writers,* ed. Edith J. Morley, 3 vols. (London, 1938), I, 369.

7. I discuss this method in greater detail in my dissertation, *"The Forme of Faustus Fortunes": Structural and Thematic Analysis of Christopher Marlowe's The Tragedie of Doctor Faustus, 1616* (Oslo, 1983), esp. pp. xiv–xxv and 328–334. See also the article entitled "The Topomorphical Approach" by Maren-Sofie Röstvig in the forthcoming *Spenser Encyclopedia,* and my "Two into One: The Unity of Gascoigne's Companion Poems," *SP,* LXXX, no. 3 (Summer 1984), 275–298.

phal"[8] position within a structural arrangement and by foregrounding its surface texture, poets tried to communicate their thematic emphases. The existence in the Renaissance of such compositional techniques is a well-documented fact as far as poetry is concerned; for drama the situation is less settled, but in recent years successful attempts have been made to apply concepts of rhetorical structure in analyses of Elizabethan drama.[9] Mark Rose suggests in *Shakespearean Design* that the structural arrangements of Shakespeare's plays are essentially rhetorical and provides several analyses in support of his thesis.[10] "Rhetorical terminology," he argues, "could provide us with a precise language for describing many aspects of Shakespearean dramaturgy."[11] As I hope to show, the same applies in the case of *Doctor Faustus.*

The example of Torquato Tasso (1544–1595) must serve as my point of departure. Tasso was the last great voice of the Italian Renaissance, a poet, dramatist, and leading exponent of literary *maniera.*[12] His pastoral drama *Aminta* (1573) and *La Gerusalemme liberata* (1581) won him fame at home and abroad, and Tasso's influence on Spenser and English poets in general is well-known.[13] But what makes him interesting in this context is his preference for and practice of *unità mista,* a concept of mixed unity which entails combining different materials into a whole characterized by thematic and formal coherence. Marlowe's phrase "the forme of *Faustus* fortunes, good or bad" suggests a similar concern.

8. See Alastair Fowler's pioneering study of the literary triumph, *Triumphal Forms: Structural Patterns in Elizabethan Poetry* (Cambridge, Eng., 1970).

9. See Mark Rose, *Shakespearean Design* (Cambridge, Mass., 1972); William Leigh Godshalk, *Patterning in Shakespearean Drama* (The Hague, 1973); Keith Brown, "Form and Cause Conjoin'd, *Hamlet* and Shakespeare's Workshop," *SS,* XXVI (1973), 11–20; Ernest Schanzer, "The Structural Pattern of *The Winter's Tale,*" *REL,* V (1964), 72–82; and Leonard H. Frey, "Antithetical Balance in the Opening and Closing of *Doctor Faustus,*" *MLQ,* XXIV (1963), 350–353.

10. See Rose's analyses of *A Midsummer's Night's Dream* and *The Winter's Tale* in *Shakespearean Design,* pp. 17–21.

11. *Shakespearean Design,* p. 60.

12. Maria Rika Maniates, *Mannerism in Italian Music and Culture,* 1530–1630 (Chapel Hill, N.C., 1979).

13. See the account by C. P. Brand, *Torquato Tasso* (Cambridge, Eng., 1965), pp. 226–307.

Mixed unity, Tasso claims, is achieved when applying the "rules . . . that are absolutely necessary in every poem, . . . in epic, tragedy, or comedy."[14] These are rules that turn the finished poem into a little world characterized by the same harmonious disposition of parts as God's own poem, the world. For "the art of composing a poem resembles the plan of the universe, which is composed of contraries, as that of music is."[15] Symmetry and antithesis are the basic elements in Tasso's message, and recent criticism has established that he followed his own recommendations.[16] But the fact that the chiastic arrangement of cantos in *La Gerusalemme liberata* is an intended structural expression of divine order should not obscure the equally interesting observation that the poem's formal patterns are akin to those discussed by Rose in *Shakespearean Design*. As Tasso's reference to the genres reveals, we here have a set of compositional rules of a general kind.

Tasso experiments with various structural designs, but nowhere does he succeed quite so well as in his centrally placed procession to Mount Olivet (XI.i–xix).[17] The effectful distribution of topoi and locotemporal references within the sequence makes this "spettacolo santo" particularly well suited to illustrate the compositional method Marlowe deploys in *Doctor Faustus*. Tasso's nineteen *ottave* present the crucial act which symbolizes the marriage between heaven and earth, when the crusaders receive absolution and once again become God's "squadre pie" (XI.xv.7). The sequence thus harbors the epic's most important *peripeteia,* or "mutamento di fortuna," as Tasso puts

14. Torquato Tasso, *Discorsi dell'arte poetica* [1587] *e Discorsi del poema eroico* [1594], ed Lugi Poma (Bari, 1964), p. 28. The quotation is from the *Discorsi dell'arte poetica.*

15. *Discourses on the Heroic Poem,* trans. Mariella Cavalchini and Irene Samuel (Oxford, 1973), p. 76.

16. Andrew Fichter observes that "taken canto by canto the *Liberata* unfolds in a pattern of bilateral, or mirror symmetry," "Tasso's Epic of Deliverance," *PMLA,* XCIII, no. 2 (1978), p. 268, while Röstvig argues that "the relationship between the two halves of Tasso's epic resembles that between the Old Testament and the New," "Canto Structure in Tasso and Spenser," *SSt,* I (1980), 182.

17. When we count the stanzas, the first nineteen stanzas of Canto Eleven (out of a total of twenty cantos) are preceded by 949 stanzas and followed by 949 stanzas. The stanza total is 1899 (949 + 19 + 949). I have used *La Gerusalemme liberata,* ed. Lanfranco Caretti (Turin, 1971).

it. He also refers to the episode containing this reversal as "the knot" (il nodo) of the plot; and in *La Gerusalemme liberata* he turns this nodal episode into a miniature "epic" in itself. It incorporates different materials, such as narrative, dialogue, songs, and prayers, at the same time as its thematic movement parallels that of the poem as a whole. Its structure is as follows:

Figure 1

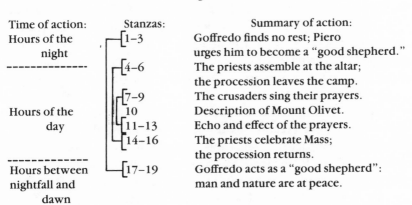

Time of action:	Stanzas:	Summary of action:
Hours of the night	1–3	Goffredo finds no rest; Piero urges him to become a "good shepherd."
	4–6	The priests assemble at the altar; the procession leaves the camp.
	7–9	The crusaders sing their prayers.
Hours of the day	10	Description of Mount Olivet.
	11–13	Echo and effect of the prayers.
	14–16	The priests celebrate Mass; the procession returns.
Hours between nightfall and dawn	17–19	Goffredo acts as a "good shepherd": man and nature are at peace.

We first note how Tasso arranges his stanzas in groups of three—"in triplicati giri" (XI.vii.6)—and in accordance with the mannerist ideal of the *figura serpentinata*.[18] The action begins in darkness and on a note of despair, and moves on to a spiritual confrontation (i.e., the hymn and the profanations) between Christians and pagans (XI.vii–ix and xi–xiii) won by the former when they resolutely go on to celebrate Mass. The sequence ends on a note of hope and reconciliation before "la matutina tromba" (XI.xix.7) announces the new day. Thus Tasso creates a frame of darkness (i–iii and xvii–xix) around the stanzas (iv–xvi) reporting the daytime events. The crusaders' movements through the landscape—from the camp up to the top of the sacred mountain and back again—quite naturally strengthen the orderliness of the sequence. Time can here be said to be both linear and cyclical: the events proceed steadily from the hours of the night to the point at which the succeeding night turns into dawn and the diurnal cycle is completed.

18. John Shearman, *Mannerism* (London, 1967), pp. 81–83.

Tasso thus depicts a temporal flux within a well-defined unit of time. The spiritual dimension of a time-span of twenty-four hours is explained by theologians: drawing on scriptual exegesis, they saw the diurnal cycle as an image of eternity and Providence.[19] Tasso, who uses typology in many episodes of *La Gerusalemme liberata*,[20] further elaborates on this dimension by introducing allusions to scriptural figures and events, such as the Good Shepherd and the Last Supper,[21] into the sequence. Tasso in this manner invests his ceremonial centerpiece with a spiritual and structural design similar to that found in the whole epic, where he arranges his episodes in place and time in accordance with what he saw as the providential plan in human affairs. As we shall see, *Doctor Faustus* reveals evidence of a similar compositional technique, but the differences are as great as the similarities.

When turning to Marlowe's tragedy, we first notice the exploitation of a richly suggestive temporal frame which comprises the whole of the play. Marlowe creates this frame by combining the twenty-four years of the compact with what appears to be the twenty-four hours of an idealized day. He achieves this by substantially altering and synopsizing the time references found in the source. Max Bluestone has commented on the way in which Marlowe's "adaptation compresses time, manipulates it freely to generate conflict," and to imitate the flow of real time.[22] Thus in the *EFB* Faustus raises the devil at "nine or ten of the clocke in the night" (ii) and dies "between twelve and one a clock at midnight" (lxiii).[23] In the play, however, the compact is made to begin and end at midnight. Several references to that time (ll. 323–324, 416, and 2040) make sure that nobody misses this point. The fact that

19. Pietro Bongo, *Mysticae numeorum significatione liber* (1584–1585 and many subsequent editions). I have used the edition printed in Bergamo in 1591. Bongo's summary of the numerological exegesis of the Fathers concerning the number twenty-four ("De Numero XXIV") occurs on pp. 443–449.

20. See Thomas P. Roche, Jr., "Tasso's Enchanted Woods," in *Literary Uses of Typology*, ed. Earl Miner (Princeton, N.J., 1977), pp. 49–77.

21. Goffredo functions as a shepherd to his flock, and in obvious imitation of Christ as the Good Shepherd, when he assembles his closest men "a mensa" (XI.xvi.7). The parallel is strengthened by the image of "il pastore" in XI.xix.4. The noctural *mensa* itself, where Goffredo presides, alludes to the Last Supper.

22. Max Bluestone, *From Story to Stage* (The Hague, 1974), p. 252.

23. P. F., *The English Faust Book of 1592 (EFB)*, ed. H. Logeman (Ghent and Amsterdam, 1900). References are to chapters.

Marlowe invents a final soliloquy that is made to coincide with the last hour of the compact further illustrates how Marlowe consciously aligns a textual unit with a well-defined unit of time. Thus the initial thirty lines of the soliloquy are made to parallel its first thirty minutes. When the second half-hour is considerably shorter linewise than the first, this seems designed to produce an effect of accelerated time and shock. The speech provides a good example of "the idea of speed."[24] The important point here, however, is the insistent presence of the clock which increases our awareness of the passage of time and its symbolic overtones.

The twenty-four years which begin and end at midnight in Faustus's study constitute the play's inner temporal frame. A second and outer frame comprises the whole of the action. This second frame lacks the very precise numerical parallel scheme of twenty-four years which accompanies the inner frame, but in this instance, too, Marlowe elaborates upon a reference to time in the prose source, where the students discover Faustus's dead body "when it was day" (lxiii). In *Doctor Faustus* these students reappear in the guise of Faustus's scholar friends, who were at "supper" (l. 1872) with him the evening before. Whereas it is certain that the discovery scene is set during the early hours of the day, no direct references in the first soliloquy of the play tell us when its action takes place. The only precise clue exists in the dinner mentioned toward the end of Faustus's conference with Valdes and Cornelius, a meal which evidently still goes on when Wagner confronts the Puritan scholars in the next scene (ll. 185 and 189–224). As dinner may be served at noon or in the evening and because Valdes and Cornelius are to instruct Faustus "after meate" (l. 185), it is more reasonable to assume that the trio's first conference took place before noon. This interpretation is supported by D. E. Dreher's discovery that "the second biblical verse Faustus cites [i.e., 1 John 1:23] was used in the Order for Morning Prayer."[25] We note, moreover, that the Valdes-Cornelius material, the dinner, like the reference to a supper toward the end of the play, are all Marlowe's own inventions, so that it

24. Annabel M. Patterson, *Hermogenes and the Renaissance: Seven Ideas of Style* (Princeton, N.J., 1972), discusses the figure of speed (pp. 163–175).

25. D. E. Dreher, "*Si pecasse negamus*: Marlowe's *Faustus* and *The Book of Common Prayer*," *N&Q*, XXX, no. 2 (April 1983), p. 144.

is very likely that the references to dinner and supper have been included to signpost different stages in the play's idealized time-scheme. In the reference to the sumptuous supper Faustus arranges the evening before he dies, I believe we witness an instance of ironic contrast with the Last Supper, where Christ gathered his disciples for a final meal.[26] This, we observe, is a different use of a typological superstructure also used by Tasso. In *Doctor Faustus* the purpose of this parellelism is to expose the protagonist to irony, not to elevate him to a Christ-figure.

The effect of this double arrangement is that an outer frame of daylight—a symbolic day indicated by the movement from morning to morning—encloses an inner circle of darkness, which again encompasses the twenty-four years of the compact, as indicated below:

Figure 2

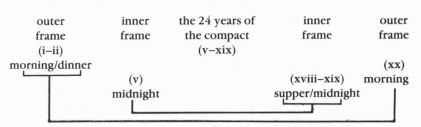

Marlowe's skillful insertion of a scheme of twenty-four years within that of an idealized day suggests that he may have been familiar with the Aristotelian argument that a tragedy should be contained within a *periodos,* or "a revolution of the sun."[27] We remember in this context that in *Tamburlaine, Part One,* V.ii.169, Marlowe refers to the unity of a poem made up of many parts as "one poem's period."[28] It is just possible that the Latin epigram printed after the Epilogue to *Doctor Faustus,* "*Terminat hora diem, terminat auctor opus*" ("the hour ends the day, the author ends his work") points to a similar alignment of temporal and literary structure. We have seen that Tasso deployed a

26. For a similar example, see W. L. Godshalk, *Patterning in Shakespearean Drama,* p. 125.

27. *Poetics* 1449b, 12–13, in *Introduction to Aristotle,* ed. Richard McKeon (New York, 1947), VI, 630.

28. I quote from *Tamburlaine the Great, Parts I and II,* ed. John D. Jump (Lincoln, Neb., 1967).

comparable technique in the centerpiece of *La Gerusalemme liberata,* and Shakespeare, so Rose has told us, was to employ a similar temporal design in *A Midsummer Night's Dream.* In addition to the "double frame" constituted by the distribution of settings in that play, Shakespeare creates a frame of light (the bright Athens panels) around its "moonlit centre-piece."[29] Thus the scenes set in daylight and inside the city walls encompass the chaotic scences set in the dark forest.

As was the case in Tasso's *Gerusalemme,* XI.i–xix, the diurnal cycle enclosing Faustus's twenty-four years in sin assumes particular significance in relation to scriptural exegesis. In *Doctor Faustus,* however, the references to the religious superstructure are made more textually prominent, and they may also have been visualized on stage by the use of artificial lighting.[30] Pietro Bongo, the sixteenth-century authority on the meanings attributed to numbers in Scripture, explains that the sun's orbit around the world—Ptolemaic style—illustrates how Christ in his capacity as *sol aeternus* illuminates and teaches us how to avoid the darkness of sin.[31] Marlowe draws on much the same symbolism, when he lets Faustus beg "faire natures eyes . . . rise againe and make / Perpetuall day" (ll. 2041–2042). The quest for "[p]erpetual day" is nothing but a prayer to Christ, the sun of eternal light, who briefly appears to Faustus in a vision which colors the heavens as red as a blood-red dawn (ll. 2049–2953 and 1463 A). The Good Angel has already given Faustus a glimpse of the circle of light in which he no longer can participate:

> *Faustus,* behold,
> In what resplendent glory thou hadst set
> In yonder throne, like those bright shining Saints,
> And triumphed ouer hell, that hast thou lost.
>
>   (ll. 2011–2014)

The "bright shining Saints" are the twenty-four elders of Revelation 4:2–4, whom Bongo cites in support of the orthodox interpretation that the diurnal cycle of twenty-four hours is a type of Christ's reign

29. *Shakespearean Design,* pp. 18–19.
30. See Keith Brown's challenging essay in favor of artificial lighting in the Elizabethan public theaters, "More Light, More Light," *EIC,* XXXIV, no. 1 (January 1984), 1–13.
31. *Mysticae numerorum significatione liber,* p. 448.

over the blessed. A similar argument is adduced by Augustine in the treatise *De libero arbitrio* III.xxv.265,[32] but I do not imply that Marlowe must have studied this treatise or Bongo's *Mysticae numerorum significatione liber* in one of its many editions. More important than the question of influence is the discovery that the temporal structure emerging in *Doctor Faustus* qualifies our reading of the play. What Tasso uses positively as a symbolic representation of Providence in human affairs, Marlowe in the vision of the elders turns into an instrument of torture. The circle of light in Marlowe's play encloses Faustus in every sense of the word and suggests a predestined universe rather than a providentially planned one. Thus the man who bid "[d]iuinitie adeiw" is dead by the time the final scene establishes the frame of light. In that scene Faustus's death is likened to the creation of light and order out of darkness and confusion: "such a dreadfull night was neuer seene,/ Since first the worlds creation did begin" (ll. 2095–2096). In this manner Marlowe ensures that his tragedy's external structure reflects its meaning, so that "structural emphases" indeed become "moral emphases."[33]

One obvious effect of the play's double temporal structure is that it contributes to the play's unity. This does not apply to the disputed central sequences, because the references to time are found exclusively in the second chorus and in the serious scenes located at the beginning and the end. Time may nevertheless be said to have a unifying effect even here, when the way in which the time schemes of the two different strands of action interact is considered. As far as the scenes of the main plot are concerned, their time scheme is seriously broken at two points, marked in the text by the second (ll. 776–801) and third (930–947 A) chorus, introducing respectively the papal and imperial sequences. The third chorus is not in the B-text. The disrupted time

32. I refer to Augustine's interpretation of Psalm 83:11: "Far better is one day in thy courts than thousands." To Augustine, "one day . . . represents the immutability of eternity," while "thousands of days" signify "a life of innumerable years spent in delight"; *On Free Choice of the Will,* ed. Anna S. Benjamin and L. H. Hackstaff (New York, 1964), p. 265.

Emrys Jones argues more generally that the number twenty-four represents "completeness," adding that Faustus's twenty-four years pass like twenty-four hours"; *Scenic Form in Shakespeare* (Oxford, 1971), p. 51.

33. Alastair Fowler, *Triumphal Forms,* p. 201.

scheme of the main plot follows logically from its episodic nature and its claim to represent a period of twenty-four years. When we turn to the comic subplot, however, it is apparent that its time scheme is quite different. True enough, it runs parallel to that of the main plot during the play's first seven scenes, where serious and comic scenes alternate.[34] But whereas the second chorus breaks up the time scheme of the preceding serious scenes and prepares for an entirely new line of action in the imperial sequence, the scene with Robin and Dick and the stolen cup (ll. 1128–1180) continues where the two left off in their previous scene (ll. 743–775). In that scene they were headed for a tavern (l. 771), while here they leave a Vintner's (l. 1130). Finally, when these comic characters reappear in the ducal sequence (ll. 1578–1636 and 1675–1768), together with the Horsecourser whom we first met in the comic scene following the imperial sequence (ll. 1523–1545), we perceive how Marlowe makes the action of the comic scenes continuous, so that an illusion of temporal continuity is created. The construed impression of continuity counteracts the disruption of the action in the main plot. Those who have seen the B-text acted will know that this theatrical illusion functions quite well on stage. Also we note that the main plot and the subplot are brought closer in the Horsecourser scene and that they are completely integrated in the scenes at the ducal court, after which the comic characters disappear from the play.

The comic subplot in *Doctor Faustus* indubitably fulfills the basic functions of an Elizabethan subplot: it both fills out the play and provides an alternative line of action which mirrors and comments upon the main plot. In addition to this, it mitigates the disruptive effects of having the play's middle section divided into three only loosely connected episodes. To visualize the interaction of the different story lines and temporal schemes, the two plots may suitably be represented by two parallel curves: the longer broken curve (A–A) represents the main plot and the shorter unbroken curve (B–B) represents the subplot. The letters C_1 and C_2 mark the places where the first and the second internal choruses interrupt the action.

34. For the argument that tragedy and comedy alternate during the first seven scenes and that no scene is missing, see "A Marlowe Discovery: The 'Lost' Clownage-scene in *The Tragedy of Doctor Faustus* (1616)," *ES* (1981), LXII, no. 2, 49–58.

Figure 3

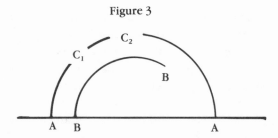

Here we can get an impression of how the comic action bridges or pulls together the play at the points where there are great gaps in the story line of the main plot. That this may partly have been the intention behind the insertion of comic scenes after scene xi and scene xiv is suggested by the fact that there are no comic scenes after scene xvii, that is, when the action of the main plot once again is continuous.

Shakespeare's superb handling of comedy and the mirror plot in *King Lear* can be used to illustrate what Marlowe attempts to achieve in *Doctor Faustus*. In Shakespeare's play the Lear-and-daughters plot and the Gloucester-and-sons plot are fully integrated in the third act. This is also the point of the action when Lear goes mad and the sympathetic Fool disappears from the play. He is no longer needed now that Lear functions as his own fool and at the same time assumes his Fool's wisdom. Similarly, the two plots in *Doctor Faustus* mingle in the ducal sequence. The clowns take over for a few moments, before Faustus silences and sends them off for the rest of the play. This occurs at a point when the action has become infested with farce and cheap spectacle, and it can be argued that Faustus's tragic folly has been fully established. The situation, then, is partly analogous in *King Lear* and *Doctor Faustus*, but the double chronology in the latter constitutes an added difficulty.[35] The different time schemes of Marlowe's plots tend to annul time, establishing a feeling of omnitemporality and spatiality. Marlowe's use of spatial form probably arises from his innovatory attempt to communicate "the extratemporal quality" of his vision of tragedy.[36] The spatiality is further emphasized by Marlowe's handling of "the places" of action.

35. The classical example of "double time" is, of course, *Othello*; for a discussion and critique of the theory applied to *Othello*, see *Scenic Form in Shakespeare*, pp. 55–63.

36. Joseph Frank, *The Widening Gyre: Crisis and Mastery in Modern Literature* (Bloomington and London, 1968), p. 58. I quote from a comment on Proust.

The distribution of settings in *Doctor Faustus* at first glance seems to lack the overall plan which informs Marlowe's treatment of time, that is, if we except that the action is circular in the sense that it begins and ends in Faustus's study. However, the clue to "the platforme of in-uention"[37] which has systematized the play's "places" of action lies not so much in the main plot, I propose, as in its political overplot. This I take to be the struggle between Pope and Emperor, which natu-rally reflects England's conflict with Spain and the papacy, as well as the domestic rivalry between Protestants and Catholics. The clue to this political overplot and its implications for Faustus's "fortunes" lies in the main settings of the action. When considering the setting, it does not matter whether a scene is set in Faustus's study or a tavern at Wittenberg, so long as the basic setting remains the same. This way of looking upon the play produces five main locations for the action which establish the following sevenfold symmetrical pattern:

Figure 4

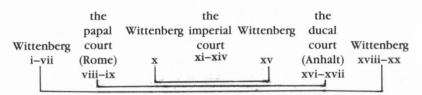

As shown in the figure above, the scenes are grouped in blocks set at the same locations. Thus the first seven scenes, which alternate be-tween tragedy and comedy, are set at various locales at Wittenberg. The next two scenes (viii–ix) report Faustus's activities at the papal court in Rome, and in the comic scene (x) with Robin and Dick which follows we are back at Wittenberg. The four scenes of the imperial se-quence contain no information about the precise location, but they are set at Charles V's court (xi–xii) and a grove near by (xiii–xiv), while the following scene (xv) where Faustus gulls the Horsecourser is set in

37. George Gascoigne's revealing term occurs in *Certayne notes of Instruction con-cerning the making of verse*, § 6, in *The Posies of George Gascoigne* (London, 1575), sig. T iii (r). That Gascoigne composed his works after such "platformes," we see in Alfred Anderau's study, *George Gascoignes The Adventures of Master F. J.: Analyse und Inter-pretation* (Bern, 1966). Anderau points out that the novel's "narrative phrases" are ar-ranged according to a pattern of recessed symmetry (pp. 78 ff.).

Wittenberg or in its immediate environs. This is suggested by the sudden reappearance of Wagner at the beginning of the scene (ll. 1569–1576) and perhaps also by the Carter's account in the next scene of his unfortunate encounter with the magician: "As I was going to / *Wittenberge* t'other day, with a loade of Hay" (ll. 1600–1601). We also note that scenes xvi and xvii are set at a ducal court and that no precise indications of location are given, although Anhalt (or Vanholt as the A- and B-texts render it), which is close to Wittenberg, may have been intended. The last three scenes (xviii–xx) are set at Wittenberg, so that the action has come full circle, as it were.

The imperial sequence occupies the middle, or "triumphal," position within this symmetrical arrangement of settings, but this position does not, as was the case in Tasso's epic, coincide with the play's textual center. Such pointillist effects are not to be expected in a stage play which combines verse and prose. When considering the central placing of the sequence in terms of setting, it is perhaps appropriate that in it Marlowe lets Faustus stage a sophisticated pageant with music in celebration of his and Emperor Charles's victory over Pope Hadrian, the pageant being the Alexander dumb show (ll. 1293–1318). This allegorico-historical mime shows how one of Charles's alleged "progenitors" defeats the effeminate Persian ruler Darius, who thus becomes a parallel to Charles's degenerate opponent.[38] It can thus be argued that the sequence featuring Charles holds the center as an effect of conscious political decorum and in accordance with the conventions of "triumphal" literature. For in the same manner as Tasso placed his procession in honor of God at the center of the *Gerusalemme,* Marlowe would seem to pay lip service to Elizabethan political iconography. Frances Yates has pointed out "the importance of the Catholic imperial symbolism of Charles V . . . for the Protestant Tudors."[39] But the conflict in the play between Pope and Emperor functions on several levels. If we first consider the political aspects, it appears that Marlowe when adapting the source has taken great care to build up a hierarchy of power in the central sequences. It is important in this context to remember Max Bluestone's observation, that "the

38. Darius's reputation as an effeminate and inadequate ruler was emblematic; see Sir Walter Raleigh, *The History of the World,* ed. C. A. Patrides (London, 1971), IV.ii.4 (p. 258).

39. Frances A. Yates, *Astraea: The Imperial Theme in the Sixteenth Century* (London, 1975), p. 57.

playwright's retension, omission, and modification of source elements . . . imply intention."⁴⁰ Marlowe invents new material for the
papal sequence, freely adapting an episode from Foxe's *Actes and Mon-
umentes,* and thus completely changes the insignificant incident
found in the source. The alterations are all geared to the purpose of
contrasting Pope and Emperor: The Pope is given the name Hadrian,
the name of a great Roman Emperor, and he sends Bruno, the pro-im-
perial pope, to the dungeons in Castel Sant'Angelo, formerly Emperor
Hadrian's mausoleum, now the Pope's stronghold. Hadrian is furthermore equipped with a "progenitour" called Alexander (l. 945), a detail that evidently is intended to parallel Charles's claim that Alexander
the Great is c ne of his progenitors. We note, too, that Faustus wishes
to visit "the Monuments" (l. 851) of Rome's imperial past before he
deals with the Pope. These details are Marlowe's own inventions and
seem especially designed to discredit the Pope as a political and spiritual ruler.

When turning to the imperial sequence, we first observe that no specific locale is given for the Emperor's Court, even though Innsbruck is
mentioned in the source. The reason for this omission is obvious. Neither that small Austrian town, nor the two imperial capitals in Germany (Augsburg and Regensburg), could compete with the status of
the Rome of emperors and popes, so a neutral setting was chosen. Further evidence of a political hierarchy in the play is seen in the epithet
"Saxon" attributed to the antipope and the appearance of the Duke of
Saxony in the entourage of Charles in scene xii. As a result of these
conspicuous references to the political, historical, and geographical
setting of the three central sequences, the play's highest ranking figure
is placed at the sovereign center while his treacherous (Hadrian) and
loyal (Anhalt) vassals occupy the flanking sequences. Little attention
has so far been paid to this aspect of the play, and even if it may be
more valuable in the context of a discussion about the integrity of the
B-text,⁴¹ it is interesting to note that Marlowe refers to the political

40. *From Story to Stage,* p. 255.

41. For my defense of the integrity of the B-text, see my dissertation, *The Forme of
Faustus Fortunes* (forthcoming as a book). As a general point, I believe it is difficult to
argue that a play that is so highly planned as the B-text is partly the product of a later
hack-writer. The central sequences are too well integrated for that to be the case. Prob-
ability-tested stylistic analyses point uniformly to Marlowe as the author of the disputed
scenes; *The Forme of Faustus Fortunes,* pp. 257–315 and 441–443.

overplot right from the beginning. In view of the fact that the political conflict in this form is wholly absent in the source, it is noticeable that Marlowe should foreground Faustus's desire "to chase the Prince of *Parma* from our Land" (l. 120).

The Pope is obviously important in relation to Faustus, since Faustus frees a reputed heretic from his prisons, but Hadrian is not quite so important as G. K. Hunter has suggested. Hunter, who rightly sees Faustus's antipapal activities "as political action of some kind" discusses the play's structure in terms of the pyramidal pattern of *de casibus* tragedy, arguing that "Faustus starts his descent through the world from the highest point, in Rome."[42] The political hierarchy built into the play's settings argues against this hypothesis, and so does indeed the rise-fall pattern of its protagonist's sociopolitical fortunes. His career is still very much in the ascendant when Faustus triumphs over the false Vicar of Christ. If we were to pinpoint the exact peak in his public career, it would have to be at the end of scene xii, when Charles rewards Faustus's "high desert" and proclaims him vice-regent of Germany (ll. 1367–1370). This often neglected appointment explains why Faustus can call the knights who attack him in the following scene "[t]raytors" (l. 1447). They do in fact attack their own sovereign. At this stage, however, it must be emphasized that the appointment and the courtly splendor of the twelfth scene are deceptive. When we take a close look at the scene's most striking event, the Alexander dumb show, it is apparent that it is a brittle theatrical illusion which fades when confronted with reality. Faustus is forced to admit that "[t]hese are but shadowes, not substantiall" (l. 1304), and Charles's rapture when seeing the Paramour's wart amply illustrates that he is a foolish character. A ruler who feels more joy at this sight than at the acquisition of "another Monarchie" (l. 1317) cannot be taken seriously. Thus it appears that Marlowe creates a hierarchy of power at the center of *Doctor Faustus* for the sole purpose of debunking it. He is fully aware of the function of a triumphal centerpiece, but he bends the device to fit his own purpose. The device which Tasso employed to vindicate an orthodox, Christian world order, Marlowe uses to undermine the image of authority. We are reminded of Harry

42. G. K. Hunter, "Five-Act Structure in *Doctor Faustus,*" *TDR,* VIII (1964), 83.

Levin's shrewd observation that the "unquestionably weak" middle of the play "corresponds to the anticlimax of the parable."[43]

The antiauthoritarian philosophy behind this ironic centerpiece clearly bears upon the theme as a whole. In the same manner as Faustus rebels against Pope Hadrian, the unjust spiritual ruler in the papal sequence, he challenges God in the main plot. Hadrian's belief in his own infallibility and power to condemn others to hell put him on a par with the professors of the doctrine of predestination, the doctrine Faustus rejects in the first soliloquy. In the imperial sequence, too, the action bears directly on Faustus's struggle against God in the main plot. Tasso had, we remember, fashioned his centerpiece into a miniature epic whose action reflects the theme of the whole work. The tragicomic conflict between Faustus and Benvolio serves a similar purpose in *Doctor Faustus*. The struggle informs all the scenes of the sequence and could be said to function as a mythological play-within-the-play which is patterned on the familiar Actaeon myth. The relevance of this myth about a man who gains forbidden knowledge and is punished by being torn to pieces is obvious. Nothing quite as brutal happens to the skeptic knight in Marlowe's play, but Benvolio, who is identified with Actaeon twice (ll. 1287–1293 and 1343), is supplied with antlers and chased by Faustus's hellhounds. There are many sides to the myth in Renaissance emblem books and mythographies. Marlowe is preoccupied with its "visionary side," as Leonard Barkan has pointed out:

> If *Merry Wives* turns the amatory side of the myth into grotesque comedy, then *Doctor Faustus* does the same for the visionary side. The skeptic Benvolio vows he will turn himself into Actaeon if Faustus can actually conjure, whereupon Faustus plants horns on the scoffer's head and calls up a legion of hell hounds to torment him. Benvolio is farcically forced into belief.[44]

In its own way, Benvolio's progress from skepticism and despair in scene xi, via his abortive challenges to Faustus, to his despair and reluctant acceptance of Faustus's power in scene xiv constitutes a tragi-

---

43. Harry Levin, *Christopher Marlowe: The Overreacher* (Cambridge, Mass., 1952), p. 147.

44. Leonard Barkan, "Diana and Actaeon: The Myth as Synthesis," *ELR*, X (Autumn 1980), 352 n.

comic analogue to "Faustus fortunes" throughout the play. In this respect the Benvolio material, which is almost exclusively Marlowe's own invention, functions formally as an ironic counterpart to the thematically expressive episode—or *nodo*—in Tasso's *Gerusalemme*. Moreover, because such an episode preferably should coincide with a major "change of fortune," it is interesting to note that Faustus's fortune begins to decline once he has reached the top in scene xii. The first serious attack on his position occurs in the next scene and the decline continues. The gradually descending social status of his adversaries bears this out: In the following order he confronts knights, soldiers, a horsecourser, a carter, a clown, a hostess, an old man, and finally the devils. It appears, then, that the middle sequences are more essential to the presentation of Faustus than hitherto assumed.

I believe it is right to see the constantly changing settings of the play as an expression of the restlessness which characterizes the protagonist's quest. At the same time, however, the many "places" of the action are ordered so that an overall impression of unity emerges—a kind of unity which recalls Tasso's "unità mista." This multiple unity also gives rise to a sense of spatiality, when—as Stephen Greenblatt comments—"space is transformed into an abstraction" and becomes a symbol of "transcendental homelessness."[45] The inherent conflict between restlessness and a fixed order can be related to Faustus's rebellion against the doctrine of preplanned damnation as expressed in the first and last soliloquies. The doctrine of predestination poses an insurmountable problem to a man whose philosophy of life is dictated by the doctrine of natural aspiration, a view of man's potential which Marlowe expresses most fully in one of Tamburlaine's celebrated speeches:

> Nature, that fram'd us of four elements
> Warring within our breasts for regiment,
> Doth teach us all to have aspiring minds.
> Our souls, whose faculties can comprehend
> The wondrous architecture of the world,
> And measure every wandering planet's course,
> Still climbing after knowledge infinite,

45. Stephen Greenblatt, *Renaissance Self-fashioning from More to Shakespeare* (Chicago and London, 1980), p. 196.

> And always moving as the restless spheres,
> Wills us to wear ourselves and never rest, . . .
>   (*Tamburlaine, Part One,* II.vii.17–26)

Several critics have connected this speech with the philosophy of Giordano Bruno, the most comprehensive study being that of James Robinson Howe.[46] But nobody has so far commented on the way Bruno and Marlowe make use of figurative rhetoric to emphasize the endless circulations which characterize "the restless spheres" and the strivings of man alike. As I argue more fully elsewhere,[47] Bruno often casts circular verbal spells in his poetry and makes no secret of this practice. In his commentary on a nine-stanza poem in *De gl'heroici furori* (1585), he explains that the poem is sung by "the nine intelligences and the nine muses, whose chorus is ordered according to the number of the nine spheres," so that to each of the stanzas correspond one intelligence, one muse, one sphere.[48] In Tamburlaine's speech (II.vi.12–29), a part of which is quoted above, Marlowe systematically deploys cosmological imagery to denote what Bruno describes as "un certo moto metafisico . . . e infinto" (II.380). To every step in Bruno's metaphysical movement corresponds one stage in Tamburlaine's speech, from "the comprehen[sion] of the wondrous architecture of the world," enabling "our souls' to "climb . . . after knowledge infinite," to Bruno's description of the soul, "questo numero . . . movente" (II.371), echoed in Marlowe's "souls . . . always moving." The ana-

---

46. James Robinson Howe, *Marlowe, Tamburlaine, and Magic* (Athens, Ohio, 1976). Other critics who have treated Bruno's possible influence on Marlowe are Benvenuto Cellini, *Marlowe* (Rome, 1937), pp. 108–114; Philip Henderson, *Christopher Marlowe* (London, 1952), pp. 12, 29–31, 44–54, and 66–67; and A. D. Wraight and V. Stern, *In Search of Christopher Marlowe: A Pictorial Biography* (London, 1964), pp. 147 and 155.

47. "Mnemonics and Giordano Bruno's Magical Art of Composition," *Cahiers Elizabethains,* XX (October 1981), 3–10, and " 'Un Certo Amoroso Martire': Shakespeare's 'The Phoenix and the Turtle' and Giordano Bruno's *De gli eroici furori,*" *SSt,* II (1981), 193–215.

48. Quotations from Bruno's Italian dialogues are from *Opere italiane,* 3 vols., ed. Giovanni Gentile and Vincenzo Spampanato (Bari, 1923–1927). The present quotation is from Paul E. Memmo's translation of *De gl'heroici furori* (London, 1585), *The Heroic Frenzies* (Chapel Hill, N.C., 1964), p. 77. The Italian text is found in *Opere italiane,* II, 325.

logues are close enough in terms of ideas and phrasing to suggest a direct influence.

What makes the connection between Marlowe and Bruno particularly interesting for *Doctor Faustus* is the way in which Marlowe organizes key words and topoi in Tamburlaine's Brunian speech. Marlowe expresses the Scythian conqueror's restlessness by applying the same circular rhetorical schemes as Bruno, namely, *epanalepsis* and *antimetabole*. He places the key words "minds" and "souls," which denote the concept of metaphysical motion, at the center of the speech, while the other key words and concepts are ordered symmetrically around this center in the following manner:

sweetness . . . crown (l. 1)
mov'd (l. 16)
man as "frame" (l. 18)
aspiring minds (l. 20)
center of speech   souls (l. 21)
world as "architecture" (l. 22)
moving (l. 25)
sweet . . . crown (l. 29)

(The numbers in parentheses indicate the position of the words within the twenty-nine-line speech.)

Marlowe completes the chiastic pattern by disposing symmetrically within the speech the topoi of man "fram'd . . . of four [warring] elements" and of the world as "architecture" composed of "wandering" "planets," thus aligning movements within the microcosm and the macrocosm. The resulting verbal artifact is characterized by the same "ordine e analogia" (II.386) as Bruno's dialogues and poems. Bruno linked such verbal and conceptual "circles" with man's endless quest for the infinite and with the principles governing the infinite universe. In another of his London dialogues, *De la causa, principio, e uno,* he provides the following diagram of the "circulo infinito":[49]

I believe it is meaningful to consider the loco-temporal patterns found in the arrangement of *Doctor Faustus* within this context, be-

49. This geometrical figure is reproduced from *Opere italiane,* I, 261, where Bruno explains that this system of many concentric circles illustrates the principle by which "il massimo e il minimo convengono in uno essere." To Bruno this principle equals the absolute unity of the divine mind (I, 259).

Figure 5

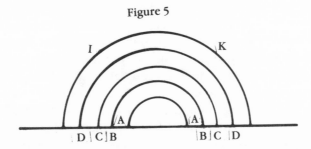

D \ C] B   B] C] D

cause Faustus, too, subscribes to the doctrine so eloquently presented by Tamburlaine. Both Bruno and Tamburlaine use the classical myths of metamorphosis connected with Jove when presenting their yearnings for the infinite.[50] "What better precedent than mighty Jove," Tamburlaine asks, and Faustus responds positively to the Bad Angel's suggestion: "Be thou on earth as *Ioue* in the skye, / Lord and Commander of these elements" (ll. 103–104). His response—like that of Tamburlaine—contains a mixture of yearnings for earthly and heavenly gains, for sovereignty and "strange Philosophy" (l. 113) alike. In the play's first comic scene, Wagner alludes to the natural restlessness of Faustus, emphasizing the idea that he is made of conflicting and "always moving" forces: "For is he not *Corpus naturale*? and is not that *Mobile*? (ll. 204–205). To Bruno the myths of metamorphosis are emblems of man's quest for the infinite and "the wheel of metamorphosis" ("la ruota de le metaforfosi," II.372) is magical metaphor through which man "from a vile creature . . . become[s] a God."[51] We remember Faustus's words when he has embraced magic:

> But his dominion that exceeds in this,
> Stretcheth as farre as doth the mind of man:
> A sound Magitian is a Demi-god,
> Here tire my braines to get a Deity.
>
> (ll. 86–89)

---

50. I analyze one of these sonnets, the "Quel dio che scuote il folgore sonoro" (II, 371), in "Mnemonics and Giordano Bruno's Magical Art of Composition," pp. 6–7. In this sonnet Bruno repeats thematic key-words acrostically ("dio . . . pastor . . . fu . . . dio . . . fu . . . pastor . . . dio") and explains that it symbolizes the vicissitudinal motion of "la ruota delle metamorfosi" (II, 372).

51. *The Heroic Frenzies,* p. 122.

These dreams about unbounded expansion and dominion are fired by Faustus's confrontation with the doctrine of predestination (ll. 64–75), and within this context we should bear in mind that Bruno's defense of man's free will and ability to turn himself into a god is also a strong reaction against Calvinism and Calvinist thinkers, as witnessed most clearly in the London dialogue *La cena de le ceneri* (1584).[52] It may not be surprising, then, that Faustus's first soliloquy parallels the argument of Bruno's opening dialogue in that work and that it incorporates at least one verbatim "quotation" from it.[53] For Faustus first desires to "liue and die in *Aristotles* workes" (l. 34), then refers to the title of one of these works ("Sweet *Analitikes,*" ll. 34–35), before he rejects shallow readings of Aristotle. His lines thus parallel Bruno's attack on Calvinist pedants. Bruno lets the scoffing character Frulla mock those who "voglion *vivere e morire per Aristoteles*; i quali non intendono né anche quel che significano *i titoli de' libri d'Aristotele*" (I.34; my italics). Like Bruno, who favors the followers of "la scuola pitagorica e nostra" (I.35), who are experts in medicine, law, and theology, Faustus who excels in precisely these disciplines, sides with "the old Phylosophers" (l. 286).

Faustus's allegiance to one of these thinkers of the past, Pythagoras, appears clearly in his last soliloquy, when the magician tries his utmost to escape his doom by appealing to "*Phythagoras Metempsycosis*" (l. 2075), a theory essential to Bruno's magical philosophy. When Faustus spends his last energy in a final incantatory soliloquy:

> It strikes, it strikes; now body turne to aire,
> Or *Lucifer* will beare thee quicke to hell.
> O soule be chang'd into small water drops,
> And fall into the Ocean ne're be found. / . . .
>
> (ll. 1284–1287)

before he is torn to pieces by the furies, it is ironical that his words should present a close parallel to Bruno's description of mystical *sparagmos* in *De gl'heroici furori*. The impasse of Bruno's frenzied lover (*furioso*) is described suggestively as follows:

52. See for instance his characterization of Calvinists as "an idle sect of pedants" and "pests of the world," *The Expulsion of the Triumphant Beast,* trans. Arthur D. Imerti (New Brunswick, N.J., 1964), pp. 124 and 126.

53. See my "Giordano Bruno and *Doctor Faustus* (B)," *N&Q,* 32 (December 1985), 463–465.

il senso . . . che non sapendo passar avanti, né
tornare a dietro, né dove voltarsi, svanisce e
perde l'esser suo; non altrimente che una stilla
d'acqua che vanisce nel mare, o un picciol spirito
che s'attenua perdendo la propria sustanza nell'aere
spacioso ed immenso.

(II.461–462)

(Not knowing where to turn, equally incapable of
going forward or backward, the mind vanishes and
loses it being like a small drop of water that
disappears into the ocean, or a little spirit that fades
away when losing its proper substance in the immènse
and spacious air; my translation.)

It is perhaps worth mentioning that in Bruno, too, this wished-for dissolution into elements occurs in the middle of the night, the reference
to the time being "è notte" (II.462). Faustus appeals in vain to the doctrine of transmigration of the soul, praying for instant metamorphosis
and liberation, and in so doing echoes Benvolio's hope that "time shall
alter this our brutish shapes" (l. 1519):

Oh *Pythagoras Metempsycosis*; were that true,
This soule should flie from me, and I be chang'd
Into some brutish beast.

(ll. 2074–2076)

Marlowe's alignment of Benvolio, the tragicomic Actaeon-figure in the
imperial sequence,[54] with Faustus may not be entirely a concidence.

54. Benvolio is most obviously an ironical name for a skeptical and irascible knight. It
is perhaps worth mentioning that one of Bruno's sonnets which bears on Faustus's quest
for the sun in the final soliloquy begins as follows: "*Bene far voglio,* e non mi vien
permesso; / Meco il mio sol non è, . . . ; II, 449 ("I long to do good, but it is denied me; /
my sun is not with me, . . . " my translation and italics). The similarity between the
opening words of Bruno's sonnet ("Bene far voglio") and the name of Benvolio, whose
"fame" is "eclipst" through Faustus's intervention (1520), may be coincidental, but is
nevertheless suggestive. Benvolio, we remember, is reported to have drunk "kindly . . .
to *Bruno's* health" (l. 1201), and Bruno in his turn has been described in terms which
point in the direction of *De gl'heroici furori*: He is sent to Germany "on a *furies* back"
(l. 1188; my italics). The year Marlowe composed *Doctor Faustus,* 1592, is also the year
in which Bruno was arrested by the Venetian Inquisition on a charge of heresy and sent
to the Pope in Rome.

The beautiful Actaeon image in *De gl'heroici furori* constitutes Bruno's fullest expression of the painful quest for the infinite, and the image is central to the dialogue quoted above.[55] By this I do not say that Marlowe intended Faustus to be "saved" and emerge as frenzied lover on a par with Bruno's virtuous hero. It is more likely that Marlowe felt the attraction of Bruno's powerful ideas as expressed in the dialogue published in London in 1583–1585, to broaden his presentation of Faustus. Bruno's controversial views on man and the universe appealed to many of Marlowe's contemporaries and could on many points enrich his account of the satanic practices of the German scholar. When one is writing about the problem of man's free will, it is certainly interesting to take into account the view of a contemporary who defiantly declared that "the act of the will is infinite."[56] Faustus's problem, however, was that he did not heed the limitation Bruno imposed upon this bold statement: the will's power is infinite solely with regard to the quest for "the good." That goal Faustus denies himself by consorting with Lucifer, but this fact does not prevent him from practicing his magic—impatiently—much in the same manner as Bruno's frenzied lover in pursuit of "curiosi studi" (II.460).

Marlowe's experiment with spatial form in *Doctor Faustus*, where loco-temporal "places are systematized so as to create a "unità mista," becomes meaningful within the context of Bruno's philosophy of the infinite. The conflict between restlessness and a fixed order found in the play finds an analogue in Bruno's emblem "Manens moveor," which employs the relentless "moto continuo" of the wheel of time around its own fixed axis to illustrate the opposite forces of hope and fear within the mind of the frenzied one (II.444–445). This is an image which suspends time as a linear process, focusing instead on time's relativistic and spatial character.[57] In *Doctor Faustus* the similar opposition in Faustus's mind between hope and despair is given a textually

---

55. Bruno devotes two dialogues of *De gl'heroici furori*, I, 4, and II, 2, to the Actaeon myth.

56. *The Heroic Frenzies*, p.71.

57. Shakespeare, too, seems to have been inspired by Bruno's attempts at suspending conventional ideas of reality, judging by his experiments in *A Midsummer's Night's Dream* and "The Phoenix and the Turtle"; see Barkan, "Diana and Actaeon: The Myth as Synthesis," p. 358, and my "Un Certo Amoroso Martire," passim.

appropriate expression, I suggest, in the opposition between the shifting settings and the fixed temporal frame of the play. The protagonist
may ask "[w]hat resting place is this?" (l. 823), but no real rest, nor certain answers to his more fundamental questions are granted. "[N]ew
exploits do hale him out agen" (l. 793), and wherever his Apuleian folly brings him, he remains like the Carter "vnder heauen" (l. 1708) and
under the crippling influence of the doctrine of predestination. A few
lines in the first internal chorus pinpoint Faustus's limited sphere of
action:

> He viewes the cloudes, the Planets, and the Starres,
> The Tropick, Zones, and quarters of the skye,
> From the bright circle of the horned Moone,
> Euen to the height of *Primum Mobile:*
> And whirling round within this circumference,
> Within the concaue compass of the Pole,
> From East to West his Dragons swiftly glide, / . . .
>
> (ll. 783–789)

"[W]hirling round this circumference," these words which recall Per-
seus's flight epitomize Faustus's restless actions and "the forme" of the
play which collects them into one shape. The symbolic time scheme
which encompasses the protagonist's whirligig "in pleasure and in da-
liance" (l. 863) produces an effect of inevitability and enclosure which
is essential in all great representations of tragic suffering. The description of the play's "places," too, is principally symbolic throughout,
and "when a meaningful sense of place finally emerges," it is "as a
place to die"—when Faustus has returned to his study at Wittenberg.[58]
Time similarly is spatialized and sought annulled until it again becomes a pressing reality when the clock strikes at midnight, establishing an absolute end-point to Faustus's life. Marlowe's careful planning
of the finale, where the suggestive splendor of the midnight scene
(xix) is followed by the squalor of the discovery scene set in the morning (xx), fully dramatizes the dilemma his protagonist faces by imply-
ing that Faustus was predestined to his end. The play's preplanned
structure, what Goethe saw as its "grosse Anlage," evokes the idea of

---

58. *Renaissance Self-fashioning from More to Shakespeare,* p. 196.

predestination. And it seems most appropriate that *Doctor Faustus,* the most powerful critique of the problems posed by the doctrine of predestination and the cult of the will in the Elizabethan era, also should reflect upon these problems by way of its conspicuously "artificial" treatment of time and place.

"His form and cause conjoin'd": Reflections on "Cause" in Hamlet

JONATHAN BALDO

His form and cause conjoin'd, preaching to stones,
Would make them capable.

Hamlet, III,iv.126–127[1]

CHARACTERS in *Hamlet* are continually hunting down causes. Claudius and Polonius seek to determine the cause of Hamlet's distemper, fearing for their own safety and their daughter's, respectively. At the beginning of the play Horatio and the sentinels are uncertain of the cause of Denmark's military preparations. And Hamlet, reflecting on the weightiness of his own cause, wonders at the lack of sufficient cause governing the actions of the Player and of Fortinbras. It would be possible to argue, as one critic has done, that in *Hamlet* "society is presented, and is present to each character, as a continuous network of causes, agents, and effects, a network of men reciprocally using and exploiting one another"[2]—except that the play seems finally more

---

1. All citations from *Hamlet* refer to the Arden Edition, ed. Harold Jenkins (London, 1982).
2. Terence Eagleton, *Shakespeare and Society: Critical Studies in Shakespearean Drama* (New York, 1967), p. 40.

75

concerned with the difficulties attending the notions of agency and
cause. Polonius is one of the first to sound the motif of "cause," thinking "that I have found / The very cause of Hamlet's lunacy" (II.ii.48–
49). Of course, there is some doubt, to observers both at court and in
the audience, as to whether Hamlet is in fact mad; that is, the "effect"
is as problematic as the "cause." But Polonius, who claims to know effect as well as cause, proceeds to subject both to the bravura of word-
play:

> Mad let us grant him then. And now remains
> That we find out the cause of this effect,
> Or rather say the cause of this defect,
> For this effect defective comes by cause.
>
> (II.ii.100–103)

Others speak in a more hesitant mood of the cause of Hamlet's distemper. Rosencrantz reports to the King and Queen, "He does confess he
feels himself distracted, / But from what cause a will by no means
speak" (III.i.5-6). And Gertrude expresses a wish that Ophelia's "good
beauties be the happy cause / Of Hamlet's wildness" (III.i.39-40).

While other characters are busy seeking to determine the cause of
Hamlet's distraction, it is curious that Hamlet himself dwells so little
on specific "causes"—at least, until the end of the play, when the dying Hamlet urges Horatio to live so that he may "report me and my
cause aright / To the unsatisfied" (V.ii.344–345). He holds a faltering
interest in his own cause ("Like John-a-dreams, unpregnant of my
cause"), and, oddly enough, for one so concerned with penetrating
beneath surfaces and peeking behind veils, it never occurs to him to
seek out the causes governing the actions or behavior of his mother
and his friends Rosencrantz and Guildenstern. Hamlet is more concerned with the disruptions of causal relationships in the action of the
Player and of Fortinbras, both of whom "act" without sufficient cause,
and in his own inaction. Hamlet's own "cause" fails to produce the expected result, to move him to sweep to his revenge:

>   I do not know
> Why yet I live to say this thing's to do,
> Sith I have cause, and will, and strength, and means
> To do't.
>
> (IV.iv.43–46)

In the following essay I propose to explore the workings of the word "cause," which I take to be a key and a complex word in the play, and to show the extent to which Hamlet's difficulties are also difficulties attending the concept of "cause." The word "cause" summarizes what is perhaps the most persistent theme of tragedy and an important conflict in the play. It designates both a willful or deliberate course of action and a causal logic that suggests that our actions are never free or unconditioned. In Part II of the essay I plan to explore some of the issues that are focused by the antithetical nature of the word "cause." *Hamlet* is also in large part a meditation on, or a brooding over, the validity of causal logic, which since Aristotle has been assumed to be an essential ingredient of drama. A pervasive concern with interpretation, I will try to show, both in *Hamlet* and among Shakespeare's characters generally, interferes with an understanding of actions and events as links in a causal chain.

I

It is probably Hamlet's friend Horatio who is farthest from the naturalistic view of action as a sequence of causes and effects. Horatio is a semiotician of sorts; rather than trying to understand actions and events by locating them along a causal chain, he "reads" events as portents, signs, representations. At the end of Act I, scene iv, after Hamlet has met the ghost of his father face to face, Horatio wonders, "To what issue will this come?" (l. 89). The question is an anxious one, suggestive of a dramatic sensibility, an intellect eager to pursue the possible consequences of actions and events, but the force of this suggestion is partly undercut by Horatio's next line: "Heaven will direct it" (l. 91). More important than his fatalism, however, is Horatio's means of understanding events: he shows less concern for the particular direction of events than for their general drift, for events are finally the signs of a divine will. Thus, when Horatio speculates on the recent appearances of the ghost, he places general significance in the foreground, particular causes and consequences in the background:

> In what particular thought to work I know not,
> But in the gross and scope of my opinion,
> This bodes some strange eruption to our state.

> (I.i.70–72)

Horatio's concern with signs and their interpretation becomes even more apparent later in the same scene, when he compares the eruption of signs and portents in Rome just prior to the death of Caesar to a Denmark haunted by the "portentous figure" of Old Hamlet:

> And even the like precurse of fear'd events,
> As harbingers preceding still the fates
> And prologue to the omen coming on,
> Have heaven and earth together demonstrated
> Unto our climatures and countrymen.
>
> (I.i.124–128)

A difficulty in Horatio's speech lies in the word "omen," which here refers to an event foretold rather than a sign foretelling an event. How may we construe the transformation of "feared events" (1. 124), events foretold by omens, into another prophetic sign, or "omen" (1. 126)? And why should a sign ("omen") need another sign, another prologue or harbinger, to announce or represent it? In Horatio's speech, "events" that have been announced by signs have themselves become signs. It may be that Horatio's antiquated conception of events—"I am more an antique Roman than a Dane," he tells the dying Hamlet (V.ii.346)—is better suited to a reading of Shakespeare's play than the naturalistic conception of events as a sequence of causes and effects. In Shakespearean drama, events have a tendency to become signs under the pressure of attempts at understanding. Information in Shakespeare's plays, seldom of value in itself, characteristically functions as pointer or sign. The importance of events within what seem to be networks of causal chains is inevitably overshadowed or eclipsed by the signifying function. In *Julius Caesar* the principal event, the death of Caesar, is something of an anticlimax. Although the death of Caesar would appear to be the signified of many signs or omens in the play, it soon becomes a cipher, another sign, another text in need of interpretation: that is, in need of being staged. And that is precisely what Brutus and Marc Antony do before their countrymen: they put Caesar on stage for the people of Rome. Why do events—e.g., the murder of Caesar—evaporate in the effort to understand them? The event can remain an event only so long as it does not offer itself up to interpretation. As soon as it offers itself up to interpretation, the event ceases to be the nexus of sequences of causes and effects, actions and consequences, and becomes instead the nexus of various signifying chains, the shadowy center of a field of representations. Therefore, paradoxically, at the moment the event offers itself up to interpretation, there ceases to be anything—any signified that is not, in a famous formulation of Derrida's, always already in the position of the signifier—to interpret.

Drama, I would argue, frequently acts to obviate this unsettling movement of interpretation. An event that would not necessitate interpretation is approximated by the device of the surprise. Suddenness and surprise, which have figured prominently in dramatic theory since Aristotle (where they are implicit in the concepts of *peripeteia* or change of fortune and *anagnorisis* or discovery), appear to forestall the movement of interpretation and reinforce the audience's perception of events qua events. In what Aristotle calls complex plots (distinguished from simple plots in that their action may be understood in causal, not merely simple sequential terms), dramatic action is composed of a continuous, unbroken chain of causes and effects and at the same time manages to take the audience by surprise:

Such an effect [fear or pity] is best produced when the events come on us by surprise; and the effect is heightened when, at the same time, they follow as cause and effect.[3]

If the audience has been prepared to expect a certain outcome or turn of events, then its responses to climactic scenes will have been already played out, will be attenuated reenactments of prior responses. Aristotle's second criterion—that events should follow as cause and effect— is necessary to balance the first, for if events are surprising without being causally related, then presumably they run the risk of seeming theatrical, or staged for their own sake. If there is nothing inevitable about a series of events, then an audience may not feel compelled to respond to such events or to their outcome, since events might very well have happened differently.

3. *Aristotle's Theory of Poetry and Fine Art,* trans. S. H. Butcher (1911; rpt. New York, 1951), p. 39 [1452a].

In Aristotle's text causal relations extend beyond the boundaries of stage and text to include relations between the play and its audience. If events in a play follow as cause and effect, then the audience's responses, too, will be rigorously determined, will constitute a (terminal) link in a causal chain. Causal relations between events in a play, therefore, like the device of surprise, promise to avert the movement of interpretation, to obviate the spectator's need to stage or put on— i.e., to interpret in the strong sense of that word—the play he is viewing. In his staging of Philippe Sollers's *Nombres* Jacques Derrida writes of the reader's need to write or to "stage" the text before him:

> There is at any rate no tenable place for [the reader or the spectator] opposite the text, outside the text, no spot where he might get away with *not* writing what, in the reading, would seem to him to be *given, past;* no spot, in other words, where he would stand before an already *written* text. Because his job is to put things on stage, he is on stage himself, he puts himself on stage.[4]

But since in Aristotle's account of causal relationships in drama the spectator's own response is an "effect," it might seem that the spectator does in fact get away with not having to "write" or "stage" the play before him; he would seem to have the prerogative denied Brutus and Marc Antony to refuse to play the dangerous game of interpretation.

In Shakespeare's plays both of Aristotle's criteria are less than successfully met or fulfilled. Comparing the English playwrights with the French and Spanish, John Dryden writes that the former "cumber themselves with too much plot," while the latter "only represent so much of a story as will constitute one whole and great action sufficient for a play; we, who undertake more, do but multiply adventures, which, not being produced from one another as effects from causes, but barely following, constitute many actions in the drama, and consequently make it many plays."[5] And Coleridge notes, as a general characteristic of Shakespearean drama, "Expectation in preference to surprize."[6] The German critic Wolfgang Clemen has shown that scenes in Shakespeare's plays frequently prepare their audiences for what will

---

4. *Dissemination,* trans. Barbara Johnson (Chicago, 1981), p. 290.

5. "An Essay of Dramatic Poesy," in *John Dryden: Selected Works,* 2d ed., ed. William Frost (San Francisco, 1971), p. 451.

6. *Shakespearean Criticism,* ed. T. M. Raysor (1930; rpt. London, 1960), I, 199.

follow, intimate or forecast what will happen in subsequent scenes.[7] Expectation enables an audience to participate in the staging of events in two senses. First, it moves the habitually passive spectator nearer to the position of the playwright, enabling him to "write" or "stage" subsequent scenes and acts in the play. Second, it shifts the audience's attention from events, for which the audience has already been prepared, to their interpretation. The element of surprise, then, hinders the dissolving of events into signs and fosters an ontology of the (singular, nonrepeated, nontheatrical) event that is undermined by the element of expectation.

Coleridge's formula—"Expectation in preference to surprize"—aptly describes both the relation of the spectators of a Shakespearean play to the action, and Hamlet's own relation to the action in the first three acts of the play. Hamlet's anticipatory posture is a means of rehearsing or staging, as it were, the action of revenge, in an effort to control not so much the course of events as the course of their interpretation: not so much to get the action of revenge right, but to get its "staging" or interpretation right. Many actions are deflected in *Hamlet,* including Fortinbras's assault on Denmark as well as Hamlet's revenge. But the course of an action's interpretation is even more easily deflected than a course of action, as Hamlet surely realizes when pondering the significance of Fortinbras's military action toward the end of the play (IV.iv.25–66) and when accusing himself before Ophelia, "I am very proud, revengeful, ambitious" (III.i.124–125), a speech which is not so much a confession of his true character as a confession that he knows how variously interpretable is any action.

Hamlet's favored posture toward the end of the play may be summarized by inverting Coleridge's formula: surprise in preference to expectation. "Rashly— / And prais'd be rashness for it" begins Hamlet's recounting of his adventures aboard ship to Horatio in the final scene of the play. Rash action appears to suspend or bypass questions of interpretation, for the rash action promises to be action in its purest form, an action performed too quickly to be adulterated with reflection, representation, posturing, or interpretation. Hamlet's praise of rashness, like the element of surprise in dramatic theory, is an

7. "Shakespeare's Art of Preparation," in *Shakespeare's Dramatic Art: Collected Essays* (London, 1972), p. 60 f.

attempt to reinstate a dramatic logic of causality and to establish an ontology of actions and events. Like the element of surprise, the Aristotelian notion of causality returns at the end of the play in the forms of "inevitability" and "providence" in Hamlet's conversation with Horatio: "There's a divinity that shapes our ends, / Rough-hew them how we will—"(V.ii.10–11); "Why, even in that was heaven ordinant" (V.ii.48); "There is special providence in the fall of a sparrow" (V.ii.215–216). Toward the end of the play, then, Hamlet himself would seem to be trying to fulfill both of Aristotle's conditions; he is a Shakespearean character trying to write for himself, or write himself into, an Aristotelian play.

II

In *Hamlet* "cause" is a compelling term in part because it neatly summarizes and perhaps even reconciles two opposing conceptions of actions and events. It suggests both *determination*—a character's determination to advance or to try his "cause"—and *determinism*, both the willfulness of a fully intentional action and the idea that actions and events are never free or unconditioned, but always determined by antecedent causes (either external or psychological). "Cause" therefore evokes with extraordinary economy a major conflict in the play: between a freely chosen or willful course of action and one determined by causes beyond a character's control. (The latter theme is sounded repeatedly throughout the play, beginning with Laertes' advice to his sister regarding Hamlet's attentions: "his will is not his own. / For he himself is subject to his birth" [I.iii.17–18].) The antithetical nature of "cause," rather than destabilizing the word, actually lends it greater stability, greater tenacity, for the negation of the word can only reinforce one of the two primary senses of the word, as may be seen when the word is applied to two of the play's three avenging sons, Laertes and Fortinbras.

When an impassioned Laertes returns to Denmark following his father's death, the King challenges, "What is the cause, Laertes, / That thy rebellion looks so giant-like?" (IV.v.120–121). Does Laertes, like Hamlet in the preceding scene, "have cause," or does the effect (Laertes' "rebellion") exceed the cause? (Laertes is, after all, avenging the death of a comic father, so the audience is likely to share some of the King's skepticism.) With his question, the King dexterously deflects attention away from Laertes' "cause" in the senses of the object or end of an action and "a movement which calls forth the efforts of its supporters" (*OED;* recall that there is a movement afoot to proclaim Laertes King). The word "cause" in these senses could be used to designate Laertes' "rebellion" as well as the *cause* of his rebellion, but the careful wording of Claudius's question denies the rebellion the status (and the impelling force) of a "cause." Claudius tauntingly suggests that Laertes has no legitimate cause in the sense of an adequate ground of action, and also that Laertes is not the agent of a fully deliberate action, since his "rebellion," like Hamlet's madness, has deleterious causes outside of his control.

Fortinbras's "cause"—in the sense of a controversy or "a movement which calls forth the efforts of its supporters"—is exemplary, even though his action seems uncaused or without sufficient cause. He epitomizes the life of ambition and purposive action, of full and sufficient causes, although his action "shows no cause" in the sense of an adequate reason or explanation:

> Two thousand souls and twenty thousand ducats
> Will not debate the question of this straw!
> This is th'imposthume of much wealth and peace,
> That inward breaks, and shows no cause without
> Why the man dies.
>
> (IV.iv.25–29)

The cause of Fortinbras's action, like the abscess, a mysterious or hidden cause of death, and like the cause of the Player's passion, is not immediately apparent. This disjunction between cause and effect has a twofold result. Fortinbras's action appears to be both willful rather than conditioned or automatic—the predictable effect of an antecedent cause—and theatrical or gratuitous, lacking purpose or cause. Later in the same soliloquy Hamlet reflects,

> . . . To my shame I see
> The imminent death of twenty thousand men
> That, for a fantasy and trick of fame,
> Go to their graves like beds, fight for a plot

Whereon the numbers cannot try the cause,
Which is not tomb enough and continent
To hide the slain.

(IV.iv.59–65)

Fortinbras's "cause" seems large indeed—a "great argument" (1. 54)—precisely because of the discrepancy between the "cause" and the "straw" that is its ostensible aim: a plot of land that is not large enough to serve either as a battlefield or as a tomb for the soldiers who will die fighting for the cause.[8]

At times the word "cause" seems to suspend the conflict between determination and determinism by temporarily reconciling the two terms. In the soliloquy that follows the appearance of Fortinbras's army, Hamlet reflects,

                                    I do not know
        Why yet I live to say this thing's to do,
        Sith I have cause, and will, and strength, and means
        To do't.

(IV.iv.43–46)

In this instance "cause" takes on a legal sense, something like "just cause," although a number of meanings of the word converge here. It absorbs from "will" and "strength" part of its meaning; Hamlet's "cause" is just, and it has sufficient force to produce the intended effect, to cause him to carry out the proposed action. Furthermore, Hamlet's proposed action is validated by an antecedent agency or cause and therefore adheres to dramatic logic: Hamlet's father's in-

8. The word "cause," the *OED* informs us, also meant "sickness" or "disease," and that is one of its primary senses in IV.iv.28, where Fortinbras as apparent symbol of health and vigorous unreflectiveness is under discussion. This meaning of the word is troubling in light of the pervasive and much discussed disease imagery in the play, since it is precisely through Hamlet's advancement of his "cause" that the disease that infests Denmark is supposed to be cured. Hamlet's advancement of his cause, therefore, if it is indeed a kind of medicine, is *homeopathic* medicine, this use of the word "cause" suggests. The use of the word "cause" to mean "sickness" or "disease" helps to account for Hamlet's taking as exemplary characters whose action appears to be uncaused (Fortinbras, the Player) and characters who have no causes in the sense of purposes or ends (Horatio, Ophelia).

junction has caused, determined, set in motion Hamlet's course of action, which would therefore "have cause" in the sense that it, unlike Fortinbras's action, may be understood as the effect of a prior cause. For Hamlet in this scene, then, "cause" represents nothing less than a suspension of the oedipal struggle and the coincidence in a single word of his father's will and his own. Fortinbras's action, on the other hand, is without cause in at least three senses: something that produces an effect or gives rise to an action; the purpose or end of an action; and, in a legal sense, just cause or adequate ground for an action. Fortinbras lacks "adequate ground" in a literal as well as a figurative sense: the ground he is fighting for is not large enough to serve as setting for the action by means of which he hopes to win that ground.

But this opposition between determinism and determination, an opposition encapsulated by the word "cause," appears, from a certain perspective developed by the play, to be a false one. Part of the play's (and its main character's) interest in theatricality derives from its power to displace some of the most prominent sets of polarities in the play: active/passive, doing/suffering, will/fortune. Acting, or theatrical representation, suspends rather than mediates these differences. It cannot be said of the theatrical utterance, gesture, or action either that it is willed or that it is caused by circumstances that exceed a character's will. Theatricality promises relief from the alternatives Hamlet poses in his famous soliloquy—to be/not to be, to oppose/to suffer—and from the conflict summarized by the word "cause" between exertion of the will and circumscription of the will either by other characters, by the governance of society ("for he himself is subject to his birth," Laertes warns Ophelia), or by fortune (Hamlet at the eleventh hour adopts Horatio's view that "there's a divinity that shapes our ends, Rough-hew them how we will"; V.ii.10–11).

Theatrical utterance—the Player's Speech, for instance—is independent of causes in at least two senses. It is not caused because it does not appear to issue from the motives of its speaker ("What's Hecuba to him, or he to her, / That he should weep for her?" II.ii.553–554). "Of that I shall have also cause to speak," Horatio prefaces his recounting of Hamlet's tale at the end of the play, referring to Fortinbras's claim to the throne. And most dramatic characters do have "cause to speak": that is, in drama utterance generally issues forth under the stress of strong motives. Dramatic speech becomes theatrical (in the pejorative sense of that word) when it issues forth without motive or cause. And more than one speaker in *Hamlet* speaks without cause: not only the Player, whose mysterious emotion seems uncaused, but also, notably, Polonius. Nor is a theatrical utterance motivated by its context, from which, like a set piece, it stands out ("One speech in't I chiefly loved," Hamlet says of the speech he asks the Player to recite, even though he praises the play in which it occurs for being seamless and "well digested in the scenes": II.ii.435–436, 442).

A theatrical, as opposed to a dramatic, utterance does not issue from the pressures exerted by its contexts either because it exceeds its contexts (it is theatrical in the sense of hyperbolic or overdone) or because it cuts itself off from its contexts by calling attention to itself (it is theatrical in the sense of self-reflexive). A theatrical speech, gesture, or action is by definition independent of what came before it. In most drama, on the other hand, utterances, gestures, or actions are never independent of an intricate network of causes and effects. In drama, language itself frequently functions as agency or cause. Dramatic language often drifts from the constative to the performative plane, to invoke a distinction made by the philosopher J. L. Austin and adopted by much recent literary criticism.[9] The independence of theatrical utterance from causes helps to account for its appeal to Hamlet, even though he vigorously forswears theatricality in his famous advice to the Players:

Speak the speech, I pray you, as I pronounced it to you, trippingly on the tongue; but if you mouth it as many of your players do, I had as lief the town-crier spoke my lines.

(III.ii.1ff.)

Hamlet's theatrical tastes, suggested by his admiration for the Player's speech and the tendency of his own speech to stray toward the hyper-

9. See J. L. Austin, *How to Do Things with Words* (Cambridge, Mass., 1975). For a concise exposition of Austin, see John Lyons, *Language, Meaning, and Context* (London, 1981), pp. 171–194. Two thoughtful critiques of Austin's speech-act theory are: Jacques Derrida, "Signature Event Context," in *Glyph I* (Baltimore, 1977), pp. 172–197; and Barbara Johnson, "Poetry and Performative Language: Mallarmé and Austin," in *The Critical Difference* (Baltimore, 1980), pp. 52–66.

bolic, are easier to account for if we understand theatrical discourse (discourse that is either overdone or self-reflexive) as discourse which appears to be independent of "causes." Such a discourse would have an obvious appeal for a character like Hamlet, who seeks to free himself from a network of causes and agencies.

But a theatrical mode of discourse does not entirely succeed in bracketing questions of "cause," precisely because of the unpredictable and ungovernable tendency of language itself—or, more generally, of "forms"—to function as "causes," as I shall try to demonstrate in the remainder of this essay.

In the closet scene Hamlet enjoins his mother on the entrance of his father's ghost,

> On him, on him. Look you how pale he glares.
> His form and cause conjoin'd, preaching to stones,
> Would make them capable.—Do not look upon me,
> Lest with this piteous action you convert
> My stern effects. Then what I have to do
> Will want true color—tears perchance for blood.
>
> (III.iv.125–130)

"Form and cause conjoin'd" suggests an ideal union in Hamlet's father of inner (purpose or "cause") and outer ("form," l. 126, or "effects," l. 130). Hamlet's speech rehearses the disruption of the unity of form and cause. The precarious conjunction of cause ("what I have to do") and form ("true color") in the son Hamlet will be shattered, Hamlet fears, by his father's look. But the disunity of (outer) form and (inner) cause is not disturbing in itself. In fact, we might conjecture that this disunity is Hamlet's motive, in this speech and elsewhere: for example, in his speech to his mother in Act I, " 'Tis not alone my inky cloak, good mother, / . . . Together with all forms, moods, shapes of grief, / That can denote me truly" (I.ii.77, 82–83). For the disjunction of form and cause preserves the integrity of the latter, and suggests that the essential character of an action—its "cause"—survives all changes of costume, mood, or "colour" ("tears perchance for blood"). To put it another way, this disjunction preserves the distinction between acting (in the sense of theatrical representation) and action (in the sense of doing).[10] The disunity of cause and form is far less disturbing than the undoing of the very distinction, an undoing which is perhaps the main concern of the play.

Actions in *Hamlet* are viewed as a signifying practice, and events as a kind of language, as already codified. Fortinbras's action appears on the one hand to be the purest in the play, untinged by hesitation and by reflection in both senses of that word—thought and representation, or "acting" in the sense of posing. But on the other hand, Fortinbras's is the most highly formalized and *codified* action in the play. Not only is his action eminently interpretable, but it seems to be performed for the sake of its interpretation. Although opaque when understood in causal terms, Fortinbras's military action is transparent when regarded as an act of signification whose "signified" is "honour." Hamlet reflects,

> Rightly to be great
> Is not to stir without great argument,
> But greatly to find quarrel in a straw
> When honour's at the stake.
>
> (IV.iv.53–56)

Because his action is so highly codified, a *parole* whose *langue* is the code of miltary honor, the interpretation of his action does not appear to be superadded to the action. His action appears to be not temporally or logically prior to its interpretation, but rather coincident with it. Fortinbras's action is ostensibly perfectly autotelic (remember Hamlet's reflection on the inconsequentiality of the plot of ground Fortinbras will gain); it represents the prospect of the reduction of action to form, so that an action may seem theatrical, intransitive, an end in itself. Counterbalancing Fortinbras's seemingly perfect formalization of action is Hamlet's attempt to reduce or eliminate the formal or representational element in action, which Hamlet thinks he has achieved in his rash actions aboard ship. The rash action, I have argued, represents to Hamlet action of the purest kind, action performed too quickly to be adulterated with "reflection": either thought or acting (theatrical representation that holds the mirror up to nature). Now the perfect

10. I discuss the distinction between action and acting in *Hamlet* in "'He that plays the king': The Problem of Pretending in *Hamlet,*" *Criticism*, XXV, no. 1 (1983), 13–26.

formalization of action—the intransitivity or autotelism of "form"—
and the teleology or transitivity implied by "cause" are not merely impossible alternatives between which any character in Hamlet who pro-
poses to act in either sense of that word is fated to move; the very
terms of the polarity lose their identity or integrity in the course of the
play.

T. S. Eliot takes the occasion of his famous criticism of *Hamlet* to develop the notion of the "objective correlative." Hamlet's feeling of disgust, according to Eliot, is without sufficient cause, or exceeds its
cause: "Hamlet is up against the difficulty that his disgust is occasioned
by his mother, but that his mother is not an adequate equivalent for it;
his disgust envelops and exceeds her."[11] The disjunction between
cause and effect, as Eliot failed to understand, is not an unwitting failure but rather a major premise of the play. It characterizes the action
and responses of other characters besides Hamlet. In the first scene,
Francisco remarks, "For this relief much thanks. 'Tis bitter cold, / And
I am sick at heart" (I.i.8–9). This, the first non sequitur of the play,
seems almost a parody of Eliot's notion of an "objective correlative":

The only way of expressing emotion in the form of art is by finding an "objective correlative"; in other words, a set of objects, a situation, a chain of events
which shall be the formula of that *particular* emotion; such that when the external facts, which must terminate in sensory experience, are given, the emotion is immediately evoked.[12]

In Francisco's utterance the "external facts" would seem to "terminate
in sensory experience": "'Tis bitter cold." But "the complete adequa-
cy of the external to the emotion" is another matter.[13] The transition
from "'tis bitter cold" to "I am sick at heart" is abrupt and left unex-
plained.

If we take a closer look at Eliot's formula, we find that it is contradictory. On the one hand it asserts the conventional nature of the "objective correlative": the "objective correlative" is the "formula" of an
emotion. The relation of the "objective correlative" to the emotion it
produces is that of an arbitrary, conventional sign to its referent. On

11. *Selected Prose of T. S. Eliot*, ed. Frank Kermode (New York, 1975), p. 48.
12. Ibid.
13. Ibid.

the other hand, this relation appears to be the immediate and necessary or nonarbitrary relation of cause to effect. Eliot provides the following example from *Macbeth:* "the words of Macbeth on hearing of his wife's death strike us as if, given the sequence of events, these words were automatically released by the last event in the series."[14] Although by nature a "formula," the objective correlative's immediate relation to the effect it produces would seem not to admit of formulation or signification. A cause, an event that follows as an effect from a cause, an action undertaken with sufficient cause (unlike the Player's Speech, and unlike Fortinbras's military action)—each purportedly has an immediate relation to its antecedent or consequence *and therefore cannot function as a sign,* which by definition has a nonimmediate relation to what it represents. It is for this reason that Hamlet, who like his friend Horatio is concerned with signs and their interpretations, is so preoccupied with the *disturbances* of causal logic in the play. In the case of Fortinbras, this disturbance is precisely what allows his "action" to signify so strongly.

Toward the end of the play, Hamlet attempts to unite these two logics—the causal and the signifying—in those meditations on divinity and providence. "There is special providence in the fall of a sparrow," Hamlet says to Horatio just after he is called to the fencing match and to his doom (V.ii.215–216). The providential event is both one that has been *caused,* and one that *signifies* providential will. It therefore obeys and promises to reconcile two seemingly contradictory logics in the play: that of causation and that of signification.

But often it is difficult for the reader even to keep distinct these two logics, and equally difficult for a character to control either action as a signifying practice (for example, Fortinbras's action, which is interpreted so freely, so variously) or language as a form of action. For language in *Hamlet* frequently appears to have overcome its secondary or representational character to become violently instrumental. Thus, on the one hand, all action in *Hamlet* tends to become formalized through repetition—for example, the treble repetition of the main action of a son's revenge for his father's death—and through the pervasive theatrical metaphors in the play, which make even the most swift, direct, and decisive action—that of Fortinbras—seem "reflective" in

14. Ibid.

the sense of formal or representational. On the other hand, language itself frequently functions as agency or cause in *Hamlet* and through-out Shakespearean drama. Hamlet vows to "speak daggers" to his mother, "but use none" (III.ii.387). And Hamlet's words act as he pur-posed, for in the closet scene the Queen cries out, "These words like daggers enter in my ears" (III.iv.95). Toward the beginning of the play, Barnardo invites Horatio,

> Sit down awhile,
> And let us once again assail your ears,
> That are so fortified against our story,
> What we have two nights seen.
>
> (I.i.33–36)

Narratives of violence promise to inflict an equal violence on their au-dience or readers. The Ghost darkly intimates to Hamlet,

> But that I am forbid
> To tell the secrets of my prison-house,
> I could a tale unfold whose lightest word
> Would harrow up thy soul, freeze thy young blood,
> Make thy two eyes like stars start from their spheres,
> Thy knotted and combined locks to part,
> And each particular hair to stand on end
> Like quills upon the fretful porpentine.
>
> (I.v.13–20)

Although there is plenty of nonlinguistic or nondiscursive violence in the play—poisoning and stabbing—many of the play's scenes hinge on a violence which is discursive: Hamlet's confrontation with Ophelia in Act III, scene i, or with his mother in Act III, scene iv, amply demon-strates the ability of language to function as "cause." Language in *Hamlet* may even be implicated in a more general violence, one more difficult to limit or control. Roland Barthes writes,

. . . Neither politeness nor torment, neither the humanity nor even the humor of a style can conquer the absolutely terrorist character of language (once again, this character derives from the systematic nature of language, which in order to be complete needs only to be valid, and not to be true).[15]

15. *Critical Essays,* trans. Richard Howard (Evanston, Ill., 1972), p. 278.

In this view Hamlet's metaphor "Denmark's a prison" (II.ii.243) is as coercive as the more explicitly violent forms of language in the play— e.g., the "daggers" that Hamlet speaks to his mother. Hamlet tacitly acknowledges this when to Rosencrantz and Guildenstern he retorts, "Why, then 'tis none to you, for there is nothing either good or bad but thinking makes it so. To me it is a prison" (II.ii.249–251). And Hamlet's speeches to Ophelia in Act III, scene i, though they certainly inflict considerable violence on Ophelia, may perform an equal violence on their speaker Hamlet, who often seems to be coerced into extravagant postures by his metaphors.[16]

Characters in *Hamlet* frequently deplore the hollowness of "words, words, words" (II,ii.192). At the end of his hollow prayer the King concedes, "Words without thoughts never to heaven go" (III.iii.98). Horatio mocks the courtier Osric, "His purse is empty already, all's golden words are spent" (V.ii.129–130). And Hamlet, in the closet scene again, prepares to reveal to his mother a deed so heinous that it makes of "sweet religion . . . a rhapsody of words" (III.iv.47–48). Words and speakers are several times compared to harlots. Following the Player's speech, Hamlet curses that he "must like a whore unpack my heart with words / And fall a-cursing like a very drab" II.ii.581–582). In the next scene, Claudius remarks in an aside,

> The harlot's cheek, beautied with plast'ring art,
> Is not more ugly to the thing that helps it
> Than is my deed to my most painted word.
>
> (III.i.51–53)

And Polonius commands Ophelia not to believe Hamlet's vows of love, which are "mere implorators of unholy suits, / Breathing like sanctified and pious bawds / The better to beguile" (I.iii.129–131). Words are among the most unreliable causes in the play in two primary senses of the word. First, they constitute one of the more ghostly or

---

16. The extreme or exaggerated character of Hamlet's postures and attitudes has been noted by many critics, most notably perhaps T. S. Eliot in his famous criticism of the play. L. C. Knights points to Hamlet's "exaggerated sense of unworthiness" and to his equally exaggerated "attitudes of hatred, revulsion, self-complacence, and self-reproach," in *Explorations* (New York, 1964), pp. 83, 87.

elusive causes in the sense of the object or end of an action. In the last acts of the play, both Fortinbras and Hamlet are fighting for the cause of words: Fortinbras for honor or reputation—"a fantasy and trick of fame"—and "a little patch of ground / That hath in it no profit but the name" (IV.iv.18–19). And the dying Hamlet urges his stoical friend Horatio not to put an end to himself so that he may tell Hamlet's story. In other words, both Fortinbras in Act IV and Hamlet in Act V are "fighting for a plot," as Hamlet says of Fortinbras: a plot of ground in Fortinbras's case, but also a narrative. This second sense of "plot" is all the more likely because until Acts IV and V, all we know of Fortinbras we know through narrative: e.g., Horatio's account to the sentinels in the first scene of the play (I.i.98ff.). Words are also unreliable "causes" in another sense: a speaker's ability to function as the agent of his language and to control its effects is opened to doubt by the play. In the graveyard scene, for instance, both Hamlet and his rival Laertes indulge in hyperbole, which may be regarded as an attempt to move language from the level of description to that of action. Hamlet's hyperboles are perhaps an attempt to achieve for language the status of agency or cause, but in Ophelia's grave, Hamlet's hyperboles appear to be inefficacious figures, forms as "bloat" as the King himself appears to Hamlet (III.iv.184).

But qualifying all of the play's reflections on the falseness of words (their status as hollow *forms*) is the play's exploration of the violent efficacy of words (their ability to function as *causes*). The passage from Barthes suggests that these two aspects of language may in fact be the same, or indistinguishable. The coerciveness of language, according to Barthes, results from its systematic, formal, conventional nature. Its coercive power, in other words, is heightened rather than attenuated by its formal or systematic character. The more formalized language becomes, the more coercive it becomes, precisely because it is no longer governed or controlled by extralinguistic referents. As Paul de Man has written with admirable (and characteristic) crispness and lucidity, "In conformity with a paradox that is inherent in all literature, . . . poetry gains a maximum of convincing power at the very moment that it abdicates any claim to truth."[17] Language, therefore, may never

17. Paul de Man, *Allegories of Reading* (New Haven, Conn., 1979), p. 50.

constitute that perfectly controlled union of cause and form—"his form and cause conjoin'd"—that Hamlet's father represents. Perhaps experiencing this paradoxical convergence of the attenuation and efficacy of words leads to madness, and perhaps it is this form of madness that stalks the protagonist of Shakespeare's greatest play.

The Iconography of Primitivism
in Cymbeline

PEGGY MUÑOZ SIMONDS

IN HIS RECENT ARTICLE "The Pastoral Reckoning in 'Cymbeline,'" Michael Taylor follows a long line of *Cymbeline* critics in mistaking a primitive setting in the Welsh mountains for a pastoral setting, and he finds Imogen's scene with the beheaded corpse of Cloten astonishingly "grotesque" within this ideal if "hard" pastoral world.[1] Although Shakespeare does indeed use pastoralism in a number of his plays, sheep and shepherds are notably lacking in *Cymbeline*, to the despair of the heroine herself. Imogen yearns for the innocence and security of a pastoral world when she laments in Act I, "Would I were /

The research for this paper was done while the author held an NEH Fellowship for College Teachers in 1982. An early version of the essay was read that same year at the meetings of the South Atlantic Modern Language Association in Atlanta, Ga.

1. *ShS*, XXXVI (1983), 97. Taylor argues rather unconvincingly that there is always some sort of "reckoning" in the pastoral mode, which helps to explain this "gruesome" scene. Although it is true that pastoralism includes the sad truth that "All greenness comes to withering," we do not ordinarily witness the kind of savagery in pastoral poetry that we see in *Cymbeline* and, for that matter, in *King Lear*. Moreover, the opposing modes of pastoralism and primitivism may occur together in the mixed dramatic genre of tragicomedy, as is iconographically clear from the title page of *The Workes* of Ben Jonson.

A neat-herd's daughter, and my Leonatus / Our neighbour-shepherd's son!"[2] Instead, the dramatist presents her with a cave and three self-proclaimed savages, or Wild Men, to contrast with the corrupt and superficially civilized world of the king and his courtiers, who use the pastoral song genre primarily as a means to seduce innocence.[3] Violence and death are everyday aspects of this wilderness life, as Imogen soon discovers, despite the natural courtesy and courage she also finds in Wales.

My purpose in this essay is to discuss the significance of Shakespeare's carefully selected iconography of cultural primitivism and to relate it to the basic Christian theme of the play and to the Jacobean court it both flatters and satirizes. I will show here that the iconography of primitivism serves three major functions in *Cymbeline*. It ironically portrays the savage life as virtuous and instructive in contrast to life in a depraved court; secondly, it focuses our attention on Shakespeare's use of the literary convention of the hunt, which permeates much of the play's action; and, finally, it endows the newly reformed court of Britain with fecundity, strength, and justice, through its human representatives, the Wild Men.

First we must recognize, however, that although William Empson believed that any alternative world was "pastoral," there is actually a sharp dichotomy between Wild Men and shepherds in iconography.[4] Of course these figures may on occasion appear together in tragicomedy, as in fact they do in Guarini's *Il pastor fido*, which opposes a lustful satyr to a princely shepherd, and in Shakespeare's *The Winter's Tale*, which introduces a brief fertility dance by satyrs into a shepherds' festival. But in *Cymbeline* there are no shepherds, only shaggy hunters, and here the alternative world to the court is distinctly primi-

---

2. All quotations from *Cymbeline* are from the Arden Shakespeare, ed. J. M. Nosworthy (London, 1979).

3. G. M. Pinciss also has pointed out the presence of Wild Men in *Cymbeline*. However, since he insists that the play is written in the pastoral mode, he sees the savages as merely symbolic of the natural in contrast to the art of the court. See "The Savage Man in Spenser, Shakespeare, and Renaissance English Drama," in *The Elizabethan Theatre 8*, ed. George R. Hibbard (Port Credit, Ont., 1982), pp. 69–89.

4. See *Some Versions of the Pastoral* (London, 1950).

tive (fig. 1). This in itself may suggest a satiric or ironic social purpose underlying the events of the play, since wildness always symbolizes the lowest level of Renaissance society, or the extreme opposite from the power and glory of the king and his court.

As the word "pastoral" itself indicates, pastoral characters are shepherds and shepherdesses, and pastoral art concerns the lives of those who domesticate and protect animals from the savage aspects of nature. In contrast, "primitivism" denotes the actions of savages or hairy (sometimes leafy) Wild Folk who live what would usually be considered a subhuman, beastly existence in the wilderness, without any of the arts of civilization, sometimes without even the gift of human speech. The shepherds of the pastoral convention are often poets, musicians, and true lovers, while Wild Men were originally depicted in the Middle Ages as fierce, lustful rapists. Shepherds protect their flocks from foxes and wolves; the Wild Man is a hunter of savage beasts and is often described in terms of the predaceous animals he hunts. Predatory himself and often a cannibal, he is a natural enemy to the domesticated pastoral world. Indeed Shakespeare's innocent pastoral characters tend to be clowns, and their simplicity makes them easy dupes for the trickery of those who enter their Edenic haunts. Shakespeare's Wild Men, on the other hand, derive from the tougher, more radical tradition of postlapsarian primitivism, which depicts a moral and physical descent from the human state to that of the brute.[5]

But the figure is notably ambivalent in iconography. The Wild Man may, like Caliban, represent man's lower nature which must be controlled, or, during the late Middle Ages and the Renaissance, he may represent what Timothy Husband describes as "a free and enlightened creature living in complete harmony with nature," who is no longer "a symbol of all that man should eschew but, on the contrary . . . [a] symbol of all that man should strive to achieve."[6] In the latter role, he becomes a conventional and thus a safe way to satirize the rigid social hierarchy of the Jacobean age, even when he goes so far as to lop off the empty head of an ungentle prince in *Cymbeline*. Nevertheless, we should note that judging and executing erring courtiers was also quite

5. See Arthur O. Lovejoy and George Boas, *Primitivism and Related Ideas in Antiquity* (New York, 1973), p. 7.

6. *The Wild Man: Medieval Myth and Symbolism* (New York, 1980), p. 13.

within the accepted tradition of the Wild Man, as a manuscript illustration from a Book of Hours (c. 1500) clearly indicates (fig. 2).

I

The first function of Shakespeare's inconography of primitivism in *Cymbeline* is to portray the wild life as virtuous and instructive in contrast to life in a corrupt court. Twenty years before the first scene opens, a malicious courtier had slandered Belarius to the king, who promptly exiled his formerly trusted adviser. Desiring immediate revenge for his dishonor, Belarius kidnapped the infant sons of Cymbeline and took them with him into a desolate exile in the Welsh mountains, where we first meet all three of them in Act III, scene iii, living in a cave.

They are simple worshipers of the goddess Natura and of the sun, Platonic symbol of the Good. By now their only clothes are those they have fashioned themselves from the skins of animals they hunt for food. Belarius is later described as having a long white beard, and the boys must be equally shaggy in appearance, since Arviragus complains of their state in terms clearly identifying them as ignorant and savage Wild Men: "We have seen nothing: / We are beastly: subtle as the fox for prey, / Like warlike as the wolf for what we eat" (III.ii.40–41). According to Hayden White, "In most accounts of the Wild Man in the Middle Ages, he is as strong as Hercules, fast as the wind, cunning as the wolf, and devious as the fox."[7]

Cymbeline's other kidnapped son, Guiderius, calls their cave dwelling "A cell of ignorance" (III.iii.33), which further suggests the traditional medieval image of Wild Folk cut off from civilization, unable to read or write. However, Belarius, who knows "the art o' th' court," sees their lives as *pious* rather than bestial: "This rock, and these demesnes, have been my world, / Where I have liv'd at honest freedom, paid / More pious debts to heaven than in all / The fore-end of my

---

7. "The Forms of Wildness: Archaeology of an Idea," in *The Wild Man Within: An Image in Western Thought from the Renaissance to Romanticism,* ed. Edward Dudley and Maximilian E. Novak (London, 1972), p. 21.

time" (III.iii.70–73). And he has tried consciously to raise the boys to a life of courtesy within nature.

Husband tells us that early medieval myths of the Wild Man describe him as a hairy hunter who often lives in a cave located on a desolate mountain or deep within the forest. His behavior tends to be brutish and violent, "not only against wild animals but also against his own kind."[8] In *Cymbeline,* Shakespeare's Guiderius displays just this natural aggressiveness in a prompt and ferocious way when he beheads the king's lustful stepson Cloten in Act IV, scene ii. In telling contrast to the hairy Guiderius, Cloten is decked out in elegant court garments he has stolen from Posthumus; yet he arrogantly calls the honest Wild Man a "thief" and "villain base" (ll. 74–75), clear evidence of the dramatist's implicit social satire. Guiderius, in turn, considers Cloten of no more value than a tailor's mannequin and coolly chops off his head, to the horror of the former courtier Belarius. The contrast in this scene between the two younger men represents an important symbolic inversion of the Wild Man topos, since in *Cymbeline* the savage is indeed a true prince, and Cloten is a crude courtly imposter who has obtained his social position at the top of the hierarchy only through his mother's marriage to the king.[9]

His opposites, the Wild Boys—despite their innate and still uncontrolled violence—are natural young noblemen, well-born but bred in the wilderness and innocent in their own lives of all courtly artifice.[10] In Act III, scene vii, of *Cymbeline,* when the wandering Princess Imogen, disguised as a page, unexpectedly meets her shaggy and still unrecognized brothers in the mountains, she wishes they were indeed her father's lost sons:

---

8. Husband, *The Wild Man,* pp. 2–3.

9. Derek Traversi notes that Cloten is "a court parody of the truly 'natural' man, enslaved to his base passions." See *Shakespeare: The Last Phase* (Stanford, Calif., 1955), p. 49.

10. They may therefore have a partly Celtic origin in the myth of Perceval of Wales, who was called "*le valet sauvage*" by Chrêtien de Troyes. According to Richard Bernheimer, "the very fact that a man was brought up in the woods may confer upon him a certain incorruptible quality which alone enables him to resist temptations to which others succumb, and thus attain aims inaccessible to them." See *Wild Men in the Middle Ages* (Cambridge, Mass., 1952), p. 19.

> Great men
> That had a court no bigger than this cave,
> That did attend themselves, and had the virtue
> Which their own conscience seal'd them, laying by
> That nothing-gift of differing multitudes,
> Could not out-peer these twain.
>
> (III.vii.54–59)

They in turn instantly love her and accept her as a "brother," although instinctively doubting her masculinity. Cloten, on the other hand, desires to rape her, much as Shakespeare's most famous Wild Man, Caliban, longs to ravish Miranda in *The Tempest*.

Unlike the "natural" young noblemen, Arviragus and Guiderius, their kidnapper Belarius is a Wild Man of a more sophisticated Renaissance variety, an educated exile from contemporary civilization.[11] When he emerges from his cave in Act III, scene iii, he may well have reminded Shakespeare's audience of Emblem 37 in Andrea Alciati's widely read *Emblemata*. The *inscriptio* or motto of this emblem, "Omnia mea mecum porto" or "I carry everything I own with me," derives from the Erasmian adage, "Sapiens sua secum bona fert" ("The wise man carries his goods with him").[12] It refers to that which we carry within us, such as learning and virtue. The adage is an allusion to Bias, one of the Seven Sages of the classical world, who left all his material goods behind him after a fire. The *pictura* in the 1551 edition of Alciati depicts a Wild Man dressed in skins which have been stitched together. In the background are a cave, trees, and the Scythian Sea, suggesting a reference to the *De Germania* of Tacitus and his ironic descriptions of the barbarians of the north as virtuous in contrast to the Romans of his own time. The *subscriptio* of the emblem reads:

The poor Hun, the most wretched inhabitant of Scythian Pontus, constantly has his limbs burnt livid with unending cold. He knows not the resources of Ceres, or the gifts of Bacchus, nevertheless he always wears precious clothing.

---

11. As the type of educated Wild Man unjustly thrust into the wilderness, Belarius seems to derive topically from the biblical Ishmael: "and he will be a wild man, his hand will be against every man, and every man's hand against him" (Gen. 16:12).

12. Margaret Mann Phillips, *The "Adages" of Erasmus: A Study With Translations* (Cambridge, Eng., 1964), p. 134.

For animal skins envelop him on all sides: Only his eyes are visible, every other part is covered. Thus he has no fear of thieves, thus he disdains the wind and rain: He is safe among men, and safe among the gods.[13]

Some editions of the *Emblemata* show the "poor Hun" as naked, a common variant of the Wild Man topos (fig. 3).

Shakespeare's Belarius appears to be a Wild Man of this virtuous Erasmian type so wistfully celebrated by Alciati. He is a soldier-scholar, who carries his learning and virtue with him into the wilderness to escape the multiple evils of life at court. He assures Arviragus and Guiderius, who complain of their savage existence, that, "this life / Is nobler than attending for a check: Richer than doing nothing for a robe, / Prouder than rustling in unpaid-for silk: / Such gain the cap of him that makes him fine, / Yet keeps his book uncross'd: no life to ours" (III.iii.21–26). One may object, however, that Belarius is also a kidnapper. In this respect, Husband informs us that the mythical Wild Man did characteristically abduct children, "but often only to fulfill parental instincts."[14] And, in fact, Belarius had considerably better parental instincts than does Cymbeline, who is described by his daughter Imogen as like the tyrannous north wind which "Shakes all our buds from growing" (I.iv.37).

The audience witnesses in Act III, scene iii, of *Cymbeline,* on the other hand, an excellent model of the proper education of princes when the Wild Man Belarius, by pointing out examples in nature, trains his royal pupils against moral abuses arising from the unnatural hierarchy of the Renaissance social order. Even the mouth of their humble cave provides a lesson in natural piety: "Stoop boys: this gate / Instructs you how t'adore the heavens; and bow you / To a morning's holy office. The gates of monarchs / Are arch'd so high that giants may get through / And keep their impious turbans on, without / Good morrow to the sun. Hail, thou fair heaven!" (III.iii.2–7). These Wild Men are indeed comfortably "safe among the gods," as Alciata had put it. The antithesis to such pious humility can be seen at Cymbeline's court,

13. See Andrea Alciati, *Emblemata cum commentariis* (1621; rpt. New York and London, 1976), pp. 203–206. All translations of Alciati's emblems in this essay have been graciously provided by Virginia W. Callahan.
14. Husband, *The Wild Man,* p. 3.

where "You do not meet a man but frowns; our bloods / No more obey the heavens than our courtiers / Still seem as does the king's" (I.i.1–3).

Defending the wild life in the kind of speech termed an *argumentum emblematicum* by Albrecht Schöne,[15] Belarius also informs the princes that in the wilderness, "often to our comfort, shall we find / The sharded beetle in a safer hold / Than is the full-wing'd eagle" (III.iii.20–21). As H. W. Crundell has noted, this peculiar image originated with Aesop, was later elaborated upon by Erasmus, and then was used by John Lyly in both *Euphues* and *Endimion* before reappearing in Shakespeare's *Cymbeline*.[16] However, Shakespeare and the educated members of his audience would probably have known as well Alciati's use of the eagle and the beetle in Emblem 169 of his *Emblemata*. Since Alciati's *inscriptio* reads "A Minimis quoque timendum" ("Even the smallest is to be feared"), the reference in *Cymbeline* should probably be understood as a warning by Belarius to the princes not to abuse their own future dependents as he himself has been abused by the tyrant Cymbeline. By extension, a gentle warning is also being sent by the playwright to his own patron, James I, who owned a copy of Alciati and could not possibly be offended by what had become a Renaissance commonplace taught to schoolboys.[17]

The *subscriptio* of Alciati's emblem tells us that,

The beetle is waging war and of his own accord provoking his enemy: And inferior in strength, he conquers through strategy. For without being recognized, he secretly hides himself in the feathers of the eagle, in order to seek the enemy's nest through the highest stars, and piercing the eggs, he prevents the hope of offspring from growing: in this way he goes away, having had vengeance for the dishonor he has suffered.[18]

Alciati's emblem sums up the situation in Shakespeare's play very well indeed, although we have no reason to consider it a direct source. In the tragicomedy, Cymbeline has unwisely dishonored Belarius, who in turn has stolen the king's male offspring from the palace (or nest) in

15. See Peter Daly, *Literature in the Light of the Emblem* (Toronto, 1979), p. 140.
16. In "Shakespeare, Lyly, and Aesop," *N & Q,* CLXVIII (January–June, 1935), 312.
17. See T. W. Baldwin, *William Shakspere's Small Latin & Lesse Greeke* (Urbana, Ill., 1944), I, 535.
18. Alciati, *Emblemata,* p. 709.

order to keep them from becoming tyrants like their father and to avenge his own wounded honor. On the other hand, Belarius—unlike the beetle—does not prevent the boys from growing; instead he educates them in what he understands to be the universal laws of nature.

The *pictura* of this emblem in the 1534 Wechel edition of Alciati shows an angry eagle at the left, his tongue extended, looking up at the beetle in a tree (fig. 4). The source of the emblem was Erasmus's adage "Scarabeus aquilam quaerit" ("The beetle seeks the eagle"). Although Erasmus retells an Aesopian fable, he adds the detail that the beetle actually pushed the eggs out of the eagle's nest. The meaning of the fable, he explains, is that no enemy is to be despised no matter how unfortunate.[19] Later, in *The Education of a Christian Prince,* the Dutch humanist states that in making use of a fable such as the eagle and the beetle, "the teacher should point out its meaning: not even the most powerful prince can afford to provoke or overlook even the humblest enemy. Often those who can inflict no harm by physical strength can do much by the machinations of their minds."[20] Belarius as teacher cannot, of course, fully explain his emblematic argument in *Cymbeline* at this point, but he does remind the boys that "it is place which lessens and sets off" (III.iii.13), and he suggests that certain responsibilities go with high position. At once Guiderius unconsciously associates himself and his brother with the eagle rather than with the lowly beetle: "Out of your proof you speak: we poor unfledg'd, / Have never wing'd from view o' th' nest; nor know not / What air's from home" (ll. 27–29). The irony of this regal association by the Wild Boy would have been immediately apparent to the educated members of Shakespeare's audience. Belarius later proclaims, " 'Tis wonder / That an invisible instinct should frame them / To royalty unlearn'd, honour untaught, / Civility not seen from other, valour / That *wildly* grows in them, but yields a crop / As if it had been sow'd" (IV.ii.176–181; emphasis added).

And life in the wilderness does indeed bring out the native virtue of the kidnapped princes, as Belarius has hoped it would. He comments on this result in a prayer to Natura:

19. Phillips, *Erasmus,* p. 262.
20. See Desiderius Erasmus, *The Education of a Christian Prince,* trans. Lester K. Born (New York, 1936), p. 147.

O thou goddess,
Thou divine Nature; thou thyself thou blazon'st
In the two princely boys: they are as gentle
As zephyrs blowing below the violet,
Not wagging his sweet head; and yet, as rough,
(Their royal blood enchaf'd) as the rud'st wind
That by the top doth take the mountain pine
And make him stoop to th' vale.

(IV.ii.169–176)

Once more there is a close parallel between Belarius's nature imagery
and the emblem tradition. Geoffrey Whitney's "Nimium rebus ne fide
secundis" ("Be not too confident in prosperity") in *A Choice of Emblemes* (1586) has the following *subscriptio*:

The loftie Pine, that on the mountaine growes,
And spreades her armes, with braunches freshe, & greene,
The raginge windes, on sodaine ouerthrowes,
And makes her stoope, that longe a farre was seene;
So they, that truste to muche in fortunes smiles,
Though worlde do laughe, and wealthe doe moste abounde,
What leste they thinke, are often snar'de with wyles,
And from alofte, doo hedlonge fall to grounde:
Then put no truste, in anie worldlie thinges,
For frowninge fate, throwes down the mightie kings.[21]

In *Cymbeline* Belarius compares the Wild Boys to the rude wind
which makes the pine "stoop to the vale" right after Guiderius has described how he cut off the head of an excessively arrogant Cloten.
Thus Cloten is the proud pine which does indeed "hedlonge fall to
grounde" when the true heir to Cymbeline's kingdom meets him like
the raging wind of fate.

II

Our recognition of the primitive mode through the presence of Wild
Men in *Cymbeline* leads us directly to what may be the principal metaphor of the tragicomedy: the hunt of love. Shakespeare's savage hunt-

---

21. (Leyden, 1586), p. 59.

ers Belarius, Arviragus, and Guiderius "do" literally for survival what Posthumus, Imogen, Cloten, and even Iachimo do metaphorically throughout the play. In fact, the entire middle section of *Cymbeline* is devoted to hunts of various kinds—including a war hunt—in the mountains of Wales, and in this focus the play resembles Guarini's *Il pastor fido,* which contains what Bernard Harris calls a "great central episode of the boar hunt."[22] Although Harris has commented briefly on the presence of hunting imagery in *Cymbeline*,[23] no one has yet, to my knowledge, analyzed the play specifically in terms of the chase. We should keep in mind, of course, that hunting was the favorite sport of Shakespeare's royal patron, James I.

Marcelle Thiébaux identifies the significance of the literary convention of the hunt as follows:

Metaphorically and symbolically. . . . the chase becomes an imperative Journey by which a mortal is transported to a condition charged with experience: a preternatural region where he may be tested or placed under an enchantment; a transcendent universe; or the menacing reaches of the self. The act of the chase may reflect not only the compulsion arising from within his own nature to undergo change, but also an external force that imposes this necessity on him: that is, the god. For we are frequently aware of some power outside the hunter himself, with which his own will is made to coincide, both of these, driving, luring, compelling him.[24]

In Shakespeare's tragicomedy, the deity is very close indeed, and, not surprisingly, he finally appears to the hero and to the audience in the dream vision. As many students of *Cymbeline* have pointed out, the doctrine of the incarnation must in some way inform the play as a whole, since the Nativity of Christ was the only "historical" event of real importance to occur during the reign of Cymbeline.[25] And, if the Nativity is indeed the hidden center of the play, then a morally fallen

---

22. " 'What's past is prologue': 'Cymbeline' and 'Henry VIII,' " in *Later Shakespeare,* Stratford-upon-Avon Studies 8 (London, 1966), p. 212.

23. Ibid., p. 216.

24. *The Stag of Love: The Chase in Medieval Literature* (Ithaca and London, 1974), pp. 57–58.

25. See Homer D. Swander, "*Cymbeline*: Religious Idea and Dramatic Design," in *Pacific Coast Studies in Shakespeare,* ed. Waldo McNeir and Thelma N. Greenfield (Eugene, Ore., 1966), pp. 248–262.

world must be properly prepared for such an event. The wilderness, which iconographically represents the fallen world, is an obvious setting for both physical and metaphysical hunts during a period of such preparation. This is so because the Wild Men who inhabit the wilderness are instantly recognizable symbols of postlapsarian humanity. According to Genesis 3:21, "Unto Adam also and to his wife did the Lord God make coats of skins, and clothed them" after the Fall.

Thiébaux tells us that four distinct types of metaphorical hunts occur in literature, although they frequently change and even dissolve into one another: "The sacred chase, the mortal chase, the instructive chase, and the amatory chase."[26] The quarry of a sacred chase lures the hero to a direct confrontation with a god (or a goddess, in the case of Actaeon), and may cause his conversion and/or his death. In the mortal chase, the hunter is led by the quarry as psychopomp from the world of the living to the world of the dead. In the instructive chase, the protagonist undergoes an initiation of some sort, during which he passes "from a condition of ignorance to one of knowledge or self-knowledge."[27] And, finally, in the amatory chase the hunter is lured by the quarry into the nets of a passionate love. All of these forms of hunting occur in *Cymbeline,* with the peculiar twist that in every instance the character thinks he is on one kind of chase, only to discover in the end that he has been on an entirely different type of hunt. In all cases, the ultimate quarry is love: love of God, love of knowledge, love of beauty, love of a spouse, or even ordinary lust for power.

To begin with a literal chase, the three Wild Men in *Cymbeline* must of course hunt for their food. But Belarius insists that they do this in the courtly form of a ritualized sport, thus bringing the chivalric rules of the chase and all of its attendant metaphorical meanings into the play. In Act III, scene iii, Belarius exhorts the Wild Boys to the chase with the shout, "Now for our mountain sport, up to yond hill!" (l. 10). Arviragus, however, yearns for military pursuits instead and complains that "Our valour is to chase what flies" (l. 42). He would much rather face a worthy foe in battle than kill a deer for supper, although hunting was actually considered an ideal way to train the best fighting

---

26. Thiébaux, *The Stag of Love,* p. 58.
27. Ibid.

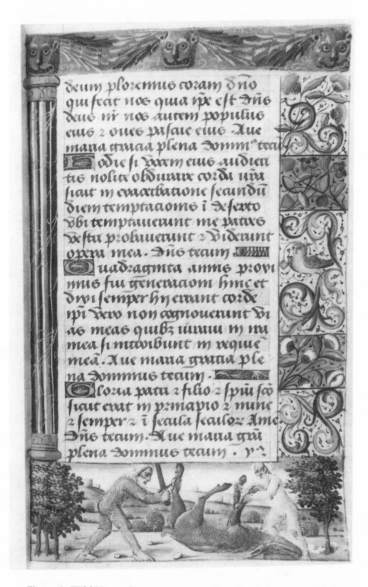

Figure 1. Wild Men as hunters quarter a deer they have just killed. The picture comes from the illuminated border of a Book of Hours, Jean de Montlucon shop, Bourges, France (Ms. 436, 14 recto): by courtesy of the Beinecke Library, Yale University.

Figure 2. Wild Men judge and execute a courtly hunter. From a Book of Hours (c. 1500), Montluçon shop, Bourges, France (Ms. 436, 76 recto): by courtesy of the Beinecke Library, Yale University.

Figure 4. The eagle and the beetle from Andrea Alciati's *Emblemata* (p. 68, 1534 Wechel edition, PN 6349 A8). By permission of the Folger Shakespeare Library.

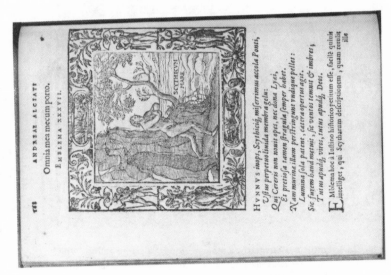

Figure 3. Emblem 37 from the *Emblemata* of Andrea Alciati (p. 168, 1581 edition, PN 6349 A8): by permission of the Folger Shakespeare Library.

Figure 5. Emblem 47 from the *Emblemata* of Hadrianus Junius, which depicts the wounded deer, as a figure of the anguished soul, fleeing from its pursuer (p. 53, PN 6349 J8 1595 copy 1). By permission of the Folger Shakespeare Library.

Figure 7. Linlithgow coat of arms with three Wild Men (pl. xi, *Wood's Scottish Peerage*, xs 468 D74 1813 v.2). By courtesy of the Folger Shakespeare Library.

Figure 6. The sacred chase from Otto van Veene's *Emblemes of Love* (1608) (p. 131, STC 24627a.5 copy 1). By permission of the Folger Shakespeare Library.

Figure 8. Title-plate for John Speed's *The History of Great Britaine* by Jodocus Hondius (STC 23045 copy 1). By permission of the Folger Shakespeare Library.

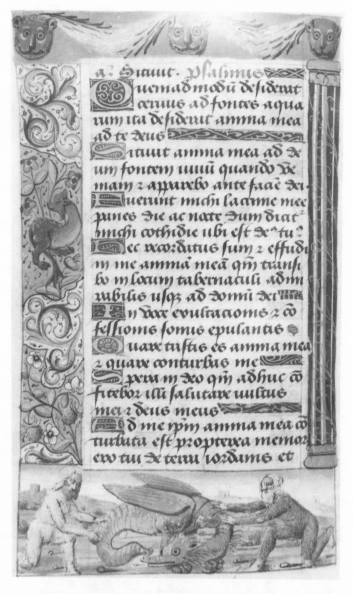

Figure 9. Wild Men subdue a dragon in a Book of Hours (90 recto, Ms. 436). By courtesy of the Beinecke Library, Yale University.

Figure 11. Wild Man as guardian pinnacle, St. Mary's Church, Mendlesham, Suffolk, England. Photograph by Peggy M. Simonds.

Figure 10. Closeup of Wild Man over the porch door of St. Michael's Church, Peasenhall, Suffolk, England. Photograph by Peggy M. Simonds.

Figure 12. Wild Man on the stem of the baptismal font in St. Peter's Church, Sibton, Suffolk, England. Photograph by Peggy M. Simonds.

Figure 13. Wild Man and lion on the stem of the baptismal font with the Evangelists carved on the basin: St. Peter's Church, Sibton, Suffolk, England. Photograph by Peggy M. Simonds.

men.[28] Belarius cuts off the boys' discontent with a reminder of the ritual nature of their hunt and with a satirical comment on the sinister aspects of a refined life at court:

> But up to th' mountains!
> This not hunter's language; he that strikes
> The venison first shall be the lord o' th' feast,
> To him the other two shall minister,
> And we will fear no poison, which attends
> To place of greater state. I'll meet you in the valleys.
>
> (III.iii.73–78)

The whooping music of horn and hounds then becomes an integral part of the theatrical performance, prompting occasional interpretations by Belarius, who remains on stage: "Hark, the game is rous'd!" (l. 98) and, finally, "The game is up" (l. 107).

This literal chase—to the astonishment of the hunters—ends as a sacred chase, since divinity hunts down men with as much persistence as men hunt for deer. Thus, while the Wild Men pursue a stag on the mountain top, the true quarry takes shelter in their deserted cave. When the hunters return home carrying their deer, Belarius announces ceremoniously, "You, Polydore, have prov'd best woodman, and / Are master of the feast: Cadwal and I / Will play the cook and servant: 'tis our match" (III.vii.1–3). But the weary Guiderius replies, "There is cold meat i' th' cave, we'll *browse* on that" (l. 11; emphasis added). With his use of the word "browse," Guiderius transforms the successful hunters themselves into three deer, who are then captured or captivated by their mysterious intruder. When Imogen, disguised as the page Fidele, suddenly emerges from the cave to face them, the startled Belarius exclaims, "Behold divineness / No elder than a boy" (ll. 16–17). This seems to be an obvious allusion to Amor or Cupid, the winged hunter of men. Such an unexpected confrontation with the "divine" beauty of Imogen-Fidele has an instant civilizing effect on the Wild Men, who piously invite her to share their humble meal.

Of course I not mean to imply here that Imogen is a type or personification of Christ; rather I believe she is a soul figure on her own painful quest for love in the wild mountains of Wales, and—in this most

28. Ibid., p. 49.

Platonic of Shakespeare's plays—her beauty and goodness seem to reflect for many of the characters in *Cymbeline* something of the sacred
quality of the Love-god soon to be born. For example, when Arviragus
first looks at Imogen, he understands at once the essence of Christ's
ethical teaching: "He is a man, I'll love him as my brother" (III.vii.44).
Further echoes of the Christian myth occur when Imogen-Fidele sick-
ens, apparently dies, and is resurrected. Moreover, she has previously
called herself "Th' elected deer" (III.iv.111), which can refer to Christ
as the quarry of man's desire but is also a frequent symbol of the human soul pursued by God.[29]

As for the wild hunters, they see Imogen as a winged creature
untimely brought to earth. "The bird is dead," mourns Arviragus
(IV.ii.197). Then, after a brief funeral ceremony for both Imogen and
the beastly Cloten, who has been judged unworthy of the new era to
come and executed by Guiderius, the three Wild Men go off on another type of hunt. This patriotic war hunt takes place on the battlefield, where they chase after the invaders of their native land and at
last reveal their true princely mettle to the courtly world.

In contrast to the earlier sacred chase of the Wild Men, the courtier
Cloten embarks on a *chasse d'amour* which soon becomes a mortal
chase. Lusting to "penetrate" Imogen, as the hunter penetrates the
stag with his arrow or lance, Cloten first unsuccessfully attempts to
gain access to her bedchamber through bribery: "'Tis gold / Which
buys admittance (oft it doth) yea, and makes / Diana's rangers false
themselves, yield up / Their deer to th' stand o' th' stealer" (II.iii.66–
69). When Imogen runs away from the court, the frustrated poacher
says, "I will pursue her / Even to Augustus' throne" (III.v.101–102).

But soon afterward, Cloten meets Guiderius in the mountains,
where the vicious hunter from court becomes the Wild Boy's prey in a
mortal hunt. As Thiébaux points out,

The encounter with the quarry or the struggle to which the quarry has conducted the hero may result in the dissolution of his former or human identity,
perhaps the loss of his life. The hunter himself becomes the hunt's object; he,

29 See Michael J. B. Allen, "The Chase: The Development of a Renaissance Theme,"
Comparative Literature, XX (1968), 306–307.

not the quarry, is sacrificed. Failing to survive the crisis to which the hunt has brought him, he is annihilated in the act.[30]

Guiderius lops off the arrogant Cloten's head with his victim's own sword, only to find the head ludicrously empty. Thiébaux informs us that in literature, "Details of the quarry's dismemberment may correspond to the hero's conquest of [a] former self, which he is now enabled to cast from him."[31] Although, in this case, the casting away of the empty head is performed by the Wild Boy, the dismemberment of Cloten does clearly resemble the "breaking up" of a deer after the hunt, since cutting off the quarry's head was part of the established ritual. Indeed *Turbervile's Booke of Hunting* (1576) states that after the prince slits open the animal's belly, "we vse to cut off the Deares heades. And that is commonly done also by the chiefe personage. For they take delight to cut off his heade with the woodknyues, skaynes, or swordes, to trye their edge, and the goodnesse or strength of their arme."[32] The brains were then usually given to the hounds as a reward, but of course Cloten had none to spare.[33]

Iachimo, the second poacher in the play, also sets off in pursuit of "ladies' flesh," although he is really on a hunt for the riches he hopes to gain by seducing Imogen and winning his wager with Posthumus. But once again the hunter becomes the hunted. After scheming his way through flattery into Imogen's bedchamber, Iachimo ignores the warning iconography of Diana bathing, which is depicted on a bas-relief over the fireplace. He continues to the bed, where he boldly gazes down on beauty bare. However, to his astonishment, the sight of

30. Thiébaux, *The Stag of Love,* p. 57.

31. Ibid.

32. (1567; rpt. Oxford, 1908), p. 134.

33. See Peggy Muñoz Simonds, "Some Courtier *Topoi* in *Cymbeline,*" *RenP* (1982), 97–112. This essay discusses the significance to the play of Alciati's Emblem 189. Under the motto "Mentem, non forman, plus pollere" ("The mind, not the form, matters"), Alciati depicts a fox holding an empty head in his paws. According to the verse, "A fox entering the property room of a stage manager, came upon a human head polished by a craftsman, so elegantly fashioned that it seemed only to lack breath, and to be alive in other respects. When that one took the mask into his hands, he said: 'O what a head is this! but it has no brains.' " The source is an adage of Erasmus based on one of Aesop's fables.

the sleeping princess makes him acutely aware of his own evil and of its ultimate results for his soul: "I lodge in fear; / Though this a heavenly angel, hell is here" (II.ii.49–50). Many commentators have pointed out Iachimo's likeness in this scene to the voyeuristic hunter Actaeon. Since this myth was frequently employed during the reign of Queen Elizabeth to warn courtiers against excessive "presumption," as Leonard Barkan has shown,[34] Shakespeare may well have intended a similar warning against intrusion on the privacy of Princess Elizabeth when he evokes the image of Actaeon profanely peeking at the royal Diana in *Cymbeline*. But there are also Platonic suggestions in this scene of the moral effect of beauty on the beholder. Although Iachimo is not at once punished, as is Actaeon, or even deflected from his wicked plot, he is indeed subtly changed by the experience. At the end of the play, he admits to Cymbeline that "I was taught / Of your chaste daughter the wide difference / 'Twixt amorous and villainous" (V.v.193–195), a lesson in feeling he had not expected to learn.

Imogen herself sets out for the wilderness at first on an amatory hunt for her banished husband. Then Pisanio makes her aware that she is also the quarry for another hunter when he shows her the letter from Posthumus ordering her murder for adultery. Her first reaction is despair: "Prithee, dispatch," she cries out to Pisanio. "The lamb entreats the butcher. Where's the knife?" (III.iv.97–98). At this moment, she closely resembles the medieval iconographic figure of "the driven soul" as a "harried stag" pursued by the vices of wrath and jealousy (Posthumus), envy and greed (Iachimo), and vanity and lust (Cloten).[35] She turns at bay to face Pisanio, who refuses to obey his master's written order to kill her. "Why hast thou gone so far," she asks, in the language of the hunt, "To be unbent when thou hast ta'en thy stand, / th' elected deer before thee?" (III.iv.109–111). Convinced of her innocence, Pisanio suggests that she disguise herself as the boy Fidele and continue alone on her love hunt for Posthumus in Wales. Imogen is not like the fleeing wounded stag of Emblem 47 by Hadrianus Junius, which has an inserted Petrarchan motto: "De diulimi struggo, et di

---

34. See "Diana and Actaeon: The Myth as Synthesis," *English Literary Renaissance,* X (1980), 334–335.

35. Thiébaux, *The Stag of Love,* p. 44.

fuggir mi stanco," or "I am consumed with anguish, and I exhaust myself with flight" (fig. 5).[36]

At this point, Imogen's amatory hunt is transformed into an instructive chase, during which she is initiated into some of the mysteries of
love. First she learns to understand the powers of her own beauty for
either good or evil. When they encounter her beauty in masculine disguise, the Wild Men immediately vow to befriend her, offering all they
have; but Cloten, who has seen her in female clothing, literally loses
his head over her, since he desires not to serve beauty but to possess it
selfishly. She learns, in addition, to love deeply—to love not only
Posthumus, despite his now obvious imperfections, but all suffering
mortality as well, no matter what their social rank or their degree of
sinfulness. The princess in disguise soon discovers that, although
"man's life is a tedious one" (III.vi.1), she can enjoy serving as a cook
for humble but good savages: "Gods, what lies I have heard! / Our
courtiers say all's savage but at court; / Experience, O, thou disprov'st
report" (IV.ii.32–34). And she observes in a similar vein that empires
"breed monsters" while "sweet fish" are found in small rivers
(IV.ii.35–36), another instance of hunting imagery. The comment is
also a satirical reminder to the audience of the dangers inherent in
King James's ambitious dreams of founding a new Augustan empire in
Britain. Most significantly, however, in mistaking the dead Cloten for

36. *Emblemata* (Antwerp, 1565), p. 53. Junius's verse (translated for the author by
Roger T. Simonds) reads as follows: "Why, Stag, pierced by the Cretan reed [= arrow], /
do you give free rein to headlong flight? / This is the lover's luck, whom flight stirs up: /
Too grievous a wound drives him out of his mind." See also *The Heroical Devises of
M. Claudius Paradin* (1591). Scholars' Facsimiles and Reprints # 391 (Delmar, N.Y.,
1984), pp. 354–355: "A Hart stroke thorough with an arrow, & eating of a branch or
leafe of Dictanus (which is an hearbe growing abundantly in Candia, or the Iland of
Crete, which being eaten of a hart, his wounds are immediately healed) with this inscrip-
tion, *Esto tienne su remedio, y non yo,* that is, the heart here hath helpe, but my wounde
is incurable, may bee a figure or simbole of love that can never he healed: alluding to
that verse of Ovid in his Metamorphosis, wherein Phoebus bewraieth his love toward
Daphnes:

> Wo to me that haggard love,
> which sets our mindes on fire,
> Cannot be healed by hearbes or rootes,
> nor druggie potions dire.

her beloved Posthumus, she learns that all men are essentially alike
and all are to be pitied in the end.

When Imogen takes medicine for her love sickness in Act IV, scene
ii, she continues to behave like the pierced stag which traditionally
seeks for dittany to cure its wound. Otto van Veen based his emblem of
the remedy-seeking stag on earlier emblems by Symeoni (1562) and
Camerarius (1595). Under the motto "No help for the louer," the verse
reads,

> The hert that wounded is, knowes how to fynd relief,
> And makes by dictamon the arrow out to fall,
> And with the self-same herb he cures his wound withall
> But love no herb can fynd to cure his inward grief.[37]

After taking the drug, prepared as poison by the Queen but made
harmless by Cornelius, Imogen falls into a counterfeit death. She later
awakens to confront not only real death lying beside her but also the
first victim of her own beauty, Cloten. Although love is a positive force
for good, at the same time it can be mortally dangerous. Thinking that
she has at last found her own quarry, Posthumus, the grief-stricken
Imogen daubs her face with the dead man's blood. The scene may indeed be "grotesque," as Taylor and others complain, but it is also entirely appropriate to the primitive world of this play. By smearing her
face with her quarry's blood, Imogen performs a familiar hunter's initiation rite called "blooding." According to tradition, the hunter of
wild beasts is ritually daubed after his first kill with the blood of his
victim, thereby acquiring its spirit as well as a heightened awareness of
the close interrelationship between the hunter and the hunted. For example, in Shakespeare's "Venus and Adonis," when the divine hunt-
ress Venus sees her slain "deer" Adonis, she "stains her face with his
congealed blood" (l. 1122). William Faulkner describes a similar rite
of "blooding" more literally in his stories "The Bear" and "The Old
People."

The irony in *Cymbeline* is that the dead man is not Posthumus at all
but the would-be rapist Cloten. Nevertheless, Imogen's heartbreak
over the bleeding corpse of her hated pursuer is, when properly per-

---

37. *Amorum Emblemata or Emblemes of Love* (Antwerp, 1608), p. 154.

formed, a very moving dramatic experience for the audience. Her embrace of the corpse appears to symbolize on a metaphysical level the soul's incredible fusion with the gross body. It is a visual stage emblem of the shocking love union between beauty and the beast which lies at the heart of all human existence and which also lies behind the mystery of the divine incarnation so soon to take place.

In contrast to Imogen, her husband Posthumus deliberately sets out right from the beginning on an instructive chase when he consents to the unholy wager with Iachimo. He initiates a metaphoric hunt for forbidden knowledge about the nature of love. Instead of having faith in his bride's sworn love for him, he wants public proof of it, which is theologically analogous to demanding proof from God that he is to be saved. According to St. Paul in Ephesians 5, the union of matrimony is directly comparable to the redemptive union of Christ with his congregation; both are mysteries and both must be taken on faith. Therefore, when the profane hunter Posthumus impiously seeks to penetrate the sacred mystery of Imogen's love, he is permitted only false knowledge of infidelity and a bloody scrap of cloth to indicate falsely his quarry's death. Like Cloten, Posthumus has understood love only as a simple matter of sexual possession rather than as a holy lure to self-sacrifice.

Although Posthumus's subsequent conversion at the sight of the bloody token sent by Pisanio is often criticized as too sudden and unconvincing, it is in fact another venerable convention in the literature of the hunt and is certainly not intended by the dramatist to be analyzed in terms of realism. In *Cymbeline* the shock of seeking a death symbol—the bloodsoaked veil which separates life from death—enlarges the hero's capacity to love uncritically in imitation of a forgiving Christ, and once again the hunter becomes the hunted. As Arthur Kirsch has said of the hunter Silvio, who accidentally wounds his loving pursuer Dorinda in *Il pastor fido,* "Her suffering by his hand transforms him, and the arrow he has loosed upon her leaves its shaft in his heart. He is the happy prey of his own hunt."[38] But Posthumus's repentance does not immediately bring him happiness. Instead it drives him to begin a new chase, this time a mortal hunt, which—after his capture by the British—transmogrifies into yet another unexpected sacred

38. *Jacobean Dramatic Perspectives* (Charlottesville, Va., 1972). p. 12.

chase. It is significant that Posthumus's deliberate search for a death of atonement leads him directly in *Cymbeline* to a vision of divinity.

But first the forces of evil must be overcome. Searching the battlefield for his own death in penitential exchange for the presumed death of Imogen, Posthumus easily defeats the evil Iachimo in a dumb show, after which he helps the three Wild Men turn back the invading forces of Rome. He tells others of the latter event in hunting language, since battles were also considered a form of the chase.[39] The Wild Boys, as Posthumus reports, halted the British retreat with the cry, "'Our Britain's harts die flying, not our men: / To darkness fleet souls that fly backwards; stand, / Or we are Romans, and will give you that / Like beasts which you shun beastly' " (V.iii.24–27). Accordingly, the British ceased running and began, Posthumus says, "to grin like lions / Upon the pikes o' th' hunters" (ll. 37–38). The enemy then flew from the fury of the Wild Boys like "Chickens, the way which they stoop'd eagles" (l. 42). However, Posthumus himself is unable to find his own quarry—that "ugly monster" death (V.iii.70)—on the battlefield.

Still grimly determined to complete a mortal hunt, he resumes his Roman armor in order to attract British revenge against an invader: "Fight I will no more, / But yield me to the veriest hind that shall / Once touch my shoulder" (V.iii.76–78). In another of Shakespeare's imaginative reversals of the chase, the hunter Posthumus consciously agrees to become the quarry of the hind. But once again the hero fails to find death, even after he is captured by the British. Instead, like Imogen, he only sleeps. His ensuing dream vision, reuniting him with his deceased family and with his divine Creator, spectacularly encompasses three different worlds at once: his own, the underworld, and the heavens. As I have argued elsewhere, the descent of Jupiter in Act V, scene iv, would probably have been interpreted by an alert Jacobean audience as an implicit reference to the historical descent of the Christian deity, who could not otherwise be mentioned or personified on a public stage in England.[40] Thus Posthumus's hunt, unconsciously a *sa-*

---

39. See Thiébaux, *The Stag of Love*, pp. 49–50.

40. See "Jupiter, His Eagle, and BBC-TV," *Shakespeare on Film Newsletter* X, no. 1 (December 1985), p. 3. Both Dante and Petrarch used Jupiter as a symbol of the Christian deity, who is still often evoked euphemistically as "Jove" in upper-class English speech.

cred chase from the very beginning, ends with an astonishing theophany and with an unmistakably Christian answer to his instructive chase for forbidden knowledge of love and salvation. According to Jupiter, "Whom best I love I cross, / To make my gift, / The more delay'd, delighted" (V.iv.101–102). This statement suggests that the true quarries of God's love hunt and those who share with Christ the agonies of the cruel capture and crucifixion of the "elected deer" on Calvary, the ultimate consummation of the sacred chase.

Before man's redemptive quarry can be born in Bethlehem, however, the major characters in *Cymbeline* must complete their hunts for love in the wilderness and help bring a momentary peace to the world. According to the motto of an emblem by Shakespeare's Dutch contemporary Otto van Veen, "The chasing goeth before the taking." The verse states, in words much like those of Shakespeare's Jupiter, that,

> Before the deer bee caught it first must hunted bee,
> The Ladie eke pursu'd before shee bee obtaynd,
> Payn makes the greater woorth of ought thats thereby gayned,
> For nothing easily got we do esteemed see.[41]

The idea, says the emblematist, derives from Pindar. Van Veen's *pictura* illustrates the divine hunt of love in which Cupid and his hounds of desire eagerly pursue a deer in flight, the symbol of an anguished human soul (fig. 6).

III

Finally, the great denouement scene (Act V, scene v) of *Cymbeline* begins with a heraldic tableau which makes striking use of the Wild Man topos and helps bring the tragicomedy to a happy close. After winning his war against the Romans, thanks to Belarius and the two Wild Boys, Cymbeline places the Wild Men next to him onstage with the words, "Stand by my side, you whom the gods have made / Preservers of my throne" (ll. 1–2). Now, Husband tells us that Wild Men began appearing in heraldry as supporters of family shields at the end of the fourteenth century and soon became popular figures in this

41. *Amorum Emblemata,* p. 131.

role.[42] The coat of arms of the Earls and Dukes of Atholl (now Murrays but descended from the Stewart family or the royal house of Scotland) is an excellent example of the two characteristic uses of the Wild Man in heraldry. First, he appears as an *emblem* within the coat of arms. Husband suggests that through this use of the figure, "The two hundred or more European families who incorporated the wild man in their coats-of-arms may . . . have wished to . . . display their hardiness, strength and fecundity."[43] Second, he appears as a supporter of the shield, probably as a type of protective talisman.[44] Thus, by surrounding himself with the Wild Men who have almost single-handedly saved both the king and Britain from the Romans, Cymbeline draws to himself their strength, their fertility, and their loyalty. Furthermore, Shakespeare has here literalized the king's heraldic metaphor "Preservers of my throne," since the two Wild Boys are actually Cymbeline's true sons and will indeed transmit his royal succession to the future of Britain. Therefore, despite the previous criticism of the British court we have noted in passing and the implied warnings to the monarch of dangerous corruption in his palace, Shakespeare is careful to end his tragicomedy on a note of Jacobean affirmation. As Frances Yates has suggested, a compliment to James I, who also had two sons and a daughter, may well be intended in the play.[45]

In fact, the possibilities are very high that Shakespeare was indeed flattering the court in the heraldic moments of Act V, scene v, since about one-fourth of all Scottish noble families employed Wild Men in their coats of arms. There are seventeen such devices illustrated in the plates accompanying Wood's *The Peerage of Scotland,* and many of these families were closely associated with the life of King James.[46]

42. Husband, *The Wild Man,* p. 186.

43. Ibid., p. 185.

44. See Richard Bernheimer, *Wild Men in the Middle Ages: A Study in Art, Sentiment, and Demonology* (Cambridge, Mass., 1952), pp. 177–178.

45. *Shakespeare's Last Plays: A New Approach* (London, 1975), pp. 41–61.

46. See John Philip Wood, *The Peerage of Scotland,* 2d ed., 2 vols. (Edinburgh, 1813). Among these families, Walter Stewart, Lord Blantyre, had a coat of arms supported by both a lion and a Wild Man. He "was bred up along with King James VI of Scotland under George Buchanan," and he later became a commissioner for the treaty of union with England (I, 213). Edward Bruce, Earl of Elgin and Kincardine, with two savages supporting his shield, was sent in 1600 to England by James "to congratulate Queen Elizabeth on her suppression of the Essex rebellion" (I, 515). On the accession of James to the English

However, I believe the most likely specific candidate for the honor was Alexander, seventh Lord Livingston, who was created the Earl of Linlithgow by King James "at the baptism of Prince Charles on December 25, 1600."[47] Lord Livingston was also one of the commissioners appointed by Parliament to negotiate the union between England and Scotland.

Since we know that the three rustics who defended a narrow lane against invading Danes in the legendary past of Scotland were ancestors of the Hay family, the parallel heroism of Belarius, Guiderius, and Arviragus dramatized in *Cymbeline* seems to be an obvious compliment to Lord John Hay, a courtly favorite of the king, as Glynne Wickham has argued.[48] The iconographical problem here is that there are absolutely no Wild Men in the Hay coat of arms. Nevertheless, it seems that Alexander Livingston, Earl of Linlithgow, was married to Lady Helenor Hay, daughter of the 7th Earl of Errol. Through this union, a female member of the Hay family did acquire a new coat of arms with one Wild Man as emblem above the shield and with two Wild Men as supporters, thus giving us the necessary *three* Wild Men seen in the play (fig. 7). Moreover, one of the charters granting the Livingstons more land in Scotland and dated 13 March 1600, "makes honourable mention of the great care and fidelity bestowed by the Lord Livingston

---

throne, Bruce accompanied his sovereign south where he became a privy-councillor and master of the rolls for life. Perhaps the most exotic of the Scottish peers, with two Wild Men as supporters of his shield, was Sir Robert Gordon of Lochinvar, Viscount of Kenmure, who was something of a Wild Man himself. After Sir Robert had made a reputation by plundering his neighbors' cattle, burning their houses, and even taking them prisoner on occasion, James VI sent out a force to arrest him. But "he deforced his Majesty's officers, making the principal eat the warrant." His father and friends managed to obtain a pardon for him, after which he became one of the king's gentlemen of the bedchamber. Later, at a royal tournament, "Sir Robert Gordon was one of the three successful champions to whom prizes were delivered by Princess Elizabeth" (II, 126–127). It seems likely that any of these noble families could have felt honored by Shakespeare in the heraldic tableau of Act V, scene v, and perhaps the dramatist hoped they would *all* see themselves celebrated as preservers of the king's throne.

47. Ibid., II, 127.

48. See "Riddle and Emblem: A Study in the Dramatic Structure of *Cymbeline,*" in *English Renaissance Studies: Presented to Dame Helen Gardner on her 70th Birthday* (Oxford, 1980), pp. 112–113.

and his lady in the education of the King's children, and the expence incurred in maintaining them and their servants."[49]

This fact appears to throw some light on Belarius's saucy demand that the king "pay me for the nursing of thy sons" (V.v.323). He then delivers the Wild Boys to their father with glowing praise:

> Here are your sons again, and I must lose
> Two of the sweet'st companions in the world.
> The benediction of these covering heavens
> Fall on their heads like dew, for they are worthy
> To inlay heaven with stars.
>
> (ll. 349–353)

According to Wood, the Livingstons primarily had the care of Princess Elizabeth, and "they discharged that trust so much to the satisfaction of King James VI [of Scotland], that, when they delivered her safe at Windsor, in 1603, they obtained an act of approbation from the King and council."[50] In *Cymbeline,* Imogen is restored to her father at the same time that he recovers his lost sons.

The venerable figure of the wild soldier Belarius as a true defender of Britain in this final heraldic tableau of the play has a contemporary iconographic counterpart as well. The image of a Wild Man labeled "A Britaine" dominates the emblematic title-page (fig. 8) of John Speed's *The History of Great Britaine* (1611). The ancient savage towers over the other four soldiers representative of Britain's military ancestry: a Roman, a Saxon, a Dane, and a Norman. Here again James is reminded of the native worth of his people, who—if they are welcomed at court—can help to preserve the throne and maintain peace in the land. Although the Wild Man in cultural history was originally a lawless figure like Caliban, by Shakespeare's time he was also a positive heraldic figure who could be trusted to maintain law and order. Indeed two of them were used in 1610 as part of the pageant offered by the city of Chester to honor Prince Henry. Instead of behaving in a primitive and lustful manner, these Wild Men essentially performed the role of St. George in pantomime. They fought against evil by engaging in battle with "an artificial Dragon, very liuely to behold," who pursued

49. Wood, *The Peerage of Scotland,* II, 127.
50. Ibid.

"the Sauages entring their Denne, casting Fire from his mouth, which afterwards was slaine, to the great pleasure of the spectators, bleeding, fainting, and staggering, as though he endured a feeling paine, euen at the last gaspe, and farewell."[51] In religious iconography, the Wild Man also faces the dragon as a symbol of the natural strength and fortitude available to defeat evil (fig. 9). To take one example, he performs this function in a spandrel on the porch entrance of St. Michael's in Peasenhall, Suffolk (fig. 10). Or we can see him poised as a guardian pinnacle, in conjunction with a crowned lion representing the monarchy, on the battlements of the north porch of St. Mary's in Mendlesham, Suffolk (fig. 11).

But we must also recall that the Wild Man, however strong and fertile, still remained for theology a symbol of fallen humanity. According to Bernheimer, since the Wild Man was not created wild by God but fell from grace and descended into brutishness as the result of his own actions, "the state of wildness was not usually regarded as irrevocable, but as amenable to change through acculturation."[52] Thus we find that the Wild Man and his vegetable counterpart the Green Man were also permitted inside English churches from the very earliest times. The great cathedrals of Ely, Exeter, and Norwich, for example, are extraordinarily rich in Green Man iconography, with roof bosses in the gates and cloisters at Norwich serving as sorrowful reminders of still unredeemed nature, even within the church itself.[53] Therefore, *inside* many churches, the Wild Man and the uncrowned lion seem to represent that aspect of fallen nature which must be overcome and controlled by the word of God, especially when they appear together on the stems of baptismal fonts (fig. 12). Above them, on the exterior of the basin, are generally carved the four Evangelists and their symbols, as representations of the saving power of the Gospels (fig. 13).

For this reason, the Wild Men in *Cymbeline* must—for their own salvation, as well as for that of the kingdom—be removed from the cave of ignorance (called a "prison" by Guiderius, in what appears to be a Platonic allusion to the prison of the body or nature) and be reintegrated

51. Quoted by Robert Hillis Goldsmith, "The Wild Man on the English Stage," *MLR*, LIII (1958), p. 485.
52. Bernheimer, *Wild Men in the Middle Ages,* p. 8.
53. See Kathleen Basford, *The Green Man* (Ipswich, 1978), p. 19.

with a now purified court and with its formal religious celebrations. Their redemption is indeed essential to the redemption of Cymbeline's entire kingdom. In Shakespeare's dramatic context, the Wild Boys may symbolize the true defenders of the reformed church in Jacobean Britain, since they almost single-handledly drive off the "Roman" invaders of the island kingdom, rescue the captured ruler, and are finally revealed as the rightful heirs to the English throne.

Thus Shakespeare's primitive Wild Men—Belarius, Guiderius, and Arviragus—serve three thematic functions in *Cymbeline*. First, their wholesome (if violent) lives within nature are an implicit negative criticism of the dangerous excesses of a luxurious life at court. Secondly, their ritual vocation of hunting both underlies and informs the major strands of action within the play. And, thirdly, they are positive heraldic supporters of both a reformed Church and a reformed State; hence— by extension—they are supporters of the dual functions of James I, sovereign of what he hoped would soon become the United Kingdom of Great Britain.

"The Master-Wit is the master-fool": Jonson, Epicoene, and the Moralists

DIANA BENET

IT USED TO BE "something of a commonplace" that Ben Jonson's "work is, in moral terms, all of a piece"; it is now something of a commonplace to assert that the author's work is, in ethical terms, a crazy quilt reflecting "the various nature of his moral thought," as Ian Donaldson writes in "Jonson and the Moralists."[1] His dramatic art, we are told, reveals that he "was not committed to the general reform of mankind," and *Epicoene* (especially) is cited as evidence of his tolerant attitude.[2] This view of the author is closely related to the prevailing opinion of the play's gentlemen-wits. Some time ago, Edward B. Partridge pointed out that the gallants, like most of the other characters in the play, are epicene figures, and Alvin Kernan flatly rejected them as the play's ethical standard, granting only that they are "not too depraved." But recent commentary has effected the apotheosis of the young men as models of "an ideal of life which can be at once vir-

1. "Jonson and the Moralists," in *Two Renaissance Mythmakers: Christopher Marlowe and Ben Jonson,* ed. Alvin Kernan (Baltimore, 1977), pp. 148, 154.

2. Judd Arnold, *A Grace Peculiar: Ben Jonson's Cavalier Heroes* (University Park, Pa., 1972), p. 7.

121

tuous and yet urbanely sociable."[3] Even now, however, the critics who propose them as the playwright's ideal of urbanity and virtue do not claim moral perfection for them. Consequently, the revision of the wits' reputation has resulted in the revision of the author's.

The critical connection between the gallants' reputation and Jonson's depends on three biographically or historically based interpretations. The first of these, and the most persistent and influential, assumes that one character (or more) represents the author's own moral stance. Jonas Barish acknowledged, some time ago, the biographical aspect that has since gone largely unremarked: *Epicoene,* he asserted, "represents the highly equivocal victory of acceptance of life, in which Jonson can exorcise the satiric spirit in himself only by magnifying it to monstrous proportions and then tormenting it beyond measure." Since, obviously, the unattractive and eventually humiliated Morose does not represent the author in the play, and since Barish assumed the presence of an authorial spokesman or surrogate, he concluded that the role belonged to the clever and successful Truewit.[4] However, as Kernan pointed out some years ago, there is no reason, initially, to confuse the Renaissance author's identity with his railer's. Indeed, there are several reasons why such an automatic identification of one with the other is unwarranted: a popular figure in Elizabethan drama, the satiric character was typically ridiculous, presented as a flawed person lacking self-knowledge. Though he was much enjoyed by his on- and off-stage audiences, he was taken seriously by neither.[5] It is as likely, in other words, that Jonson created Morose as a variation

3. "Yet even these normal men are somewhat ambiguous, sexually," Partridge remarks, referring especially to the "allusion to the homosexual relationship of the boy and Clerimont." *The Broken Compass: A Study of the Major Comedies of Ben Jonson* (New York, 1958), p. 170; Alvin Kernan, *The Cankered Muse: Satire of the English Renaissance* (New Haven, Conn., 1959), p. 185; W. David Kay, "Jonson's Urbane Gallants: Humanistic Contexts for *Epicoene,*" *HLQ,* XXXIX (1976), 257.

4. Jonas A. Barish, *Ben Jonson and the Language of Prose Comedy* (Cambridge, Mass., 1960), p. 148. (Edmund Wilson, of course, first suggested that Morose represented an aspect of Jonson.) On Truewit: "The two ways of responding to the kind of reality projected by Jonson—the satirist's impulse to reject it with a cry of outrage, and the 'realist's' impulse to embrace it or at least accept it with a cynical shrug—reach a kind of uneasy suspension in Truewit" (p. 148). See also pp. 176–177.

5. Two well-known examples are Shakespeare's Jacques and Thersites. See Kernan, *Cankered Muse,* pp. 148 ff.

on a stock character whose current popularity guaranteed laughter as it is that he created him as a conscious or unconscious rejection of his own satiric inclinations, as most of the gallants' admirers have silently assumed.

The second and third reasons given for Jonson's supposed moral tolerance and idealization of the gallants are practical: the author gave the habitually disruptive private-theater audience before whom *Epicoene* was performed a flattering image of itself to keep it attentive and quiet; in addition, Jonson's closer acquaintance with fashionable society after 1605, as the author of James's masques, inspired him to present a sophisticated, courtly ideal.[6]

No one denies the practicality or flattery of the man who addressed James as the "best of poets" (*Epigrams* 4) or, later, the unpopular Henrietta Maria as "Hail Mary, full of honours" (*Underwood* 66).[7] Moreover, the image of a genially tolerant Jonson is appealing. But it is credible only as one of the two faces of a literary split personality, for in his poetry Jonson consistently presents himself as a reformer, an outspoken moralist who is no friend to folly in any social sphere. In particular, the *Epigrams,* published in 1616, only seven and two years, respectively, after the first productions of *Epicoene* and *Bartholomew Fair* (the other play frequently characterized as morally relaxed), do not omit harsh criticism of "courtlings" though Jonson still enjoyed his position at court.[8] The collection also testifies to Jonson's command of praise or flattery in the service of commending his friends and aristocratic patrons or inspiring them to strive toward their represented (and ideal) selves. But that is precisely the point: when this poet wishes to praise or flatter, he typically creates ideals who are ethically irreproachable characters—and the gallants in *Epicoene* are uni-

6. "Here Jonson provides his audience with a pleasing image of itself while directing its mockery to a gallery of deviants from the aristocratic ethos." Michael Shapiro, "Audience vs. Dramatist in Jonson's *Epicoene* and Other Plays of the Children's Troupes," *ELR,* III (1973), 410; "Yet Jonson's own experience brought him closer to the fashionable life he had criticized so severely, especially after 1605, when he became the leading maker of masques for the Jacobean court." Kay, "Urbane Gallants," p. 255.

7. Quotations of the poems are from *Ben Jonson: Poems,* ed. Ian Donaldson (London, 1975). Quotations of *Epicoene* are taken from the Herford and Simpson edition, with *i* and *j, u* and *v* regularized, and with abbreviated names given in full.

8. See *Epigrams* 11, 15, 52, 62, 72, and 90.

formly and obviously flawed men. Most assuredly, these dramatic characters are not, as a recent critic suggests, "kindred spirits" of "the noble men and women Jonson praises in his poems," and the author does not, in *Epicoene* or elsewhere, "recommend folly, within limits, as the only wisdom."[9]

The suggestions that Jonson's admission into the courtly sphere dictated an ideal image of its inhabitants in the gallants, and that this image is the dramatic counterpart of the ideals he created in his poems misrepresent both the playwright and the poet. I refer to Jonson's nondramatic poetry not because I assume that the same ethical standards that inform it necessarily inform his fictive and entertaining comedies. However, there is the author's own statement that his dramatic, like his poetic, aim is "to profit and delight" his audience, "to tax the crime"; more important, there is the play. *Epicoene* itself shows that the playwright taxes the crimes of a frivolous society through the gentlemen-wits, who are anything but virtuous ideals. The modern preference for crazy quilts notwithstanding, Jonson's work is, morally, all of a piece. I concede that an obtuse or dishonest playwright is, perhaps, a more interesting character: in his "prologues, inductions, dedications, choruses, epilogues, apologetical dialogues," Jonson "seems oddly tight-lipped, unable either to perceive the rich and various energies of his own work, or alternatively to concede that he does perceive them. Jonson's prime, and at times sole, concern seems to be to assure us that his work is morally impeccable."[10] But, again, as I shall demonstrate, the basis for my faith in the author's stated intention and for my estimation of the courtly gentlemen is the play itself.

There have been dissidents in the past,[11] but during the last ten years, the prevailing critical voice has implicitly asked who represents

9. Shapiro, "Audience vs. Dramatist," p. 411; Barish, *Language of Prose Comedy,* p. 184.

10. Donaldson, "Jonson and the Moralists," p. 146.

11. Among those who have not thought the gallants were Jonson's ideals or spokesmen are C. G. Thayer, *Ben Jonson: Studies in the Plays* (Norman, Okla., 1963); Gabriele Bernhard Jackson, *Vision and Judgment in Ben Jonson's Drama* (New Haven, Conn., 1968); Ian Donaldson, *The World Upside-Down: Comedy from Jonson to Fielding* (Oxford, 1970); and Allen C. Dessen, *Jonson's Moral Comedy* (Evanston, Ill., 1971). More recently, the only reader who rejects the wits as ideals is Peggy Knapp, in "Ben Jonson and the Publicke Riot," *ELH,* XLVI (Winter 1979), 577–594. Knapp's article is very informa-

Jonson's ethical stance in *Epicoene,* and assumed that, since it is not the carping Morose, it must be Truewit, Dauphine, Clerimont, or two, or all three of them. This equation of author and characters has yielded the obvious conclusion: because the wits do not reform, but tolerate, some fools, Jonson is no reformer but a playwright comfortably tolerant of the faults he dramatizes. As we shall see, however, it is not necessary to look for Jonson in his dramatic characters. Just as he does in the Carey-Morison Ode (*Underwood* 70) and *A Celebration of Charis* ("Her Man Described by Her Own Dictamen," *Underwood* 2), he finds a way to make his own presence felt in *Epicoene.* The dual purpose of this essay, then, is to discredit the reputation currently and undeservedly enjoyed by the gallants of *Epicoene* as Jonson's spokesmen or virtuous ideals, and to argue the author's literary moral consistency.

A brief review of the author's practice in the period from 1598 to 1614 will help us to place *Epicoene* morally by focusing our perspective on the Jonsonian constants that underlie its subtleties. These remarks refer to the plays from *Every Man in His Humour* to *Bartholomew Fair,* all works that include gentlemen-wits. Most commentators on Jonson's major comedies refer to three principal groups of characters in opposition to each other: the fools, the railers, and, between the two extremes, the wits.[12] But what we might call Jonson's master

---

tive on the social changes that represented an erosion of values to Jonson. She does not note, as I shall do, the internal evidence in *Epicoene* by which the author indicts the wits. Knapp suggests that Jonson feared that his dramatic art linked him with the decadent "new man" like Dauphine (p. 591). Quoting Overdo's "fine stoical speech" (*Bartholomew Fair,* IV.i.43–46), Knapp also remarks that "It would be hard to phrase a passage closer to Jonson's own ideals, and the phrasing 'Author of mine own rest' links Overdo's role as public servant with Jonson's own" (p. 590). My argument is that the author's ethical stance is entirely separate from that of any of his characters.

12. "The most important structure in *Every Man in His Humour,* and the comedies which follow, is the opposition of three major groups of characters." Arnold, *Cavalier Heroes,* p. 9. Though I shall refer to the revised *Every Man in,* it is accurate to date the period under discussion from 1598, the date of the play's first version, because the changes Jonson made were not radical: "some speeches have been lengthened and some shortened, profane oaths have been eliminated, and the Italian names have been Anglicized—but by far the most striking difference between the plays is the setting." Ralph Alan Cohen, "The Importance of Setting in the Revision of *Every Man in His Humour,*" *ELR,* VIII (1978), 183.

recipe for comedy is more easily discernible if we look at the full complement of character-types that constitute the prototypical Jonsonian cast: the wits, the fools, the manipulator-actors, the antagonist-railers, and the authority-ethical figures.

There is little to say about the wits and the fools. Generally, the wits are clever and articulate men who are amused by (but not interested in correcting) the obvious folly of the fools; usually they are not deceived by the manipulator-actors. It is their function to witness, sometimes encourage, and comment on, the self-evident vanities of the fools. The latter are either dull-wits who invite deception and ridicule or pretenders to a higher status of a more impressive character than they can justifiably claim, or both. Their dramatic function is to display in exaggerated fashion the faults of the society around them. The manipulator-actors are always dishonest in some degree. They are motivated, invariably, by financial gain or self-advancement, though they sometimes also enjoy manipulation for its own sake, as evidence of their skill, cleverness, or power. Their function is to create the complications that throw the plays' societies into disorder or confusion. The authority-ethical figures settle the conflict that moves the plot, establish an orderly society, and/or merely provide the standard against which the other characters are measured. Finally, the antagonist-railers are failed normative characters. By virtue of their own position, identity, or awareness, men like old Knowell and Downright should themselves be authority-ethical figures, but their failings disqualify them. Whether or not they rail, they are always antagonistic, opposed to the protagonists, whether these are the wits of the manipulator-actors.

Every Man in His Humour, Volpone, and *The Alchemist* include the entire cast of types, and a glance at the first will demonstrate how Jonson characteristically deploys his types to convey ethical implications. Conflict exists between the wits and the antagonist-railers (the father of one wit and the elder brother of the other). Knowell's punctilious overprotectiveness and Downright's excessive and diffuse anger account for the conflict and unfit them as the authority-ethical norms. When Knowell moves to threaten the wits (in a minor way), Brainworm, the manipulator-actor, moves to help them. He is not very dishonest. But he hopes "to insinuate with [his] young master" (II.iv.10), to secure his position for the future by ingratiating himself with Edward. The wits and the manipulator-actor join forces and, together, they outwit the fools and the antagonist-railers for the sake of "sport." Their machinations succeed to such a degree that the result is thorough confusion, a confusion that can be righted only by an authority-ethical figure who remains almost completely outside of the action and society of the play. Clement dismisses the unsalvageable fools and settles by fiat the conflict between the wits and the antagonist-railers, forming a harmonious little society.

Two things are especially noteworthy in the preceding summary: the wits are not given the normative function or the ordering power that belongs to the authority-ethical figure; and, when they act in league with Brainworm, they, too, become manipulator-actors. Quite apart from encouraging the fools, the wits also manipulate the antagonist-railers and the other characters, as when, for example, Wellbred sends first Kitely and then Dame Kitely on a fool's errand to Cob's house. *Every Man in* deals with folly, not vice, so the fraternity of the wits and the manipulator-actor does not brand Edward and Wellbred as vicious. But it does suggest an ethical carelessness or unconcern quite in keeping with the gallants' youth and enjoyment of the fools around them. Invariably, the manipulator-actors (who include, in the other major comedies, Mosca, Volpone, Face, Subtle, Doll, and the Fair people), or those who assume the role, are reprehensible or (at the least) morally lax characters in Jonsonian comedy.

The movement of characters from one category to another or the link between one group and another is typical of Jonson's comedies. Consistently, the playwright uses this movement to reveal something about a character's nature or ethical standing that may or may not be immediately apparent. Its effect is significant. What has seemed to be the moral variety among types of characters breaks down to disclose, instead, an ethical similarity beneath the different faces, manners, and stations; and such shifts are so many authorial rebukes to the reader or spectator, as the case may be, for judging the characters too soon or too rigidly.[13] Of the comedies Jonson wrote in the period from 1598 to 1614, only *Epicoene* and *Bartholomew Fair* do not embody all of the

---

13. I am indebted to one of the readers of this essay for the suggestion about the significance of the characters' shifts from one category to another.

different types in separate characters. Nevertheless, even when one of the pure types is omitted, his function is still performed, his attitude brought into play, by one (or more) of the characters who belongs primarily to another category.

The character who belongs to more than one category is clearly more complex than his fellows, and is revealed in greater detail. In *Bartholomew Fair,* for example, Adam Overdo is primarily an authority-ethical figure by virtue of his position; but he is also an antagonist-railer by his antagonism to the Fair personnel, and a fool by nature. Through him, Jonson suggests that the power and the will to reform are not enough in the absence of common sense and moral intelligence. He implies the futility of reform in a world where authority itself is tainted with vanity and folly. The types, in other words, immediately disclose the characters' superficial natures beneath the intricacies of plot; the similarities or shifts among types eventually lay bare their true natures. They do so when the import of a character's speech and action is obvious, or when it is more problematic. Our awareness of the consistently amoral nature of the manipulator-actor in Jonson's comedies, and of the playwright's habit of defining his characters ethically by means of the generic types to which they correspond will help us to understand *Epicoene* and its gentlemen-wits.

In *The Silent Woman,* there are wits, fools, and an antagonist-railer, but no pure manipulator-actor or authority-ethical figure. Jonson supplies the missing types or attitudes by creating characters who combine functions: the wits subsume the role of manipulator-actor and, eventually, invite some of the fools to collaborate with them in their manipulation. The gallants also arrogate the role of authority-ethical figure and, again, invite some of the fools to join them in that function. The implications of this combination of character-types have not been explored. A review of the scholarship on the wits discloses that a good deal of it focuses on the question of who, exactly, is the hero of *Epicoene.*[14] Though this question is irrelevant to my argument, the var-

14. I do not mean to equate the following authors' perspectives, only to indicate the lack of consensus. For Truewit, Mark A. Anderson, "The Successful Unity of *Epicoene:* A Defense of Ben Jonson," *SEL,* X (1970), 354; Huston D. Hallahan, "Silence, Eloquence, and Chatter in Jonson's *Epicoene,*" *HLQ,* XL (February 1977), 120. For Dauphine, Halla-

ious efforts to answer it constitute a survey of negative opinions on the wits; readers who favor one of them usually identify the failings of the other two. Thus, Dauphine is faulted with his attraction to the Collegiates, and with his cruelty to Morose, Daw, and La Foole; Clerimont is thought to be tainted by his association with the Collegiates, by his possible bisexuality, his indolence, and his lack of judgment; and Truewit—who provokes the strongest opinions—is variously described as "an opportunist and a troublemaker," a "zany" and "chameleon clown" who shows "an excessive commitment to the role of prankster." Truewit is also guilty of egotism.[15]

Though the enumeration of the gallants' imperfections is impressive, readers still argue that they represent Jonson's ethical ideal in the play. Judd Arnold refers to "their sense of superiority to the sad average, a superiority that breeds a joyous sense of freedom," and remarks that theirs is "the inevitable triumph of the cavalierly aloof, intellectual aristocrat over the hopeless, helpless mass of fools." Michael Shapiro suggests that Jonson presents them "as coherent images of the way true aristocrats relate to the fallen world," and W. David Kay remarks that the "ideal of conduct they embody" is "an attempt to create a model that can combine gracefulness with wisdom, participation in the world and detachment from it."[16] A reexamination of the play, however, indicates that a reformulation of these statements is in order. In *Epicoene,* there is no clear-cut triumph of wits over fools because both groups of characters exhibit the same shortcomings. The gallants are not detached but full participants in their world, as befits men who are coherent images only of their society's folly.

If the extent and meaning of the gallants' faults have been disputed, the other characters' faults are clear enough. Apart from their social

han, p. 120; Robert K. Knoll, *Ben Jonson's Plays: An Introduction* (Lincoln, Neb., 1964), pp. 113–114; and Jackson, *Vision and Judgment,* p. 61. For all three wits, Arnold, *Cavalier Heroes;* Kay, "Urbane Gallants"; and Shapiro, "Audience vs. Dramatist."

15. Seriatim: on Dauphine and Clerimont, Kay, "Urbane Gallants," pp. 255–256; and Knoll, *Jonson's Plays,* p. 114. On Truewit: Knoll; John Ferns, "Ovid, Juvenal, and 'The Silent Woman': A Reconsideraton," *MLR,* LXV (1970), 252; Shapiro, "Audience vs. Dramatist," p. 415; and Kay, "Urbane Gallants," p. 255.

16. Arnold, *Cavalier Heroes,* p. 7; Shapiro, "Audience vs. Dramatist," p. 411; Kay, "Urbane Gallants," p. 266.

pretensions, the fools are guilty of indiscretion, lying, and lechery, or, more precisely, professions of lechery. Morose, whose age and experience should make him an authority-ethical figure, is guilty of being a railer and a verbose would-be tyrant. His misanthropy seems to stem from his inability to control the world around him to his own, warped satisfaction. All of these failings (and others) are exhibited by the gallants—or attributed to them—by one another.

Indiscretion is Dauphine's complaint against Clerimont and Truewit when he lumps them with the other gossips who have exacerbated his conflict with Morose: "They are such as you are, that have brought mee into that predicament, I am, with him" (I.ii.5–6). Dauphine accuses Clerimont alone after he hears his friend tell Truewit about Morose's marriage plans and Epicoene's existence (I.ii.1), and Clerimont playfully turns the tables when he chides Dauphine for revealing the Collegiates' attentions: "O, you must not tell, though" (V.ii.51). The fools' lies are paralleled by the wits'. I will have more to say about the gentlemen's falsehood in another context, but one example of it may be given here. Daw and La Foole tell the Collegiates that Dauphine is very poor, that his uncle's marriage means bad financial prospects for him, and that he cheated La Foole at cards. Haughty asks, initially, "Is that his keeper, that is gone with [Morose]?" and La Fool responds, "It is his newphew, madam" (IV.iv.158–159). Moments later, Clerimont reports the woman's question to Dauphine, and Truewit adds: "And the brace of Babouns answer'd yes; and said thou were a pittiful, poore fellow, and did'st live upon posts: and had'st nothing but three sutes of apparell, and some few benevolences that lords ga' thee to foole to 'hem, and swagger" (IV.v.9–13). Truewit's capacity as a troublemaker is evident in his exaggerating lies. Against the fools' lechery or lecherous talk, there are: Clermont's frustration at not being admitted into the College, Truewit's disquisition on the "acceptable violence" in which a man uses force with a woman who expresses no interest in his caresses, and, of course, Dauphine's "love" for all of the Collegiates. Clerimont comments on his friend's lechery when he calls him a "stallion" (IV.i.140).

At least one of the gallants shares Morose's faults. If he is a railer, Truewit's antifeminist tirade strongly suggests that the young wit has the same talent in readiness. If Morose loves to hear himself talk, so does Truewit: Huston D. Hallahan has shown that the younger man is by far the most talkative character in the play.[17] And as for Morose's inclination toward tyranny, we need only remember Truewit's petulant determination to have entire control of the plot against the fools. When Dauphine offers some embellishments to improve it, Truewit's testy rejection of help is immediate: "I pray forebear, I'll leave it off, else" (IV.v.148–149). If he cannot control the plot, he threatens to withdraw, just as Morose has done in larger measure, but for the same reason.

One could go on enumerating the gallants' faults, but enough has been said to show that they share the fools' shortcomings. Jonson has drawn parallels between these types with remarkable care. Nowhere has he been so meticulous in letting the young men reveal themselves, however, as in his depiction of the means they use to expose Daw and La Foole. We are used to thinking that the fools get what they deserve, because "The two effeminate courtiers fabricate the tale of seducing Epicoene simply to impress their hearers."[18] But this judgment is inaccurate and unfair. La Foole and Daw answer, the first time that Clermont asks them if they have had sexual relations with the Collegiates, "No, excuse us, sir" and "We must not wound reputation" (V.i.68–69). Clerimont then leads them to the topic of Epicoene and their conversation is instructive:

CLERIMONT

Come, you have both had favours from her? I know, and have heard so much.

DAW

O, no, sir.

LA FOOLE

You shall excuse us, sir: we must not wound reputation.

CLERIMONT

Tut, shee is married, now; and you cannot hurt her with any report, and therefore speake plainely: how many times, yfaith? which of you lead first? Ha?

LA FOOLE

Sir JOHN had her mayden-head, indeed.

---

17. Truewit speaks 967 lines in the play, Morose 463. But Hallahan sees Morose's talk as ineffectual chatter and Truewit's as eloquent authority. See "Silence, Eloquence, and Chatter," pp. 126–127.

18. William W. E. Slights, *"Epicoene* and the Prose Paradox," *PQ,* XLIX (1970), 183.

DAW
O, it pleases him to say so, sir, but Sir AMOROUS knows what's what, as well.
(V.i.81–91)

The fools are cajoled into saying what the vulgar Clerimont wants them to say; even so, their "admission" is nothing like his version of it when Dauphine asks if they "have lyen with her": "Yes, and tell times, and circumstances, with the cause why, and the place where. I had almost brought 'hem to affirme that they had done it, to day" (V.ii.77–79). Later, at the great moment of their final exposure, Daw and La Foole deny that they have had sexual favors from Epicoene. Only repeated threats of violence at the hands of Clerimont persuade the cowardly duo to say what the wits want. They say what they are forced to say, in other words, and then are banished for having said it. In the reproachful words of Daw, "Is this gentleman-like, sir?"

One of Jonson's most masterly devices in characterization is what we might call the gratuitous detail. These details are swift touches that, though inessential for the advancement of plot, are richly suggestive in the delineation of character. There is a fine example of this ever. in *Every Man in His Humour,* in which the gallants are most blameless (and most dull): Bridget tells Wellbred that his efforts with her on Edward's behalf savor too much "of the squire," with the pun on "pander" (IV.viii.131). In *Epicoene,* there is the matter of the purchased knighthood. Jonson's attitude about this phenomenon is everywhere apparent in the *Epigrams.* The last two lines of "To Sir Luckless Woo-All" are characteristically scornful about the title-buyer: "The knight-wright's cheated, then: he'll never pay. / Yes, now he wears his knighthood every day." Though Truewit refers disparagingly to Sir John Daw's purchased title (I.ii.76), he never refers to Dauphine's—only the irate Morose does that: "he would be knighted, forsooth, and thought by that meanes to raigne over me, his title must doe it" (II.v.101–103).

We are justified in assuming that Dauphine purchased his knighthood because Morose's locution, "would be," indicates his nephew's active pursuit of the title (rather than his attainment of it for any service) for the sake of impressing him. Though Morose is certainly prejudiced, his remark gains credibility because he is alone, talking to himself. Moreover, no other mention is made of how the youth might have acquired his title honorably—say, when the Collegiates are singing his praises (IV.vi). In this snobbish milieu, even La Foole is anxious to establish that his knighthood devolved upon him "since it pleas'd my elder brother to die" (I.iv.61). The old man's indignation at Dauphine's challenge to his authority by means of a recently acquired title may well have reflected a social reality. Lawrence Stone remarks that the sale of many knighthoods in the early seventeenth century created "the curious situation whereby numbers of young gentlemen were swaggering about London as knights, while their fathers in the country were obliged to content themselves with the humbler title of esquire." In any case, the gratuitous detail serves its purpose: linking Sir Dauphine wi h Sir John Daw, it suggests that the gallant whose name means *"well-born heir"*[19] is named ironically to point to his foolish social pretensions and to his effort to usurp the authority of an elder relative.

The common origin of Dauphine and Daw's titles in their wallets suggests that the gallants may share the fools' "values" as well as their faults, and this is indeed the case. Barish points out that the Collegiates "are as conscious as Truewit of the ticking of the clock, but they draw Clerimont's moral, that youth is meant for indulgence, and old age for fasting and prayer."[20] The women and the gallants would also agree that numerous lovers are desirable. But the most unexpected instance of shared values surprises the reader in the fourth act (vi.24–37). There the Collegiates indicate that they are entirely in accord with the taste and outlook so memorably expressed in Clerimont's poem, "Still to be neat." They praise Dauphine's "carelessnesse" in dress and decry the artificiality of the other extreme. He is "yet not so superlatively neat as some . . . that have their faces set in a brake"; his every hair is not in place, and he is not like those men "That weare purer linenn than our selves, and professe more neatnesse than the *french hermaphrodite*!" Dauphine eventually changes his mind about the attractiveness of artificiality, but then the Collegiates use cosmetics despite their stated preference for the natural look like Dauphine's. As seem-

19. Lawrence Stone, *The Crisis of the Aristocracy: 1558–1641* (1965; abridged ed., New York, 1967), pp. 40–41. Knoll (*Jonson's Plays*, pp. 113–114) points out the meaning of Dauphine's name, but does not suggest that it is ironic.
20. Barish, *Language Prose Comedy*, p. 178.

ing distinctions between them break down, gallants and fools together contribute to the "uncertainty" about proprieties and standards that marks the play as a whole.[21]

Recent commentary on *Epicoene* notwithstanding, it would be perverse of the gallants to maintain a disapproving detachment from the little society with which they have so much in common, and they do not. One of the forms that the wits' participation in the world takes is especially interesting. In the first scene of the play, Truewit rattles off a list of the trivial, time-wasting activities of fashionable men, and ends by remarking that he follows them too, "for companie" (I.i.40–41). This would seem to disqualify him as an ethical ideal, but the only one of his admirers to comment does not think so: "Fully aware of the banality of the pursuit he has catalogued, he nevertheless participates in them for the sake of human fellowship. Those who are truly detached can enter into the world without fear of being contaminated and can even help others achieve the same detachment."[22] This faith in an uncloistered virtue that sallies forth to cavort with fools, cordial though it is, is not Jonson's. In the "Epistle to Katherine, Lady Aubigny" (*Forest* 13), he is emphatic: "For others' ill, ought none their good forget." When the alternative is bad company, solitude is safety: "In single paths dangers with ease are watched; / Contagion in the press is soonest catched" (11. 57–58). On the basis of the foregoing evidence of the shortcomings and values shared by wits and fools, we might say that the fear of contamination is meaningless when the ailment is already universal.

If the wits were detached in the general sense, they would not torture Morose; they would not plot to expose two of the male fools in retaliation for their supposed verbal abuse of Dauphine, or to rid the young knight of rivals for the Collegiates' affections. But the strongest argument against their moral detachment from their society's folly is

21. See Donaldson, *World Upside-Down,* p. 34.

22. Shapiro, "Audience vs. Dramatist," p. 414. Typically, moral detachment is not a positive value in Jonson's work. The courtier who speaks most of "On Something that Walks Somewhere" (*Epigrams* 11) remarks that no man should hope for the "least good" from him, "For I will do none; and as little ill, / For I will dare none." Jonson's opinion is expressed succinctly: "Good Lord, walk dead still." In the poems as in the plays, the person who fails to take an ethical stance is a ghost, a mere shell.

their alliance with the fools against whom they have no particular grudge, or from whose expulsion they have nothing to gain. I mentioned earlier that the wits take over the role of manipulator-actor. They invite all of the fools to adopt the same role when they invite their help in Morose's torture, and again (and most especially) when they take the Collegiates into their inner circle by enlisting them against Daw and La Foole. Dauphine cautions them, "doe not confesse in your countenance, or outward bearing to 'hem any discovery of their follies" (IV.vi.79–81). Such alliances between the wits and the fools indicate in yet another way the underlying ethical similarity that links the two types.

The gallants take on the function of the authority-ethical figure, and in this role also they voluntarily include the fools: they invite Cutbeard and Otter (as the canon lawyer and the divine) to play, as they do, at judging and punishing. The absence of a genuine authority-ethical figure means that the "re-ordered" society at the end of the play is a sham, an ironic gesture that only recalls the harmonious vision it mimics. The final scene stresses not the wits' moral detachment but their full and continuing participation in the foolish society of the play. They are pretending a nonexistent respect for the Collegiates. In the company of the ladies, Cutbeard, and the Otters, they anticipate the shabby reward they have earned by "protecting" the women against the luckless Daw and La Foole.

Only their manipulative cleverness distinguishes the young men from the others; apart from that, they are faithful images of their society's folly. *Epicoene* is about the success of Dauphine's hoax, whose purpose is to secure his rightful inheritance from a malicious hate-ridden man. Morose's discomfiture is secondary to this central purpose, but it becomes the predominant motive during the greater part of the play. The hoax succeeds in its primary and secondary purposes, but if we consider its success, we cannot ignore its mercenary nature and its questionable gains: Dauphine does not have to wait until the death of his uncle for the money with which to continue courting the Collegiates or to "Harken after the next race-horse, or hunting match; lay wagers, praise *Puppy,* or *Pepper-corne, Whitefoote, Franklin"* (I.i.34–36). The major issues of the play, identified by Mark A. Anderson, are: "the deception and falsification present in society, the reliance by society upon reputation rather than true character, and the means by which one can live 'successfully' in this society."[23] Far from being Jonson's ethical spokesman, the gallants, as we have seen, are very much a part of their society's deception and falsification. Their true characters, beneath the veneers of sophistication and cleverness, are compounded of the same flaws and vanities that are more visible (because more exaggerated) in the fools. Their success gets Dauphine ready cash and wins for all of them the Collegiates' admiration; but, certainly, the wits do not merit the reader's admiration as ideals of virtue.

The values in the play are implicit. As Kernan wrote of *Volpone,* the opening scene of *Epicoene* is "a masterful example of Jonson's indirect method of establishing the ideals of nature and society as moral reference points, while at the same time revealing their present state of corruption."[24] Truewit's statements in the first scene of the play, about the value of time and the shame of wasting it in folly and vain pursuits, establish the standard that he and the other gallants (and the rest) disregard. Clerimont puts a stop to his friend's talk by warning him that reading Plutarch's "Morals" will spoil his wit. Jonson could not have indicted the gallants more clearly—unless it was in Truewit's remark to Haughty later in the play (III.vi.48–49): often, he remarks more truly than he knows, "he that thinkes himselfe the master-wit, is the master-fool."

Of Jonson's major comedies, *Epicoene* and *Bartholomew Fair* show the greatest blurring or integration of what seem, initially, distinct character-types. Overdo's combination of three types has already been mentioned. Even Grace, who might be considered an authority-ethical figure, eventually allies herself with the manipulator-actors. She prefers to marry an intelligent rogue—any intelligent rogue—rather than a dull-witted fool. And she marries under the foolish illusion that she can reform the rogue. This lack of clear-cut differentiations

23. Anderson, "Successful Unity of *Epicoene,*" p. 352.
24. Kernan, *Cankered Muse,* p. 186. Similarly, Thayer, *Studies in the Plays,* p. 19: "the audience is educated by watching the comic characters remain essentially *un*educated, even though the material for their moral and intellectual improvement is implicit in the action and language of the play."

between the character-types, when it is perceived at all, has been interpreted as Jonson's way of suggesting with equanimity that moral distinctions are superfluous or relatively unimportant; it has led to the conclusion that *Epicoene* is a play that "delights in most of the frivolities it criticizes," in which Jonson's "comic vision is good-naturedly tolerant," and to similar conclusions about *Bartholomew Fair.*[25]

The identification of Jonson with characters like Morose and Adam Overdo has persuaded readers that the author "as a reformer would, by his own dramatically conceived standards, fall into the category of the zealously inspired fool—doubly foolish because he has so clearly defined the impossibility of his task";[26] it has further persuaded them that the author's moral stance can be equated wtih the wits'. In the comedies from 1598 to 1614, however, only the finale of *Every Man in His Humour* is a genuine effort to present a harmonious society purged of its follies through the agency of a normative character; only in Clement did Jonson create an adequate authority-ethical figure. From that point on, his comic vision gradually darkens as his insight into the complexities of the human character is more fully expresssed. In *Volpone,* we see a stage in the breakdown of the moral order when the Scrutineo only just manages, despite the greed of its members, to apprehend the villains. From this precarious situation, the next stage follows almost inevitably: Jonson advances to the little worlds of *The Alchemist, Epicoene,* and *Bartholomew Fair,* where there *is* no authority-ethical figure or where it is laughably inadequate. *Epicoene* (like *Bartholomew Fair)* deals with folly and not vice. This distinction and the laughter the play evokes counteract an overstatement of the bleak moral perspective it implies; but they do not preclude or invalidate the moral perspective. By the values and flaws the wits and fools share, Jonson suggests the universality of folly beneath the superficial distinctions of cleverness and manner. By the absence of a true authority-ethical figure in *Epicoene,* the wits' arrogation of the role, and

25. Claude J. Summers and Ted-Larry Pebworth, *Ben Jonson* (Boston, 1979), p. 72. Summers and Pebworth's discussion of Jonson's treatment of sexual roles in *Epicoene* explores an important dimension of the play. See also Barbara Baines and Mary C. Williams, "The Contemporary and Classical AntiFeminist Tradition in Jonson's *Epicoene,*" *Ren P, 1977,* pp. 43–58. On *Bartholomew Fair* see, for example, Summers and Pebworth, *Ben Jonson,* p. 98.

26. Arnold, *Cavalier Heroes,* p. 7; similarly, Donaldson, "Moralists," p. 154.

their invitation to the fools to assume the same, Jonson indicates that this is an effete society without safeguards against its own excess of folly, a world without moral controls or standards.

Having rejected Truewit and the gallants as the author's virtuous ideals or ethical spokesmen, are we left again with the "Morose Ben Jonson" described by Edmund Wilson as the censorious, "unsociable and embittered personage" through whom the dramatist torments himself "for what is negative and recessive in his nature"?[27] A partial answer to this question may be found in one of Jonson's favorite poetic strategies, the negative definition. Examples abound, as in "An Epistle to Master Arthur Squib" (*Underwood*. 45), where the device is used in self-description: "I neither am, nor art thou, one of those / That hearkens to a jack's pulse, when it goes." One of the attractions for Jonson of the discredited railer is not that the character allows him to castigate his own reforming impulses, but that it enables him to characterize himself and his own function by negative definition. He distinguishes between himself and his railers pointing out, in effect, that he, Ben Jonson, does not rail; tactfully, he calls our attention to his balanced perspective. Though Jonson sees faults everywhere he looks, he chooses to instruct his audience by making them laugh at their faults rather than by attacking them. The superior playwright has nothing to lose by directing scornful laughter also at the maladroit and ill-natured railer.

As a type, moralists have an undeserved reputation as humorless and gloomy folk. More of them than it is generally supposed know that "there are actions that may be at once reprehensible and diverting, just as there are other actions that may be morally blameless and yet emotionally uncompelling"[28]; moralists are not necessarily averse to enjoyable or entertaining forms of instruction. Jonson himself proves this through his comedies. He does not show one moral face in his poetry and another in some of his plays; in both, his aim is "to tax the crime" in order "to profit and delight" his audience, as he remarks in the second prologue to *Epicoene*. We can understand the nature of his own work only if we do not identify him with any of the characters in

27. Edmund Wilson, "Morose Ben Jonson," in *Ben Jonson: A Collection of Critical Essays*, ed. Jonas A. Barish (Englewood Cliffs, N.J., 1963), pp. 65, 66.
28. Donaldson, "Jonson and the Moralists," p. 156.

his play. There is, anyhow, no compelling reason to do this; Jonson appears in *Epicoene* in his own person. Intellectually pretentious women, Truewit tells Morose, nowadays compare *"DANIEL* with *SPENSER, JONSON* with the tother youth" (II.ii.117–118).[29] The fame of the true poet negotiates even the chasm between the real and the imagined worlds—Jonson does not need a dramatic alter ego. If anyone has one of these in the plays, it must be the reader, who is expected by the author to uncover, as fearlessly and successfully as possible, all the enormities he can find.

29. Jonson also "appears" in *The Alchemist* among the poets "that writ so subtly of the fart" (II.ii.63), and in *Bartholomew Fair* among the "Mermaid men" (I.i.30).

Perkin *without the Pretender:*
Reexamining the Dramatic
Center of Ford's Play

VERNA ANN FOSTER

IN MOST RECENT CRITICISM of John Ford's *Perkin Warbeck* the pretender's personal kingliness receives more enthusiastic endorsement than Henry's official royalty. The human values of civility, chivalry, idealism, and integrity represented by Perkin are contrasted with the political skills, generally viewed as machiavellian pragmatism, of Henry VII.[1] A theatrically oriented reading of the play, however, suggests that an audience would view the two men in a very different light. As a dramatic character rather than the focal point of a set of values, Perkin is a good deal less admirable than many of Ford's critics have claimed and,

---

A portion of this article originated in my unpublished Ph.D. dissertation, "The Dramatic Art of John Ford: Varieties of Mode and Effect" (University of London, 1977).

1. See Peter Ure, ed. *The Chronicle History of Perkin Warbeck,* The Revels Plays (London, 1968), pp. liv–lxxxiii; Jonas A. Barish, *"Perkin Warbeck* as Anti-History," *EIC,* XX (1970), 151–171; Philip Edwards, "The Royal Pretenders in Massinger and Ford," *Essays and Studies,* XXVII (1974), 18–36; Anne Barton, "He That Plays the King: Ford's *Perkin Warbeck* and the Stuart History Play," in *English Drama: Forms and Development,* ed. Marie Axton and Raymond Williams (Cambridge, Eng., 1977), pp. 69–93; Dorothy M. Farr, *John Ford and the Caroline Theatre* (London, 1979), pp. 105–124; Joseph Candido, "The 'Strange Truth' of *Perkin Warbeck,*" *PQ,* LIX (1980), 300–316. My quotations are taken from Ure's edition of *Perkin Warbeck.*

more curiously, less admirable than much of what goes on in the play implies that he is supposed to be. In the theater Perkin's moral superiority to Henry is less important than Henry's dramatic superiority to Perkin.

The only production of *Perkin Warbeck* (to the best of my knowledge) since 1745, in fact, demonstrated the centrality of Henry to the play bearing his rival's name. Reviewing the Royal Shakespeare Company's *Perkin Warbeck* at The Other Place in Stratford-upon-Avon in 1975, J. M. Maguin wrote, "To play *Perkin* without the Duke would almost prove, I am afraid, a sober and acceptable heresy!"[2] The play's directors, John Barton and Barry Kyle, using theatrical imagery in the manner of Barton's brilliant *Richard II* of a couple of years earlier, explored the ways in which *Perkin Warbeck* comments on the nature of monarchy. Both the directors and Terence Wilton, "tantalisingly ambiguous" (*Birmingham Post,* 8 August 1975) as Perkin Warbeck, carefully maintained the mystery of Perkin's identity. The theatrical imagery connected with Perkin, however, made its own comment on the pretender as a player king and, indeed, on all kingship as a form of playing (*Guardian,* 8 August 1975). Perkin appeared at first disguised in a whitish monk's robe but wearing a thin circlet of gold on his head. For the marriage celebration the monk's robe was replaced by a shining white prince's outfit, and Katherine and Perkin appeared surrounded by light. During the course of the play the gold circlet grew gradually bigger, becoming a full-sized crown ironically just before Perkin's defeat and capture.[3] But despite the directors' focusing attention on Perkin through appropriate and exciting visual effects, several reviewers found that Wilton's Warbeck, "haunting if remote" (*Birmingham Post*), was eclipsed by Tony Church's Henry VII: "the central figure of Warbeck is totally overshadowed by the chuckling, human portrayal of the English king by Tony Church, a masterly performance against which Terence Wilton's brave imposter has little chance of survival, or even interest, in his lost cause" (*Sunday Tele-*

2. J. M. Maguin, "1975—John Ford's *Perkin Warbeck* at *The Other Place*: Review Article," *Cahiers Elisabéthains: Etudes sur la Pré-Renaissance et la Renaissance anglaises,* VIII (1975), 66. I should emphasize that my conclusions about Perkin and Henry were arrived at independently of the RSC production discussed here.

3. Ibid., p. 67.

graph, 10 August 1975).[4] No doubt some of the difference in vitality and interest was due to the manner in which the parts were played, but by no means all, nor even most, of the disparity can be explained in this way. Rather, Maguin is on the mark in asserting that the central character of the play and the most persuasive actor in it is not Perkin, but Henry.[5]

Ford's presentation of Henry will be discussed below. Prior consideration must be given to the dramatist's peculiar characterization of Perkin Warbeck, whose ambiguity lies not only in who he is but also in what he is. There are, certainly, many cues in the play to suggest that Perkin is supposed to be its central figure, that he is supposed to be admirable, and perhaps even tragic. Most recent critics have followed these cues in their interpretations of the play. But over the history of Ford criticism there have always been some critics who have expressed uneasiness with the pretender, finding him flawed or insubstantial in some way.[6] This critical response can be substantiated from the evidence of the play no less than the more familiar favorable verdict on Perkin. Indeed, there is rather more evidence of Perkin's failings than of his strengths. The cumulative effect of Perkin's performance is to leave us still with the silky, inconsequential youth of Ford's sources, whom the dramatist has not transformed as much as has often been supposed.

If one is not merely to say that Ford has in some way failed in his characterization of Perkin, the pretender's role in the play needs redefiinition. Perkin, it will be argued, is both flawed and insubstantial, but the play that bears his name is neither. Perkin's failings suggest that

4. See also *Daily Telegraph,* 8 August 1975; *Financial Times,* 9 August 1975; *Quarterly Theatre Review* (Autumn 1975), 62–63.

5. Maguin, *"Perkin Warbeck* at *The Other Place,"* pp. 68–70.

6. A. W. Ward, *A History of English Dramatic Literature to the Death of Queen Anne,* III (London, 1899), 85, remarks of Perkin that "it cannot be said that the dramatist has made a real character out of his materials." Clifford Leech, *John Ford and the Drama of His Time* (London, 1957), while finding Perkin to belong to Ford's "elect" (p. 97), suggests that there is "a touch of the facile" in the dramatist's "presentation of Perkin's resolution" (p. 96). Michael Neill, " 'Anticke Pageantrie': The Mannerist Art of *Perkin Warbeck," Ren D,* VII (1976), 143, says that Katherine "supplies Perkin's own shadowy performance with the substance it otherwise lacks." See also Mark Stavig, *John Ford and the Traditional Moral Order* (Madison, Wis., 1968), pp. 168–184.

Ford was not, after all, setting up a simple contrast between human (or true kingly) values and the realpolitik that destroys them. As the RSC production demonstrated, Perkin's lack of substance, for which there are both practical and dramatic reasons, subverts his claim to the central position of the play assigned to him by most critics. What, then, is Perkin Warbeck and how does he fit into Ford's play?

It is true that in the stage effects associated with him, in his language, in the responses he evokes from other characters, in his marriage, and in his death, Perkin certainly appears to be something remarkable. Yet at the same time Ford is constantly showing us Perkin's weaknesses, undercutting his pretensions, reminding us that the pretender is only a player king, and, one might add, insistently setting him up for an unfavorable comparison with Henry. Perkin's dramatic importance finally lies not so much in himself as in his contribution to an excitingly theatrical exploration of monarchy. And Perkin's limitations as a character are essential to Ford's theme.

Ford's presentation in *Perkin Warbeck* of a pretender who has no basis for his claim in either right or power but who does possess regality of manner adds a new dimension to the English history play. The presence in Ford's play of such a character as Perkin makes the emphasis on the king as a man who plays a particular role more marked than it is even in *Richard II,* on which Ford's play was clearly to some extent modeled. Richard's theatricality and the theatrical imagery associated with him intensify his own and Shakespeare's attempt to understand his identity as man and king.[7] Perkin's theatricality and the theatrical imagery attached to him serve rather to emphasize his roleplaying. In *Richard II* Shakespeare explores the metaphysical relationship between the private man and the kingly role allotted to him in life. Ford is doing something different. In *Perkin Warbeck* he concentrates on the manner in which the kingly role is played rather than on its relation to the man playing it. Perkin's role-playing serves to focus attention on the way in which Henry and James, in turn, play their own kingly parts.

The sense that Perkin is playing a part comes across with his first appearance, partly because he is so very different from the "eager

7. See Anne Righter, *Shakespeare and the Idea of the Play* (London, 1964), pp. 113–138.

whelp" (I.i.120) Henry has led us to expect. Ford for his skeptical audience and James for his skeptical court put on a show of pomp and ceremony: Dalyell presents Perkin to Crawford, who presents him to Huntly, who presents him to the king, all to the accompaniment of "sprightly music" (II.i.38) from oboes. Ford's stage directions present Perkin as a romantic figure—in a later scene he leads in Katherine, *"complimenting"* (II.iii.71.1)—but never, it should be stressed, as a majestic one. The background music provided by oboes for the meeting between Perkin and James is more romantic than regal, and while the entrances of Henry and James are sometimes preceded by a royal "flourish," Perkin's never is.[8] Ford's stage effects may seem to be calculated to give grandeur to Perkin, but actually they are carefully limited.

In fact, there is a dichotomy in the stagecraft of *Perkin Warbeck.* That associated with Henry and James derives from the stage traditions of the English history play and gives us kings doing (or appearing to do) what kings are supposed to do. For example, at the beginning of the play Henry is *"supported to his throne"* (I.i.0.2–3) by representatives of the lords spiritual and the lords temporal. James at one point appears with Durham and Hialas *"on either side"* (IV.iii.0.1.), the traditional grouping of the king and his wise counselors. At the beginning of Act III Henry appears in emblematic warlike garb, *"his gorget on, his sword, plume of feathers, leading-staff"* (III.i.0.1–2). Henry and James use pageantry to a point; Perkin does not. When Henry is "supported" to his throne, the act symbolizes a real relationship between the king and his nobles—that one of the supporters is a traitor is an irony incident to monarchy. But when James ceremoniously receives Perkin in his court, the act means that the Scottish king is putting on a show for the edification of his nobles. Perkin's wedding celebration is even more explicitly a show, and that his marriage is not is a tribute to the character of Katherine. Despite their superficial glamor, there is a hollowness, a stage-managed quality about the visual effects associated with

8. Noted by W. B. Markward, "A Study of the Phoenix Theatre in Drury Lane, 1617–38" (Ph.D. dissertation, University of Birmingham, 1953), p. 509. The importance of sound effects should not be underestimated. According to the *Daily Telegraph,* the RSC's marvelous fanfares for Henry and James allowed them to steal "most of the early dramatic thunder."

Perkin.[9] Or even worse. The ungainly masque of *"four* Scotch Antics, *accordingly habited"* and *"four wild* Irish *in trowses, long-haired, and accordingly habited* (III.ii.111.1–3) presented in honor of the marriage of Perkin and Katherine symbolizes the disruption Perkin has caused in Huntly's family and in Scotland.

If the stage spectacle centering on Perkin is essentially an empty show, his speeches are part of that show. Through the comments of other characters Ford at once suggests that we should admire Perkin's language for its moving grace and dignity and also underscores its artificiality. From James and Katherine we hear praise: "He must be more than subject who can utter / The language of a king" (II.i.103–104) and "You have a noble language, sir" (III.ii.163). But even James and Katherine have reservations, and the fact that Perkin's regality of utterance has to be commented on at all emphasizes that there is something unlikely about it. Other characters comment critically on Perkin's language: "here are kingly bug's-words" (III.ii.111) is Huntly's embittered opinion. Durham tells James that Perkin "juggles merely with the fawns and youth / Of an instructed compliment" (III.iv.27–28). And Henry himself observes that Perkin is only acting a part.

In fact, the total effect of Perkin's discourse lends support to Henry's view that "The player's on the stage" (V.ii.68), though not necessarily with the deliberateness that Henry at first imputes to Perkin. The pretender's utterance is consistently more formal and usually less concrete than that of Henry and James. Ford slightly exaggerates the formality of Perkin's language so that it becomes noticeably unreal, though not incredible, the result perhaps of "an instructed compliment." To some extent the dramatist makes us admire the unreality of Perkin's speech as a purer form of discourse than that of Henry and James. Perkin's opening address to James is a perfect example of his rarefied utterance: "Most high, most mighty king! that now there stands / Before your eyes, in presence of your peers, / A subject of the rarest kind of pity" (II.i.40–42), etc. The inverted syntax of the first majestically periodic sentence contributes to both the suspense and the melodic grace of Perkin's presentation to himself, while his exten-

9. Michael Neill, "The Mannerist Art of *Perkin Warbeck,"* pp. 139–140, points out that Perkin's first three appearances are introduced, and in the first instance framed, by a stage audience.

sive use of amplification helps to give weight to what he is saying. But while through his language Perkin, actorlike, creates himself as prince, the studied, unrelaxed fineness of his speeches belies what he claims to be.

The characteristic mode of Perkin's discourse is autobiographical narrative. Almost every speech that he utters is implicitly if not explicitly an assertion of his identity. The autobiographical mode is entirely appropriate to Perkin's opening address to James. The factual or pseudo-factual nature of his first speech gives its dignity a substance that we do not always find in his speeches later in the play. In fact, Perkin's finest and most memorable speeches are generally those in which the narrative voice can be used effectively. For example, in the one lovely private scene with Katherine (III.ii), Perkin's farewell to his new bride transforms them both into the leading characters from some medieval romance. Perkin is constantly creating little stories about himself for the benefit of an audience. Even when he is supposed to be expressing feelings, he tends to talk *about* his emotional and moral attributes rather than realizing them in his language. The result is that Perkin's expressions of feeling seem disembodied, however beautifully they may be worded—"haunting if remote," as one reviewer described Terence Wilton's Perkin Warbeck. Perkin says to Katherine, "For love and majesty are reconciled / And vow to crown thee empress of the West" (III.ii.161–162). Here Perkin's personification of his feelings as abstractions creates a distance between the speaker and the lover so that we have the sense of emotion described rather than felt. On his landing in Cornwall Perkin asserts but hardly demonstrates his courage by describing the behavior of lions and then saying that he is like a lion: "The lion faints not / Locked in a grate; but, loose, disdains all force / Which bars his prey; and we are lion-hearted" (IV.v.26–28). The weak connective "and" fails to justify the comparison. And even when just before his death there is no longer a disparity between Perkin's behavior and the attributes he describes himself as possessing, he is still telling his own story:

> But let the world, as all to whom I am
> This day a spectacle, to time deliver,
> And by tradition fix posterity,
> Without another chronicle than truth,

> How constantly my resolution suffered
> A martyrdom of majesty.
>
> (V.iii.70–75)

Perkin again abstracts and personifies his feelings ("my resolution suffered") as if he were watching and describing his own attributes in action, as if he were part of the audience he creates for himself.[10]

The reason for Perkin's constant recourse to narrative is not far to seek. His "story" gives him something to say. Having decided to give his audience a Perkin who appears to believe totally in himself but who is not Duke Richard, Ford precluded himself from exploring his character's heart and mind, for Perkin cannot be made to feel or think either like "Osbeck's son of Tournay" (V.iii.24) or like Richard of York. Hence the thinness of his ideas and the remoteness and limited range of his feelings. Perkin's equanimity may at first appear as an admirable stoicism. But as Maguin noted in his review of the RSC production of *Perkin Warbeck,* Perkin's failure to show emotions appropriate to the various changes in his fortunes, in the theater especially, emerges as a "solemn monotony" and a "dramatic hollowness rather than the dramatic expression of an unshakeable human determination."[11] For example, Perkin conveys his gratitude to James with as much grandeur and nobility when he is told to leave Scotland as when he first arrives. And at the end of the play he asserts that he will be death's king with the same fortitude and assurance (and ease) that have marked his pronouncements that he would be England's king. "His lofty spirit soars" on all occasions and in pretty much the same vein. Ultimately, the effect of Perkin's unrelenting eloquence is to emphasize the lack of substance behind his role-playing and to make him seem, in Henry's words, like a "smoke of straw" (I.i.115) as he submits with equal grace now to James, now to Frion, finally to death.

The disparity between Perkin's words and deeds during much of the play further underscores his insubstantiality. At the very end of Act II, scene ii, Henry says, "tis now a time / to.execute, not talk" (II.ii.160–

---

10. My discussion of Perkin's expression of feeling is indebted to Joseph A. Porter's illuminating analysis of Richard II's language in *The Drama of Speech Acts: Shakespeare's Lancastrian Tetralogy* (Berkeley and Los Angeles, 1979), pp. 11–51. See J. L. Austin, *How to Do Things with Words,* 2d ed. (Cambridge, Mass., 1975).

11. Maguin, *"Perkin Warbeck* at *The Other Place,"* p. 67.

161), and at the opening of the next scene we hear Crawford and Dalyell commenting with surprise on Perkin's power over words. The juxtaposition is telling. As soon as he has to "execute" rather than "talk," Perkin looks less impressive than he at first appears, as many critics have noted, particularly in his behavior on the border and in his flight from Taunton. In the border incident Ford follows Bacon and Gainsford in making Perkin's plea to James to spare his "dear, dear England" (III.iv.67) look affected and sentimental, especially as Perkin, with a self-pitying glance at the fates of deposed princes in general (borrowed from Gainsford),[12] has to acquiesce finally in James's decision to despoil the north of England. "An humble-minded man" (III.iv.83), the Scottish king sarcastically comments. Though Ford does not stage Perkin's flight from Taunton, Katherine's shocked question, "Fled without battle given?" (V.i.58), emphasizes the dishonor of her husband's behavior. Perkin's deeds fail to support the claims of his rhetoric.

Some critics have sought objective verification of Perkin's royalty of spirit in his ability to win the love and loyalty of Katherine.[13] The simple grandeur of Ford's portrait of Katherine does bestow by implication some greatness on Perkin, but though his marriage is the most "real" thing about him, its nobility derives much more from what Katherine is and does than from Perkin himself. Katherine's initial emotional response to Perkin, certainly, emphasizes his magnetic charm and supports the favorable impression he at first makes on the audience. But Perkin's retention of his wife's affection and faith and her proud self-abasement when he is in the stocks are tributes to Katherine's character rather more than to his own. Perkin speaks to and of Katherine very beautifully, but it is Katherine who is in all ways the stronger and more discriminating character. Avoiding the question of her husband's identity, she gently asserts only her complete faith to him as his wife: "You have a noble language, sir; your right / In me is without question" (III.ii.163–164). And it is Katherine who insists

12. Thomas Gainsford, *The True and Wonderful History of Perkin Warbeck* (London, 1618), pp. 73–74. See also Francis Bacon, *The History of the Reign of King Henry the Seventh* (London, 1622), p. 160.

13. See Barish, *"Perkin Warbeck* as Anti-History," p. 160; Edwards, "The Royal Pretenders in Massinger and Ford," p. 27; Neill, "The Mannerist Art of *Perkin Warbeck,"* pp. 133, 143.

here and later when James dismisses Perkin from Scotland that she
should accompany him. Perkin asks James if he may be permitted to
keep his wife; Katherine asserts before her king, "No human power
can or shall divorce / My faith from duty" (IV.iii.102–103).

Katherine creates for Perkin his greatest triumph when in the last
scene of the play the richly clad princess stoops to kiss the (presumably by now ragged) prisoner in the common stocks. The moment is
strikingly theatrical, but also, unlike previous displays centering on
Perkin, filled with meaning—by Katherine, affirming in defiance of
the English nobles the one indisputably real act in Perkin's life:

> You abuse us:
> For when the holy churchman joined our hands,
> Our vows were real then; the ceremony
> Was not in apparition, but in act.
>
> (V.iii.112–115)

Perkin can do nothing for Katherine comparable to what she has done
for him. He brings disgrace upon her, and she transforms disgrace into
a sublime affirmation of her marriage. But even in her affirmation the
juxtaposition of the dangerous word "apparition" with its opposites
"real" and "act" underscores the ambiguity of Ford's presentation of
Perkin.

Even the scenes that redound most to Perkin's credit do nothing to
increase his regality. Perkin is more admirable in facing death than in
striving for the throne. But though his defiance of the cowardly Lambert Simnel rings true as the utterance of the man he claims to be, no
other English king or claimant to the English throne in the historical
drama dies with such easy willingness as Perkin Warbeck:

> Death? pish, 'tis but a sound, a name of air,
> A minute's storm, or not so much; to tumble
> From bed to bed, be massacred alive
> By some physicians for a month or two,
> In hope of freedom from a fever's torments,
> Might stagger manhood; here, the pain is passed
> Ere sensibly 'tis felt.
>
> (V.iii.199–205)

These are lovely "Fordian" lines, and superficially Perkin's resolution in facing death resembles that of some of the characters in Ford's tragedies, except that they have their own painful reasons for dying so that their rhetoric has a complexity that Perkin's lacks. The point is that Perkin's speech is not appropriate to the competitor for a kingdom. Richard IV has no reason to accept death in this stoical manner, though Perkin Warbeck might have. Right to the end of the play through Perkin's own speeches and through the responses to him of other characters (the honor he finally receives from the Scottish nobles, scornful wonder from the English ones), Ford invites us at once to admire Warbeck and to question our admiration for him.

Perkin's ambiguity has long intrigued critics, but it is not actually the most theatrically exciting kind of ambiguity. Perkin is ambiguous not because he is dramatically double in some way, but because he is indeterminate, wishy-washy, all surface. There is nothing there because Ford does not ever take us behind the princely persona, and cannot do so if he is to keep open the factual question of Perkin's identity. Henry VII is no more introspective than Perkin, but because Ford presents him as constantly aware of the part he is playing, the English king does emerge as a complex personality to the extent that we are not always sure which is man and which mask. Perkin is all mask. The emptiness at the heart of Warbeck, however, is not an emptiness at the heart of the play, for he is not its central character. That role belongs to Henry VII. Throughout the play Henry overshadows Perkin, and in ways that are as damaging to the pretender as his own limitations. In the final analysis Perkin is, after all, "a shadow / Of majesty" (V.ii.32–33), a player king, an illuminating foil to Henry and James, a theatrical comment on the nature of kingliness. For himself he is nothing. Ford makes Henry, by contrast, a worthy representative of England's most powerful dynasty.

Anyone growing up in the Elizabethan age, including Ford himself, would have learned from the Tudor myth promulgated in school, in the histories of Hall and Holinshed, and in Shakespeare's history plays to regard Henry VII as the savior of England after the dreadful years of civil strife between the houses of York and Lancaster.[14] So it is not sur-

14. See R. L. Storey, *The Reign of Henry VII* (London, 1968), pp. 3–4, and his review of Desmond Seward, *Richard III,* in *TLS,* 13 May 1983, p. 484.

prising that Ford makes his Henry very impressive, though he chooses the realistic mode of Bacon's history of the monarch rather than investing his king with the glamor of Shakespeare's Henry Tudor. Henry opens and closes Ford's play and has many more speeches (ninety-seven versus fifty-four) than Perkin, while in the total pattern of the play the *de casibus* action centering on Perkin is but one strand in a series of events that show how Henry VII remains secure on his throne through shrewd government. From the very beginning Ford presents the several historical crises—Stanley's defection, the Cornish risings, Perkin's claim—at one time or another from Henry's point of view, so that his perception of events in large part unifies the play and also helps to control our response to what is happening. The ostensibly embattled Henry is actually the play's presiding genius—a point well made by the RSC production, in which Tony Church's king managed "to remain central even when retreating to the shadows of the stage's corners" while his nobles carried out his wishes.[15]

Like Perkin, Henry is a player king, but of a very different order. Perkin's role-playing makes us conscious of Henry's, clarifying the nature of the English king's success. Henry knows what a good king is supposed to do, and he makes great show of doing it. Sometimes he may be hypocritical, but it is rarely easy to determine his motives. Henry is not a villain-king like Richard III, but he does share in the stagey self-consciousness of his Shakespearean predecessor so that we derive considerable intellectual excitement from watching him perform. Perkin tells Henry that "Truth in her pure simplicity wants art / To put a feignèd blush on" (V.ii.80–81). Perkin's rebuke aptly invokes both his own "simplicity," even if it is not "truth," and the kind of doubleness observable in Henry throughout the play. This doubleness derives from the dramatist's partial whitewashing of Bacon's Henry, and it is the source of the dramatic complexity and the theatrical appeal of Ford's Henry.

Though Bacon apparently intended Henry VII as a pattern for Prince Charles, to whom his *History of the Reign of King Henry the Seventh* is dedicated, he nevertheless discusses the Tudor king's failings and

15. Maguin, *"Perkin Warbeck* at *The Other Place,"* p. 69.

sometimes comments critically on his motives.[16] Ford, by contrast, incorporates in his play no authoritatively voiced criticism of Henry's behavior, but in more subtle ways through Henry's own dialogue he leaves the king's motives open to the kind of speculation that Bacon engages in. Ford makes sure that Henry displays and the English nobles draw to out attention the qualities—such as wisdom, mercy, fore-sight—that ideal kings were supposed to have, and the dramatist carefully avoids mentioning the grievances that Tudor Englishmen held against their king. Where Bacon makes it clear that Henry used the trouble from Scotland as an excuse to levy unnecessary subsidies,[17] Ford gives Henry a plausible speech defending the legality and the political wisdom of the taxation that led to the Cornish rising: "Yet, Urswick, / We'll not abate one penny what in parliament / Hath freely been contributed; we must not; / Money gives soul to action" (III.i.26–29). But there is an urgency in Henry's self-justification ("Yet, Urswick," "not . . . one penny," "we must not") that suggests his historical rapacity.[18] We can look upon Henry here as an ideal king who consults parliament or as a man pretending to be such a king in order to use parliament to get what he wants. This ambiguity makes Henry appear more intelligent and interesting than if he were simply a good parliamentarian or merely a Machiavel, and it complicates our response to him. We are in the stimulating position of wanting to be on Henry's side but not quite knowing if we ought to be. It is not surprising that one reviewer of the RSC production of *Perkin Warbeck* found the play "almost Brechtian" (*Birmingham Post*).

Repeatedly, Henry's doubleness creates dramatic tension. When he hears from Clifford of Stanley's treachery, Henry melodramatically draws attention to his own feelings: "Urswick, the light! / View well my face, sirs; is there blood left in it?" (I.iii.87–88). At this point in the play Tony Church chose to be "a magnificent actor-king, an artful forger of his own emotions."[19] But whether we are supposed to feel

16. See Bacon, *Henry VII,* dedicatory epistle. For the relation between fact and fiction in Bacon's *Henry VII* see Judith H. Anderson, *Biographical Truth: The Representation of Historical Persons in Tudor-Stuart Writing* (New Haven, Conn., 1984).

17. Bacon, *Henry VII,* pp. 162–163.

18. See Candido, "The 'Strange Truth' of *Perkin Warbeck,*" pp. 302–305, on Henry's obsession with money as it emerges in his language.

19. Maguin, *"Perkin Warbeck* at *The Other Place,*" p. 70.

sympathy for Henry as a man betrayed by his best friend or to take an intellectual pleasure in his manipulative skill—or both—remains an open question. In any case, Henry's sincerity hardly matters because he is able to hold his audience. Where Perkin distantly describes his feelings, Henry dramatizes his emotion, embodying it in his ashen appearance and in the immediacy of his exclamations: "what have I deserved / To lose this good man's heart, or he his own?" (I.iii.118–119). We are more involved here with Henry than we ever are with the remote Perkin, even though our sympathy for the king is qualified by a suspicion that it may not be altogether called for.

Again, in the matter of Stanley's execution Ford's subtle reworking of Bacon's Henry renders the king's character the more intriguing. Bacon suggests that Henry thought Stanley too powerful and in any case wanted Stanley's estates. Ford nowhere hints at these ulterior motives for Stanley's execution. His Henry, indeed, makes great show of mercy, but whether he really wishes to be merciful is another matter. His repeated request ("I hope we may reprieve him from the sentence / Of death; I hope we may" [II.ii.13–14]), coming as it does after he has received an affirmative answer to his first question ("Have ye condemned my chamberlain?" [II.ii.1]), and his deliberate absenting himself from the scene do not ring true. Rather Henry seems to be manipulating his nobles' responses to himself and Stanley so that, after all, Bacon's remark that the king waited six weeks before condemning his chamberlain in order "to shew to the World, that hee had a conflict with himselfe what hee should doe"[20] offers a more plausible explanation of Henry's behavior in the play than the English nobles' belief in his mercy. Whether Henry here and elsewhere in the play is "forging" his emotions or making the best use of those he actually has, Ford gives his audience the theatrical excitement of watching the English king pulling his own strings.

This sense of a superior intelligence adjusting the royal mask and observing the results contributes to Henry's dynamic stage presence. Where Perkin is so caught up in his role that his eloquence becomes rather unrelenting, Henry's detachment and manipulativeness find their most appropriate expression in the low-key but theatrically po-

20. Bacon, *Henry VII*, p. 134.

tent mode of irony. Henry's irony works very well for him as it emphasizes his assurance and renders absurd any idea that he might be un-
seated. Of the Cornish rising Henry says, "we must learn / To practise
war again in time of peace, / Or lay our crown before our subjects'
feet; / Ha, Urswick, must we not?" (III.i.11–14). And the king's jocular-
ity at Perkin's expense undercuts his rival's pretensions in the most
damaging way—it entertains us—and elicits a loyal response from his
own nobles, men whose intense seriousness in matters of battles and
honor amusingly highlights the superiority of Henry's own pragmatism by which battles can sometimes be avoided altogether:

> HENRY
> . . . king Perkin will in progress ride
> Through all his large dominions; let us meet him
> And tender homage; ha, sirs? Liegemen ought
> To pay their fealty.
> DAUBENEY
>   Would the rascal were,
> With all his rabble, within twenty miles
> Of London.
> HENRY
>   Farther off is near enough
> To lodge him in his home
>
> (IV.iv.36–42)

Though Henry is no more given to self-analysis than Perkin, his irony
effectively takes us into his confidence, allowing us to understand
something of his own complexity and to share his insights into the motives of others. When Surrey reports James's remark that the English
king is better able than himself to pay for the damage done in the north
of England, Henry wryly acknowledges James's slipperiness: "The
young man, I believe, spake honest truth; / A' studies to be wise be-
times" (V.ii.18–19). And his comment on Perkin, "The player's on the
stage still" (V.ii.68), articulates our own impression of what Perkin in
some important sense is. In *Perkin Warbeck* Ford makes us stand, if
uneasily at times, behind Henry VII by bringing us closer to him than
to any of the other characters and by limiting our emotional commitment to Perkin, his chief rival for our interest.

Even, perhaps especially, in playing "the King's Part," it is Henry, not Perkin, who excels, for Perkin, after all, does not appear to know that he is performing. Henry is a more consummate artist than either James or Perkin because his private personality is integrated with his role, not at odds with it, like James's, or lost in it, like Perkin's. Henry's grief over Stanley's defection comes across at least to some extent as a genuine private emotion, but at the same time it is incorporated in his kingship as his sorrow wins the respect of his nobles for his humanity and "gentleness" (II.ii.50). Similarly, Henry's ironic perspective on events, an inevitable consequence perhaps of his self-conscious doubleness as man and king, lends an air of naturalness to his discourse and simultaneously makes him appear to his nobles the more assured of success. Henry knows how to use his personal characteristics to strengthen his kingship so that he never seems to be acting a part to anyone but the audience. No one needs to say that Henry looks or speaks like a king. There is more appearance of strain in James's role-playing. He tries harder to be kingly, speaking of his royal compassion (II.i.18–34), making Surrey the offer of single combat that wins from the conventional, honor-conscious English earl the praise "so like a king a' speaks" (IV.i.36). James's effort to do the kingly thing makes itself noticed just as Perkin's royal manner receives such attention. But James is constantly coming out of his regal character, insulting his nobles or doing something dishonorable with glib hypocrisy. Perkin, of course, has no option but to stay in character because if he is not Duke Richard, he is nothing. Perkin's performance comments critically on James's less artistic because only intermittent essays at regality, and, more important, it throws into relief Henry's own skillful manipulation of the king's part.

Ford's Henry is impressive as the classic politic Tudor. In many ways he could also serve as a model for his Stuart descendant Charles I. Ford shows Henry succeeding in most of the areas in which Charles I was running into trouble. Henry scores military and diplomatic successes, as Charles did not. Henry pays his soldiers, as Charles could not. The economy of Henry's England is prosperous, and the king does not waste money on any "undeserving favourite" (IV.iv.50)—perhaps there is a glance here at the hated Buckingham, who was assassinated in 1628. Henry raises money with the consent of parliament, Charles by unpopular extraparliamentary means and in opposition to parliament's wishes. In Henry and his nobles, Stanley apart, Ford presents a picture of the kind of unity invoked as a matter of course by all early seventeenth-century political thinkers.[21] Whether, in fact, Ford, like Bacon, saw himself as providing a lesson for his own times is impossible to know. But if *Perkin Warbeck* is to be seen as offering a reproach to the government of Charles I, as Philip Edwards and Anne Barton have suggested, the reproach surely lies not in the ineffectual Perkin as the glamorous evocation of an earlier and better style of monarchy, but rather in the competence of Henry VII, which his descendant might do well to emulate.[22]

This is not to say that Henry is an "ideal" king.[23] But neither is he simply a Machiavel. Rather, it is Henry's potential to be either or both that makes Ford's portrait of the English king seem at once so politically realistic and so rich in theatrical possibilities. Henry is more dynamic, more complex, more ambiguous, and in the end more human than the play's titular hero. Being human, Henry solves the problems that he faces by methods that are inevitably flawed. One thinks of the murky betrayal of Stanley, the behind-the-scenes tampering with James through Hialas, the execution of the young Earl of Warwick, and the stocking of Warbeck himself. Ford does not ask us to excuse these acts; rather in painting Henry warts and all, he makes him much more interesting and credible than a mere stereotype of an ideal king; more capable, too, of retaining an audience's interest than Perkin Warbeck, who seems to illustrate, not embody, some ideal of kingship, but whose much-proclaimed virtues, never quite real to begin with, tend to dissolve in every crisis but the last.

In his own mind Henry is England's "best physician" (1.i.11) who has by the end of the play "purgèd" his state of "corrupted blood" (V.iii.219). Ford does not entirely corroborate the English king's san-

21. See S. R. Gardiner, *History of England from the Accession of James I to the Outbreak of the Civil War* (London, 1884), VII, 25–28, 224–225; J. P. Kenyon, *The Stuart Constitution* (Cambridge, Eng., 1966), pp. 9–11; Conrad Russell, *Parliaments and English Politics 1621–1629* (Oxford, 1979), pp. 35, 54.

22. See Edwards, "The Royal Pretenders in Massinger and Ford," and Barton, "He That Plays the King."

23. For the view of Henry as an "ideal" king see Irving Ribner, *The English History Play in the Age of Shakespeare* (Princeton, N.J., 1957), pp. 299–305; and Donald K. Anderson, Jr., "Kingship in Ford's *Perkin Warbeck,*" *ELH*, XXVII (1960), 177–193.

guine view of events. A purge is strong medicine, and there has been more waste of human potential than Henry acknowledges. But Henry does solve England's immediate problems in a way that looks forward to one of the major political events of Ford's own lifetime: the union of England and Scotland, invoked by the Bishop of Durham as an as yet mysterious "blessing" (IV.iii.17) of providence to stem from the marriage of James of Scotland and Henry's daughter Margaret. In almost the last lines of the play Henry tells the Scottish nobles that their business "shall find success / Such as your king importunes" (V.iii.212–213). Henry is onstage at the end of the play in part to pronounce an epilogue on the unhappy Perkin Warbeck, but especially because Ford has written a history play and Henry is the real subject of the history. In the final moments Perkin recedes into the distance like "some unquiet dream" (V.ii.8) of the contention between York and Lancaster, leaving the stage to Henry, the dramatic center of Ford's play, who now emerges also as the fulcrum of succeeding events of English history down to the time of *Perkin Warbeck's* presentation. In the dramatic chronicles of English history *Perkin Warbeck* as "Henry VII" appropriately fills the gap between *Richard III* and *Henry VIII*.

"Such Noise as I can Make":Chastity and Speech in Othello *and* Comus

MARY LAUGHLIN FAWCETT

A babling Nymph that Echo hight, who hearing others talke,
By no meanes can restraine hir tongue but that it needes
                                                    must walke,
Nor of hir selfe hath powre to ginne to speake to any wight,
Espyde [Narcissus] dryving into toyles the fearfull stagges
                                                    of flight.
This Echo was a body then and not an onely voyce.
Yet of hir speach she had that time no more than now the
                                                    choyce,
That is to say, of many wordes the latter to repeate.
                            Ovid, *Metamorphoses,* III. 443–449[1]

IN OVID'S TALE, Echo helped Jove conceal his dalliances by decoying
Juno into talk; in retaliation, Juno made Echo even more of a talker,
but one who can only repeat what has been said by another. Despite
this handicap, when Echo fell in love with Narcissus, she still managed
to woo him, by turning his words of rejection to serve her purposes of
pursuit. Instead of "entreat[ing]" Narcissus "with gentle wordes some

---

1. *Ovid's Metamorphoses: The Arthur Golding Translation,* 1567, ed. John Frederick Nims (New York, 1965), p. 75. All references in the text are to this edition.

favour for to get," she must use the more direct methods of chase and repetition. Her disability, by taking power out of her own mouth, turns her language *un*gentle, even self-assertive; her first, echoic word is "I" (He: "Is there any body nie?" and she: "I"). While initially her voice, by itself, attracts Narcissus (after all, it is also his voice), when she tries to put her arms around him, he runs, and runs all the way into narcissism. The touch of the *body* of the speaking woman is much less agreeable than the sound of her invisible, unbodied voice. So strong is Echo's voice, that it survives even her body's dissolution:

> The bloud doth vanish into ayre from out of all hir veynes,
> And nought is left but voyce and bones: the voyce yet still
> remaynes.
> (ll. 495–496)

Taken as a paradigmatic couple, Echo and Narcissus warn women and men of the dangers they run in loving not wisely but too well. Turn the dial slightly in one direction, and we see them as the "ideal couple"—the supportive, nearly silent wife together with the self-confident man; in the other direction, they become the shrewish, nagging wife yoked to the henpecked husband.[2] When we focus on Echo alone, we see in Ovid's story the dangers which women run in loving and speaking. At first, Echo chattered and distracted her hearer, but her unsubdued speech must be *fixed,* anchored, and appropriated. Remembering Juno's part in the story, we understand that Echo's impotence of speech results from something women do to each other, to compensate for the sexual free choice and opportunity of the male (here, Jove). Masculine voice—in its father-origin (Jove) and its lover-object (Narcissus)—indirectly circumscribes female free speech. The

2. John Hollander distinguishes two traditions of Echo. In the earlier, she is the beloved of Pan, sometimes his wife; Hollander calls this the "credential" or "affirming" Echo. In the Ovidian tradition, she is the one who loves and pursues; her speech is hollow, "mocking," and fragmented. In making such a distinction, Hollander circumvents moralizing "negative readings" of Echo; he rescues her from an apparent unimportance, making her a "regent of discourse." *The Figure of Echo: A Mode of Allusion in Milton and After* (Berkeley, Calif., 1981), pp. 11–17. However, in his discussion, the value assigned to the speech of each Echo still derives from an assessment of its *male* originator, whether Pan or Narcissus.

story further tells us that female speech expresses simultaneously both sexual knowledge (Echo *knows* of Jove's dalliances) and its frustration (she can never capture Narcissus). If the linkage between knowledge and frustration is inevitable, then the only way "out" for a woman is chastity and silence—a radical fiction which would cancel desire both of body and of tongue. Such a chaste, silent woman would have no story to tell, and none could be told about her. She would live unknown, beneath the "glassy, cool, translucent wave" of nonspeaking nonnarrativity.[3]

Thus Echo, who favors dalliance, pursuit, and the ready answer, is really antithetical to the chaste women, yet she has not seemed so. Instead, in Renaissance sermons and advice manuals, Echo was cited as the ideal of feminine chaste speech. In 1630 John Dod and Robert Cleaver defined the true, subject role of the chaste woman by saying: "As the echo answereth but one word for many, which are spoken to her; so a Maid's answer should be in a word." The wife must be "chaste and shamefast [,] modest and silent [,] godly and discreet."[4] Contemporary manuals of domestic propriety advised women to be chaste and silent, to "use their tongues lesse, and their needles more." Some writers realized that both speech and silence could be dangerous in a woman. William Gouge agreed that "too much speech implieth an usurpation of authoritie";[5] yet he recognized that silence might be a refuge from authority and thus indicate subversion. "Stoutness of stomacke and stubbornnesse of hearte, . . . is an extreme contrarie to loquacitie."[6] These writers postulate an ideal balance between speech and muteness. In such tracts, comments about this ideal are gender-specific; *women* must achieve this balance.

Iago's definition of the "deserving woman" perfectly accords with Gouge's. Such a woman is, he says, one who "had tongue at will, and

3. Quotations from *Comus* are from Merritt Y. Hughes, ed., *John Milton: Complete Poems and Major Prose* (New York, 1957). The line numbers in the text are taken from this edition.

4. Quoted in David Aers and Bob Hodge, " 'Rational Burning': Milton on Sex and Marriage," *Milton Studies,* XIII (1979), 6. See also George Steiner, "The Distribution of Discourse," in *On Difficulty* (New York, 1978), p. 71.

5. Quoted in Suzanne W. Hull, *Chaste, Silent, and Obedient: English Books for Women, 1475–1640* (San Marino, Calif., 1982), p. 47. See also pp. 47–56 and 145–216.

6. William Gouge, *Of Domesticall Duties: Eight Treatises* (London, 1622; facsim. Amsterdam, 1976), III, 282.

yet was never loud"; she is one who "could think, and ne'er disclose her mind" (II.i.149, 156).[7] Such an "ideal" woman could easily become a manipulator, could in fact become an Iago, for he is the one whom such a definition best fits. Male attempts to find the right balance between women's silence and speech find their funniest parody in Ben Jonson's *Epicoene, or the Silent Woman.* There, the loudest, most long-winded men continually proclaim the ideal of the silent wife; just when the wife, Epicoene, turns out to be a talker, she also turns out to be a *man.* Voice is, indeed, a "masculine property."[8] Such a parody of the problem shows us that we cannot dismiss the ideal, whether Gouge's or Iago's, as merely a matter of social propriety or sex-role stereotyping.

The connection between women's speech and chastity was, as these documents suggest, an important Renaissance topic. Males who claimed the right to define or prescribe women's speech habits sound as if they are concealing from themselves fears about female dominance, sexuality, and resistance to authority. Perhaps anxieties about the function of speech are attached primarily to women because women represent bodily existence with all its mysteries; chastity is a male construct which attempts to give shape to those mysteries. From the point of view of the woman, such prescriptions, such balancing acts, are dangerous. Complete silence is equivalent to death, and Echoism carries the possibility of psychic disintegration. As "onely" body, woman is mute and undefended; as "onely voyce" she is frustrated and continually seeking.

Othello and *Comus,* two works not often thought of together, can provide us with a rich field for exploring the intertwined themes of chastity and speech; in both works we see how, for women, speech peels away from the sexual state of chastity. Words cannot defend the chaste woman, and they may turn actively against her. Desdemona and the Lady, so different in behavior, in assumptions about the world

7. Quotations from *Othello* are from the Arden edition, ed. M. R. Ridley (London, 1969).

8. Margaret Homans, *Women Writers and Poetic Identity* (Princeton, N.J., 1980), p. 3. Throughout this essay, I have chosen "speech" over "voice" because "speech" suggests a more willed, formal utterance; its consonants give it an explosive sound. "Voice" refers to the sound as well as the sound-producer, and implies that the speaker is a vehicle for a natural power of utterance.

and their places in it, make the same exchange—they are silent in exchange for having had the last word. In both works, although in different ways, it has been hard for critics to hear the main female character.
These two works are rarely compared, perhaps because of differences
in date, genre, and placement in the writer's career, because of difference in the kind of woman presented (wife, Maid), or because of different thematic concerns of critics who write about Shakespeare and
Milton. But precisely because the comparison is strange, even far-
fetched, any similarities which turn up will illustrate what I call, following Maynard Mack, the "inward structure" of speech and chastity.[9]
Behind patterns in plot progression and trains of imagery, Mack noticed parallel developments of the hero figure across several tragedies.
I think we can see parallel "inward structures" in these two works by
different authors in the speech of the main female characters, because—despite differences between tragedy and masque—both works
are meant to be heard.

Five such inward structures appear in *Othello* and *Comus,* parallels
which emerge once we begin to listen to the central female character
speak and, equally, observe her silences. First, each work goes to some
lengths to posit chastity as an essence and to define it by an energetic
rejection of its opposite. Second, both works show how the idea of
chastity has affected the central female character and her sense of her
own autonomy, and how men surrounding her try to limit her sphere
of action. Third, both works present the verbal development of the
woman as a movement from early echoism to a wider verbal arena.
Fourth, in both works, at the climax, the central woman is muted and
her voice replaced by another woman who speaks for her. Finally, in
both works the chastity-speech theme is appropriated by the male artist. After all, silence can be no ideal for him; he must have "tongue at
will" to "disclose [his] mind." As Angus Fletcher has said of *Comus,*
the artist's depiction of chastity and chaste speech may "support [his]
sense of his own heroic vocation."[10] Depicting the chaste woman, the

9. See Mack's pioneering 1960 essay, "The Jacobean Shakespeare," reprinted in Alvin Kernan's edition of *Othello* (New York, 1963), p. 210 and passim. My concern in this
essay is not thematic, but rather structural.

10. *The Transcendental Masque: An Essay on Milton's Comus* (Ithaca, N.Y., 1971),
p. 209. This fine book treats many of the issues I discuss here, and I am indebted
throughout. Fletcher's discussion of virginity as a metaphysical condition is especially

artist can adopt the role of protector, praiser of the innocent, and prescriber of moral values. His use of the theme of chastity, whether mute or echoic, can deflect nervous vigor into his own, male speech. Pathos, consolation, and most important, self-transcendence may result for *him*.

I

Desdemona and the Lady are different sorts of women, at different stages in their lives, yet they are both defined as preeminently chaste, and each work presents the reader with a background definition of that state. A virgin, like the Lady in *Comus,* is physically intact. Like Desdemona, "the second type of virginity is the chaste love of matrimony"; thus Milton quoted Calvin who quoted Chrysostom.[11] Married or not, the chaste woman keeps away from unallowed sexual intercourse and even from sexual curiosity. Yet her will is *not* in abeyance; she must not be merely ignorant. Her will is exercised in order not to act, think, or speak in certain ways. The idea of chastity posits an entelechy—an inner, vital principle of growth and order, like the garden enclosed which was Mary's symbol. The chaste personality, seen as such an enclosure, will let in only sense experiences, and will not wish to augment or limit what is properly offered.

Definitions of virginity and chastity as positive qualities are not nearly as energetically expressed as is the failure of the ideal. Here, for example, is the Elder Brother:

> when lust
> By unchaste looks, loose gestures, and foul talk,
> But most by lewd and lavish acts of sin

---

interesting. Criticism of *Comus* often discusses chastity, of course, usually as a theological theme. See A.S.P. Woodhouse's 1941 article and Rosamund Tuve's 1957 interpretation, both reprinted in the useful collection edited by John Diekhoff, *A Masque at Ludlow: Essays on Milton's Comus* (Cleveland, 1968). See also William Kerrigan, "The Heretical Milton, *ELR,* V (1975), 144, for a connection between chastity and death anxiety.

11. *Complete Prose Works of John Milton,* ed. Don M. Wolfe (New Haven, Conn., 1957), II, 249. Hereafter abbreviated as *CPW.*

Lets in defilement to the *inward* parts,
The soul grows clotted by contagion,
*Im*bodies and *im*brutes.[12]

(ll. 463–468; emphasis added)

In this overdetermined passage it sounds as if lust is generated from within the body, by its own "looks," "gestures," and "talk"; like a seed implanting the womb's menstrual space, the conception or "clot" begins to grow in the "inward parts," leaving behind it "thick and gloomy shadows damp . . . link'd" to the soul like an afterbirth. A sense of sexual disgust and hatred of woman's biology is here transferred from the "lavish act" to the preexistent condition of the woman's soul. "Foul *talk*" is one step toward letting defilement in. Chastity and unchastity, then, are both matters of access—just enough, too much, not enough, or the wrong kind.

Fragile as such an entelechy may seem, its existence is an article of faith for male characters in both *Othello* and *Comus;* when they believe in it, they believe in a crucial connection between spirit and the natural world, an *essential* connection. Othello comes to value this essence in images which show that the chaste Desdemona is rare, whole, rich, and abundant: "She's fram'd as fruitful / As the free elements"; she is the "pattern of excelling nature"; she is "the fountain from which my current runs"; she is "one entire and perfect chrysolite." For him, chastity is not sterile; it is a guarantee of the world in its fullness and relatedness. Such expressions testify to Othello's sense of his own exclusion. The belief in this essence is the one given of the play. In *Comus,* also, chastity puts essence at stake. For the Elder Brother similarly the chaste soul is also essential, in a passage noted for its religious heterodoxy:[13]

12. Hughes notes here that "imbrutes" is used later to describe Satan's transformation into the serpent. See also Milton's description of sexual physiology in the divorce tracts:

in menstrous bodies, where natures current hath been stopt, . . . suffocation and upward forcing of some lower part, affects the head . . . with dotage and idle fancies.

(*CPW,* II, 278–289)

13. Kerrigan, "The Heretical Milton," pp. 134–135.

> Till oft converse with heav'nly habitants
> Begin to cast a beam on th'outward shape,
> The unpolluted temple of the mind,
> And turns it by degrees to the soul's *essence,*
> Till all be made immortal.
>
> (ll. 459–463; emphasis added)

For the elder Brother, as for Milton, the existence of chastity within one woman is a kind of guarantee of relatedness and transcendence linking this world with heaven.

In both works, the central, "good," woman, because she *embodies* the essence, must be a polemical creation. Her chaste presence in the work shows its audience that absolute virtue is possible in the world, and that, further, it can be actualized in the work of art. As Emilia claims of Desdemona's virtue: "If she be not honest, chaste, and true, / There's no man happy"; further, "the purest of her sex / Is foul as slander" (IV.ii.17–19). The Elder Brother rests even more on his confidence that "virtue may be assail'd but never hurt." His cosmic scheme of things depends on the efficacy of chastity, the essence of all virtue:[14]

> If this fail,
> The pillar'd firmament is rott'ness,
> And earth's base built on stubble.
>
> (ll. 597–599)

II

This heavily invested quality is carried by women who do not recognize its weight or calculate its effects on others. Both Desdemona and the Lady believe that they belong first to themselves, and that they may give themselves away freely. They assume an identity between speech and body or will. The Lady says, "that which is not good, is not delicious / To a well-govern'd and wise appetite" (ll. 704–705). This identity between body and will is also characteristic of Desdemona,

---

14. Louis Martz speaks of the schoolbook learning and "ambitious rhetoric" of the brothers, but there is conviction behind these words. *Poet of Exile* (New Haven, Conn., 1980), p. 11.

from her opening choice through her death. When Othello's jealousy finds her hand too hot and moist, she claims her own self-origination: " 'twas the hand that gave away my heart." She wills to "love him dearly," even though "he do shake me off" (IV.ii.159–160). A remnant of the assumption of autonomy remains at the end, when she both claims responsibility for her own death ("nobody—I myself") and reestablishes her sense of relatedness ("Commend me to my kind lord").[15] Desdemona's speech is still in process at her death; unlike Othello, she does not present herself in finished speeches; instead, these fragments sketch in an autonomy which is also a generous relatedness. Such speech, so ineffective on the surface, results, according to this reading, from the nature of her chastity.

Despite this assumption of autonomy, each woman is challenged by a male antagonist who describes a woman's sphere in a way that diminishes, delimits, or caricatures its possibilities, while he appears to praise the successful woman. Significantly, neither Desdemona nor the Lady tries to argue against the limits set by male definition. Neither woman fully answers her antagonist; both evade participating in a dialogue with terms established by the male.

Iago's "praise" of women consists in denying them any *essential* qualities; women are, he says, "players in your housewifery; and housewives in your bed" (II.i.112). When he characterizes the "fair and deserving woman," in the passage cited earlier, he limits the appropriate role for a woman: "To suckle fools and chronicle small beer." Desdemona's only reaction to this caricature is, "O most lame and impotent conclusion." While this reaction does point to the basis for sex-role stereotyping, the oedipal anxieties of the lamed male, it simply rejects Iago's definition without proceeding to refute it or to challenge his right to make it. She remains "chaste" by *not* engaging with the definition, and thus by default she seems tacitly to grant him the right to define her sphere.

Comus's depiction of woman's sphere is even more constricting than Iago's. For Comus, there are only two kinds of women, those with "homely features" who should "keep home," and those with attractive features who "must be shown / In courts, at feasts, and high solemnities" (ll. 745–746). His imperatives assert his right to judge

15. "Kind" has the root meaning of "kin."

which is which: "Beauty is nature's coin, *must* not be hoarded, / But *must* be current." For two kinds of women, two kinds of life—dull housewifery or sexual use and display. The Lady counters his assertions with a response which evades his false dichotomy by taking the argument to another level. Instead of discussing kinds of women, she subsumes the plight of the individual woman, caught in Comus's bifurcation, into the even dispensation of a superfemale, Nature, the "good cateress":

> Imposter, do not charge most innocent nature,
> As if she would her children should be riotous
> With her abundance; she, good cateress,
> Means her provision only to the good
> That live according to her sober laws
> And holy dictate of spare Temperance.
>
> (ll. 762–767)

The Lady transforms Comus's mutually exclusive opposite roles into a hierarchical, familial pattern. Yet she recognizes that her language cannot convince *this* listener: "Fain would I something say, yet to what end?" (l. 783)

Comus is unreachable; Iago is, for Desdemona, the wrong person to address. Her speech deconstructs itself even as she speaks it, and its denials can be heard as so many admissions:

> If e'er *my will did trespass* 'gainst his love
> Either in discourse of thought or *actual deed,*
> Or that mine eyes, mine ears, or any *sense*
> *Delighted* them in any other form,
> . . . .
> Comfort forswear me!
>
> (IV.ii. 154–161; emphasis added)

Denial words sound like only so many bits of punctuation in between the really telling admissions:

> If to preserve this vessel for my lord
> From any hated *foul unlawful touch*[16]

16. Two editions show "any other foul unlawful touch." If this is a slip of Desdemona's tongue, it indicates even greater ambiguity.

> Be not to be a *strumpet, I am* none.
>
> (IV.ii.85–87; emphasis added)

Certain words, such as "whore," "trespass," "delightful," or "strumpet," have more force than the surrounding emphatic syntax of denial.[17] The words convey such an immediate, visceral picture that semantic structure cannot contain or negate them. Further, language by its nature implies commensurability: things equal other things when they are put into words. "Strumpet" mysteriously equals "I." "Noses, ears, and lips" are all interchangeable in the world of words; language chops the woman's body into "messes" and, by breaking up the parts, renders defenseless the integrity of the chaste system. Language also implies continuity; an action which can be *said* can also be repeated. Othello asks himself: if with me, then why not with Cassio? If she left her father, then might she not leave me? If I gave her the handkerchief, then might she not also give it away? What is interchangeable and continuous in the world of words will turn against the woman who wishes to defend herself; language cannot speak of such matters without revealing the ranging, analogous possibilities. From the woman's point of view, this connection between chastity and speech means that, when chastity is questioned, language can never confirm it. There is an absolute gulf between physical integrity and speaking. Talk, whether "foul" or not, can only let evil in, not let the truth out.

III

When we look at the kind of verbal energy which the central woman exercises, we find a more complex relationship between the two works, involving parallel and mirroring movements. At the beginning

17. It has been hard for critics to hear Desdemona's voice by itself. For instance, Heilman's book on *Othello* has three chapters on Iago, two on Othello, and none on Desdemona. When G. Wilson Knight says that both Othello and Desdemona "assert the positive beauty of created forms—hence Othello's perfected style of speech," the reader barely notices this abridgment of the problem, this metonymy of Desdemona's voice into Othello's, so characteristic is it of most discussions of the play until recently. Robert B. Heilman, *Magic in the Web* (Lexington, Ken., 1956), and G. Wilson Knight, *The Wheel of Fire* (New York, 1966), p. 116.

of each work, the woman has not been noted for plain or loud speaking. Neither Desdemona nor the Lady initiates speech until it is necessary in the dramatic context, and, as we will see, both begin by relying on echoic speech when they do talk. Once they become engaged in the testing situation, however, both women display vigorous verbal energy, energy which seems at first to overcome the masculine hesitancies and threats which surround them.

When the Lady finds herself alone in the woods, she begins as an anxious listener. She even imagines, in a fascinating passage, invisible voices calling *to* her, "calling shapes" and "airy tongues that syllable men's names." Her response is to remind herself of abstractions such as Conscience, Faith, and Hope. When she calls out, however, it is not to these powers, but rather to Echo, not Ovid's living Echo but the dispersed sound of the dead spirit. The Lady's appeal reminds us of the hidden and involuted quality of echoic sound; like the canals of the inner ear, Echo's responses come from somewhere "unseen / Within [an] airy shell."[18] Since, at this point, the Lady is completely isolated, it seems as if she lives on the other side of a boundary, "by slow *Meander's* margent green." So placed, the Lady says:

> I cannot hallo to my Brothers, but
> Such noise as I can make to be heard farthest
> I'll venture.
>
> (ll. 226–228)

Since the males in this poem "hallo" back and forth without hesitation (see lines 481–490, for instance), her assumption that *she* cannot is noticeable. "Such noise as I can make" indicates a self-limiting decision, a self-muting, closely tied to her status as a virgin.

Similarly, in Othello's account of his courtship, Desdemona also begins as an echoic presence. Othello's past, as he spins it into narrative, is made up of hard elements, such as "rough quarries," only partially

---

18. Hollander, p. 61, points out that the song to Echo "deepens and transforms the mythical personification of Echo, . . . by being aware of earlier versions of her and attempting to move through and beyond" them and their "easy, and familiar [acoustical] effects." Milton "internalized textual echoing in the song itself." Further, we note that Milton, unlike Browne, Peele, and others, does *not* have Echo answer; ironically, Comus's appearance *is* the Lady's Echo/echo.

excavated or finished off. The tale emerges into humanity only when he finds a listener in Desdemona. Strikingly, Desdemona's listening participates in the quality of his tale. She "would . . . seriously incline" her head to hear tales of "men whose heads / Grew beneath their shoulders," in another sort of inclining. Just after Othello has described the "Cannibals that each other eat, / The Anthropophagi," he speaks of Desdemona "with greedy ear / Devour[ing] up my discourse."[19] Such a listener so partakes of tales that she almost takes part in them. Her response to the stories is nearly wordless, and utterly nonnarrative:

> She swore i' faith 'twas strange, 'twas passing strange;
> 'Twas pitiful, 'twas wondrous pitiful
> . . . .
> She lov'd me for the dangers I had pass'd,
> And I lov'd her that she did pity them.
>
> (I.iii.159–168)

Here the teller and the listener are in a fitted, congruent relationship. The essence of what was spoken has been conveyed directly into the receiving mind, which registers an immediately feeling of sympathy, and that sympathy in turn provokes the teller's love. The man, it seems, is indirectly in love with his own tale, which is his own identity, and directly in love with the feelings it engenders. We are reminded of Narcissus listening to his own words and looking into the flat mirror of the pond. Desdemona, at first, believes in the pure, Edenic transparency and reflexiveness of words: "I saw Othello's visage in his mind."

Both central women move strongly from this early echoism to claim a larger verbal arena; as a result, each of them is open to the charge of shrewishness at first, yet each falls victim to the unspeakability of her chastity. Desdemona, for instance, in the first act, addresses the nobles of Venice strongly, allotting exactly four-and-a-half lines to each of her

---

19. Stephen Greenblatt notices the significance of the latter of these two passages; he connects it with the theme of narration throughout the play. Othello and Desdemona become caught up in Iago's plots because they have "already experienced submission to narrativity" in a scene such as this. *Renaissance Self-Fashioning* (Chicago, 1980), p. 237.

obligations, to her father and to her husband. The balanced, delibera-
tive, assured quality of this speech silences her father, who can only
respond, "God be with you. I have done." Later, on Cyprus, Desdemona enters into a different kind of verbal arena, engaging in fashionable
word-play with Iago; she can "beguile / The thing I am by seeming otherwise" (I.i. 122–23). In resolving to help Cassio, she moves even further into playful, beguiling, insistent speech:

> my lord shall never rest,
> I'll watch him tame, and talk him out of patience;
> His bed shall seem a school, his board a shrift.
>
> (III.iii.22–24)

She eagerly invites Cassio to "stay, and hear me speak."[20] If these passages provoke any unease in listeners, then or now, they do so because
of the tacit assumption that loudness (rhetorical self-presentation and
the power to initiate speech) is an index of moral imbalance in a woman.[21] We might choose to hear, instead, sexual self-confidence and a
sense, tragically mistaken, that there is a place for her voice in the
world, and that the world she lives in now ("his bed . . . his board") is
a place in which she may speak.

The Lady in *Comus,* since she is not married, is free from such di-
lemmas about the proper context for her speech, nor is she surrounded by males who judge the propriety of her speech. It is, rather, male
opposition which releases her vigorous verbal resources. Her very immobility frees her speech:[22]

> Fool, do not boast,
> Thou canst not touch the freedom of my mind

20. Edward A. Snow points to Desdemona's verbal ebullience in this passage as evidence that the marriage has been happily consummated. "Sexual Anxiety and the Male
Order of Things in *Othello,*" *ELR,* X (1980), 406.

21. For other discussions of women and speech, see Martha Andreson-Thom,
"Thinking About Women and Their Prosperous Art," *ShStud,* XI (1978), 259–276, and
Marjorie Pryse, "Lust for Audience: An Interpretation of *Othello,*" *ELH,* XLIII (1976),
461–477.

22. Stanley Fish, in "The Temptation to Action in Milton's Poetry," *ELH,* XLVIII
(1981), 516–531, gathers examples from Milton's poetry of sitting or standing in readiness; he discusses their significance, although he does not treat *Comus.*

> With all thy charms, although this corporal rind
> Thou hast immanacl'd, while Heaven sees good.
>
> (ll. 663–666)

While Comus may be the master of "dear Wit and gay Rhetoric," the Lady has, or might use, the power of higher "sacred vehemence" to serve her cause, the "serious doctrine of Virginity." Her vigorous words deflate Comus, who fears that they are "set off by some superior power"; he cannot imagine that they come directly from her.

IV

When the strong voices of the central woman become muted near the end of each work, the role of speaker is taken over by *another* woman, as if the power of speech has been displaced back a generation. This pattern of silencing and replacement is curious; it asks us to listen for a silence, to hear what is not said as clearly as what is said.

The Lady's silence in the last two hundred lines of *Comus* has gone unremarked, and yet, if we consider it, it is astonishing.[23] She has, in her last lines, asserted a power of speech while at the same time refusing to claim it as her own: "Thou are not fit to *hear thyself* convinc't; / Yet should I try . . . "(ll. 792–793; emphasis added). After this firm claim of potential verbal power, she speaks not another word. Nor does the text completely account for her silence. Comus has threatened, of course, that her nerves will be "chain'd up . . . in Alabaster" (l. 660). Strikingly, when she is released, we hear no report of her thoughts during her immobility. Nor does Sabrina's speech fully take the place of the Lady's, as I hope to show later. The reader who questions her silence must conclude that chastity cannot speak about her imprisonment and liberation. We see the Lady as a body on the stage, moving through the dances which end the masque, but her experience remains unvoiced, in sharp contrast to Echo, who remained a voice

---

23. For instance, Leslie Brisman, who is at pains to discuss the theme of silencing in *Comus,* points out the difference between Comus's bestial stasis, or "arrest," and the Lady's idealized "real arrest—that is, arrest in song" (referring to her earlier song to Echo), but he makes nothing of her silence in the last two hundred lines of the poem. *Milton's Poetry of Choice and Its Romantic Heirs* (Ithaca, N.Y., 1973), p. 121.

long after she ceased to be a body. The listener who can hear her silence will be aware of the Lady's final self-enclosure.

The dancing Lady ought not to be an image of failed speech, but of transcended or perfected speech, but perhaps it is no longer possible to hear her silence in quite this way. It is intriguing to note that Milton added the Lady's strong "Yet should I try" lines when he published *Comus* under his own name in 1645; previous editions had been anonymous. In naming himself, he also strengthened the Lady's claim to speech powers. Two years earlier, in the first of the divorce tracts, Milton developed and elaborated the idea of a good marriage as a *conversation,* giving this word the sense of a mutual and intimate speaking. He praises "apt and cheerful conversation," the "understanding and conversing part," and "an intimate and speaking help" as tests of true marriage; he argues that "unconversing inability of minde," "numnesse of mind," and "dead vacation of all acceptable conversing" ought to be grounds for divorce.[24] "Conversation," in this period, had a wide range of meanings; Milton's use of it in this speaking sense opens up the flat, one-dimensional ideal of the modest, nearly silent woman extolled by Gouge or Dod and Cleaver to reveal a kernel of insentience and infertility within silence. Yet, in *Comus,* the Lady must be silent at the end simply *because* she is chaste. So we are left with a sad disjunction between speech and chastity.

Desdemona's silencing is more gradual and more absolute, until at the end she also is only body. Her rhetoric frays into ambiguities, occasional sarcasm, an old song, and then silence. We have already noted that her energetic self-defense ("If e'er my will did trespass") can be

---

24. *CPW,* II, 235, 249, 248, 269, and 331. Milton describes a divorce trial as *noisy:* as a "*clamouring* debate of *utterless* things" (*CPW,* II, 348; emphasis added). In *Tetrachordon,* he asks, "why then shall divorce be granted for want of bodily performance, and not for want of fitness to intimate conversation?" (II, 348). Further, in the matter of divorce, Milton sounds like the beseiged and silenced Lady, surrounded by a Comus-like "panick" noise of scruples:

human error had led . . . [us] to walk on between a precipice of unnecessary mischief on either side: and starting at every fals alarum, wee do not know which way to set a foot forward . . . through the confused ringing in our ears, of *panick* scruples and amazements.

(II, 343)

read as confession. Othello's mind has been reached by the picture
Iago has helped him to see and, as in the case of the Echo story, such
sights destroy the tissue of discourse:

> Would you, the supervisor, grossly gape on,
> Behold her topp'd?
> It were a tedious difficulty, I think,
> To bring 'em to that prospect [sight], damn 'em then,
> If ever mortal eyes did see them bolster
> More than their own; what then, how then?
> What shall I say?[25]
>
> (III.iii.401–407)

Iago has brought Othello to an overlook, where he can see down into
his own mind, and after this sight, words become just words, words,
words. "She *says* enough, yet she's a simple bawd / That cannot *say* as
much" (IV.ii.20–21; emphasis added).[26] In the face of the picture he
now sees, words become only surfaces of deception. Desdemona re-
treats from assertions of her chastity. She, who has prided herself on
her power to speak, and has been known as "free of speech," responds
to Emilia's sympathy with:

> Do not talk to me, Emilia,
> I cannot weep, nor answers have I none,
> But what should go by water.
>
> (IV.ii.105–107)

While the central woman is being silenced, another woman takes
her place and provides vocal testimony to the power and value of
chastity. The other woman intervenes in the action obliquely, inter-
secting with the testing situation, but coming from a world closed to
the central woman. I am thinking, of course, of Emilia, Desdemona's

---

25. *Iago* uses echoic speech here, when he repeats himself in this way. In this iteration of questions, and in his constant use of "honest," Iago reminds us of Lévi-Strauss's
observation that repeated sounds ("da" to "dada," for example) indicate "intent on the
part of the speaker." *The Raw and the Cooked* (New York, 1969), p. 339. Echo certainly
illustrates this point well.

26. Othello, in fact, has taken chastity as his *own* word, and he laments its destruc-
tion: "my name, that was as fresh / As Dian's visage, is now begrim'd" (III.iii.393–394).

servant and a woman of the world, and of Sabrina, the ultra-virgin and a woman of another world altogether. The two are absolutely unlike as characters, but they serve the same function; they indicate the same "inward structure" of the speech-chastity theme.

From the beginning, implicit in the situation of the central woman is her motherlessness.[27] She is neither supported nor circumscribed by a mother's presence. Perhaps chastity can be more clearly delineated when there is no woman of full generational gnosis existing on the same stage as that of the central, chaste figure, whose isolation more poignantly emphasizes the value of her chastity than if we were reminded of her possible future as the bearer of children. But the mother who is absent from the beginning is supplied, symbolically, near the end; the second woman stands outside the conflicts which threaten the central figure. She, perhaps, reassures us that chastity does exist, that it is valuable, despite the endings which it brings.

Emilia's intervention in the action of *Othello* provides a relief for the audience, because she has a *loud* part. She will "speak as liberal as the north." With a rush of invective and "iteration," she scours the scene:

> Let heaven, and men, and devils, let 'em all,
> All, all cry shame against me, yet I'll speak.[28]
>
> (V.ii.222–223)

This relief exacts a cost, however—a cost which must be paid because Emilia is married and speaks out against her husband: "So speaking as I think, alas, I die."

Sabrina's intervention in *Comus* comes only after the efforts of her brothers and the Attendant Spirit have failed. We note a curious disjunction here. The carefully prepared and introduced masculine instrument of salvation, Haemony, plays little part in the rescue itself. Although it is not much to look at ("unsightly," "unknown and like es-

---

27. Desdemona's mother is mentioned only in the speech to the Venetian nobles and in passing just before the "Willow" song; the Lady's mother is simply the "Lady bright" of l. 967.

28. See Carol Thomas Neely's excellent comments on this scene and on the relationship between women in *Othello,* in *The Woman's Part: Feminist Criticism of Shakespeare,* ed. Carolyn Lenz, Gayle Greene, and Carol Thomas Neely (Urbana, Ill., 1980), pp. 231–232.

teem'd," even the Shepherd Lad who gave it was "of small regard to see to"), the Attendant Spirit says that it has a "sovran" potency, and "strange vigorous faculties" which will allow the brothers to invade Comus's dominion and make his retenue "shrink." A phallic power is being described here, along with masculine anxiety about its efficacy. But despite this careful presentation, Milton elides the confrontation between the two forms of phallic power, the root the brothers have (good, familial masculinity) and the rod which Comus wields (bestial, orgiastic masculinity).

The solution to the impasse of masculinity is to "unsay" the charms already in place, to reverse Comus's rod:

> without his rod revers't
> And backward mutters of dissevering power,
> We cannot free the Lady that sits here.[29]
>
> (ll. 815–817)

This unsaying must be done by a woman, but not by the Lady, who has abjured strong rhetoric. What is needed is a new woman, one who says little but about whom much can *be* said. Sabrina brings with her an entire orderly mythological world which has consigned aggressive masculinity to the safely distant past; Locrine, Brute, Nereus, Oceanus, Glaucus, Tethys, and Thetis, among others, together signify passion transcended, murder made good, spells unlocked. Precisely because Sabrina is complete chaste, having undergone a "quick immortal change" "through the porch and inlet of each sense" (ll. 839–841), she can become a perfectly benevolent substitute for masculine power; she

---

29. Keats made an interesting application of this moment in *Comus*. He told of his difficulty in reconciling his notion of the ideal woman with the realities he saw around him. He confesses to his rather prudish friend Benjamin Bailey:

I have not a right feeling towards Women— . . . I must absolutely get over this—but how? The only way is to find the root of the evil, and so cure it "with backward mutters of dissevering Power."

He and the other romantics inherited the problem of the literary treatment of women from *Comus;* Keats especially feels himself alternately in the position of the Lady, Comus, and the brothers. *The Letters of John Keats,* ed. Hyder Edward Rollins (Cambridge, Mass., 1958), I, 341.

comes on the scene with phallic potency. The Attendant Spirit calls her:

> Rise, rise, and heave thy rosy head
> From thy coral pav'n bed,
> And bridle in thy headlong wave,
> Till thou our summons answer'd have.
>
> (ll. 886–889)

Such feminized phallicism *can* mediate between the familial masculinity of the brothers and the orgiastic masculinity of Comus, especially since her intervention is temporary, and she returns to feminine, courtly duties, "to wait in Amphitrite's bow'r." (Like Emilia, she is thus essentially a servant.) Sabrina speaks only fourteen lines of poetry and sings only one song; she leaves most of the words to the Attendant Spirit, Milton's stand-in. *He* is given powers of flight and possibility at the end of the poem: "I fly . . . Up in the broad fields of the sky" and "I can fly, or I can run / Quickly to the green earth's end" (ll. 979–1014). Sabrina returns to her domestic bowers. Feminine speech is subsumed into a larger, transcendent masculine verbal power.

V

Both Shakespeare and Milton, I think, believe in the existence of a feminine ideal which redeems the fallen physical body; both accept chastity as a *power.* Shakespeare, however, implies a strong criticism of masculine notions of this power. Both Iago the reductivist ("The wine she drinks is made of grapes") and Othello the idealizer ("If it were now to die / 'Twere now to be most happy") are seen to be acting out masculine anxiety arising from their overvaluation of the ideal of chastity.[30] The more Othello praises the *idea* of chastity, the more unlikely any em*bodi*ment of that idea comes to seem to him. Desdemona's chaste inability to argue her case effectively leaves all the words in the mouths of Iago and Othello.

---

30. For this approach, see, in addition to Snow's article, Kenneth Burke, "*Othello:* An Essay to Illustrate a Method," *HudR,* IV (1951), 165–230.

Milton does not question the existence of an ideal chastity; instead, he appropriates its powers, especially its verbal powers, to himself as an artist. Thus, he can seem to refuse with one hand the sensual abundance offered by the magician Comus, while he takes up with the other hand the essence which will replace it: "sure something holy lodges in that breast" (l. 246). This feminine inwardness has magical powers for the poet who uses it. As the Elder Brother believes, chastity is not really self-denial at all; it is a means of privileged access to higher knowledge—and as such it rewards a *poet* amply. The Angels who attend the truly chaste woman "in clear dream and solemn vision / Tell her of things that no gross ear can hear" (ll. 457–458). It is a short step from these Angels and such "converse with heav'nly habitants" to the nightly visitation from the Muse Urania, as Milton invokes her in *Paradise Lost,* Book VII:

> Up led by thee
> Into the Heav'n of Heav'ns I have presum'd,
> An Earthly Guest, and drawn Empyreal Air,
> Thy temp'ring.
>
> (VII.12–15)

Access to this higher knowledge will, he hopes, "drive far off the barbarous dissonance / Of Bacchus and his Revellers," a crew much like Comus's. This nightly visitation presents poetic inspiration as a kind of consummation, as do, even more strongly, those lines which are the Lady's last:

> Yet should I try, the uncontrolled worth
> Of this pure cause would kindle my rapt spirits
> To such a flame of sacred vehemence,
> That dumb things would be mov'd to sympathize,
> And the brute Earth would lend her nerves, and shake,
> Till all thy magic structures rear'd so high,
> Were shatter'd into heaps o'er thy false head.
>
> (ll. 793–799)

The action of this hypothesized chaste language would be a kind of universal orgasm—and Comus immediately feels "a cold shudd'ring dew . . . all o'er."[31] Chastity in the woman Milton depicts becomes, for the male artist, a principle of self-transcendence and pure, radical, revolutionary verbal power.

31. The notion that the power of speech can be considered phallic may find some support in the use of "nerves" here. The *OED* gives as an obsolete meaning, "penis." Milton used this sense when he wrote, in *The Doctrine and Discipline of Divorce*, of the inordinate consideration given in divorce proceedings to "the disappointing of an impetuous nerve" (*CPW*, II, 249).

Notes on Contributors

JONATHAN BALDO is an assistant professor of English at the Eastman School of Music, University of Rochester. His essays on Shakespeare and Shelley have appeared in *Semiotica* and *Criticism,* and he is currently completing a book on Shakespeare.

DIANA BENET is an assistant professor of English at Georgia State University and the author of *Secretary of Praise: The Poetic Vocation of George Herbert* and *Something to Love: Barbara Pym's Novels.* She is Contributing Editor of the *Elegies* volume of *The Variorum Edition of the Poetry of John Donne,* a work in progress.

ROY T. ERIKSEN is professor of English literature at the University of Tromsö, Norway. His revised thesis, *The Forme of Faustus Fortunes,* has recently been published by Humanities Press/Solum. His verse translation of Marlowe's play, and a book on Renaissance formal poetics, *One Poem's Period,* are forthcoming.

MARY LAUGHLIN FAWCETT is an adjunct professor of English at George Mason University, Fairfax, Va. She has published articles on *Titus Andronicus* and *The Mysteries of Udolpho.* She is currently writing on the itemization of the female body in Renaissance poetry.

VERNA FOSTER is an assistant professor of English at Loyola University of Chicago. She has written several articles on Marlowe, Middleton, and Ford.

181

JAMES P. HAMMERSMITH is an associate professor of English at Auburn University. He has written essays on Shakespeare, on textual criticism, and on the history of printing and proofreading in Renaissance England. He is currently editing Shakespeare's *Poems* for the New Variorum Shakespeare.

CHARLES W. HIEATT is a Senior Lecturer at the Cambridgeshire College of Arts and Technology (Cambridge, England). He is currently working on a book, in collaboration with A. Kent Hieatt and Anne Lake Prescott, on the influence of Edmund Spenser's *Ruins of Rome* on Shakespeare's poetry and plays.

SUSAN MCCLOSKEY is an assistant professor of English at Vassar College and has published several essays on seventeenth-century drama. She is now at work on a book about Renaissance dramatic worlds.

PEGGY MUÑOZ SIMONDS is a professor of English at Montgomery College, Rockville, Md. Her articles have been published in *Shakespeare Quarterly, Theatre Journal, Texas Studies in Literature and Language, Renaissance Papers, Shakespeare on Film Newsletter,* and *Mosaic.* She is currently at work on a book-length study of *Cymbeline* using the iconographic approach.